And the more one elaborates
upon the departure from Egypt, the
more praiseworthy one is.

—*The Haggadah*

Contents

Acknowledgments   ix

Bedikat: One Candle to Illuminate Your Search   xi
A Note to the Reader

1. *Dayyenu:* It Would Have Been Sufficient   1
How We "Keep" Passover. I introduce myself and
explain this book. What is a sufficient seder?

2. *Shulchan Arukh:* The Prepared Table   16
A Festive Passover Meal. When to have your seder,
who to invite, being a guest. The seder plate and the
seder table. A basic Pesach. The hidden and awful
depths of the kabbalah.

3. *Mutus Liber:* The Mute Book   55
Ritual Actions of the Seder. The choreography of
the seder ritual without the Hebrew lyrics. Actions
speak louder than words.

4. *Barukh Attah:* Blessed Art Thou   89
The Benedictions. Hebrew as a holy tongue.
Kavvanot, our mystical intentions.

5. *Mah Nishtannah Ha-Layla Hazeh:*
Why Is This Night Different?   114
The Texts of the Haggadah. Deconstructing the
Haggadah. Four or more questions about history and
myth. Telling the story. Choosing a Haggadah.

6. *Echad Mi Yode'a:* Who Knows One?   195
The Power of Numbers. Numerology. *Gematria.*
Notarikon. Acrostics. Mnemonics. Acronyms.

7. *Shir Ha-Ma'alot:* A Pilgrim Song   207
The Songs of the Seder. Learning to sing the songs.
Sheet music and recordings.

8. *Kol Dichfin Yehseh Ve-Yehchul:*
Let All Who Are Hungry Enter and Eat   227
The Foods of the Seder. The feast. Recipes. Cookbooks.

9. *Ha Lachma Anya:*
This Is the Bread of Affliction   250
Shopping for Passover. Commercial Passover foods,
horseradish root, lamb shankbones, *shemurah* matzo,
good kosher wine. Ritual objects.

10. *Ve-Higadetah Le-Vinchah:*
And You Shall Tell It to Your Children   260
Children and Passover. Getting kids involved. Children's
books, toys, audio and video tapes, software, *afikoman*
prizes.

11. *Mi-Bet Avadim:*
Out of the House of Bondage   280
Women and Passover. Passover with equality for women.

12. *Be-Chol Dor Va-Dor:* In Every Generation   286
Creating Your Own Family Haggadah.

13. *La-Shanah Ha-Ba'ah Bi-Yerushalayim:*
Next Year in Jerusalem   295
The Cycle of the Jewish Year. Keeping Passover fresh every
year. Passover in relation to the cycle of the Jewish year.

Dates of Passover Through 2012   312
Glossary   313

Acknowledgments

I must first acknowledge our people who, for well over 3,300 years, have been creating and evolving the seder ceremony, an unusual mixture of custom and law that epitomizes being Jewish and the Jewish experience. It is at once ancient and contemporary, solemn and joyous, scholarly and popular, a feast and a lesson.

That evolution leads in a direct line to my grandparents and parents, especially Mark Scheinbach, our *ba'al ha-seder;* my father, Daniel Steingroot, *alav ha-shalom;* and my mother, Ruth Steingroot, who specifically instructed me in the meaning of Passover and brought me into *Kelal Yisrael,* the Community of Israel. I owe a special debt to my mother, who in addition to many other gifts, has provided me with her recipes over the years.

My sister, Marcy Steingroot, proofread the manuscript and assisted with the research. My brother, Jay Steingroot, provided information on *kashrut.* My *machetunim,* Dr. David and Ruth Friedman, have been like second parents to me throughout the writing of this book and, indeed, ever since I stood under the *chuppa* with their daughter twenty-six years ago today. It was a remark from my mother-in-law on the night of the first seder this year that led me to notice the dialectic between matzo and wine discussed in chapter 3.

I should next make mention of Cody's Books and my Passover customers there. Through Cody's I got the chance to learn more about this remarkable holiday while trying to answer the public's questions about it. A tip of the Steingroot *shtraymel* to HarperSanFrancisco and my editor, Caroline Pincus, for giving me the chance to realize my ideas.

My wife, Kathy—"the other side of my heartbeat," as Diz said of Bird—not only titled this book and acted as my in-house editor, besides taking care of problems like getting me a new laser printer and an ergonomic chair, but has been my *soror mystica* and virtual co-author as our thought has developed over three decades in uniquely individual, mutually fructifying, yet parallel ways. She continually provided me with helpful insights that strengthened the book. "Her mouth is full of wisdom . . . Many women have done well, but you surpass them all" (Proverbs 31:26, 29). My biggest debt is to my son, Jacob, for whom it is all done. It was in having a child that I returned to keeping Passover and took my place in the chain of generations. Not the smallest of his assistances was that he taught me how to use my computer, without which I could not have completed this work. May he be privileged to enter the Promised Land, which we have only seen from afar.

Ira Steingroot
August 28, 1994
21 Elul 5754

Bedikat:
One Candle to Illuminate Your Search

A Note to the Reader

On the night before the first seder, it is traditional to search (*bedikat*) the house for any remaining leaven or bread crumbs (*chametz*). The search is conducted by the light of a single candle. This book is like a large house with many rooms and many connecting passageways that may lead to new chambers or back again to previously searched compartments. Along the way, crumbs have been scattered: Sometimes, as you read, you may find them immediately; at other times you may feel you need to retrace your steps. Do not worry. What is not fully explained at first will reappear in another room later, entered through another corridor.

The transliteration of Hebrew, Aramaic, Yiddish, and Ladino words used in this book generally follows the practices of the *Encyclopedia Judaica* or Leo Rosten's *The Joys of Yiddish,* though I have overridden those practices when I felt uncomfortable with the results. I have substituted *ch* instead of an *h* with a dot under it to indicate the guttural sound in words like Chasid and *charoset,* and *tz* instead of a *z* with a dot under it to indicate the sibilant sound in *tzimmes* and *tzaddik.* I have avoided the confusing *th* ending often used in words like *sefirot* and Shavuot. I have used both Hebrew and Yiddish versions of words according to context; for instance, the Hebrew Shabbat for the day of rest in a general sense, but the Yiddish Shabbos for my own experience of the Sabbath. Hebrew plural endings have been used throughout, so that I refer to one matzo and three matzot (feminine plural), or one Chasid and two Chasidim (masculine plural). Most foreign terms are briefly defined on their first appearance. For a fuller explanation, see the glossary at the end of this book.

When a date would be unclear without a point of reference, I have followed the Jewish practice of adding B.C.E. (before the common era) and C.E. (common era). I know this is a euphemism, but it nonetheless breaks the monopoly on time that we usually accord to Christian Western European conceptions. Likewise, the word Bible refers to the Old Testament only. Passages from the Bible and the Haggadah have been translated so that they are gender neutral: child instead of son, parent instead of father, ancestor instead of forefather, and so on. Passages from medieval and modern authors have been left untouched. Finally, Passover customs from around the globe are mentioned in the book; but although there are great similarities in the way the festival is celebrated throughout the Jewish world, the primary focus has been on the common practices of Ashkenazim, the Jewish people of Eastern Europe, since that is both my own experience and that of the vast majority of American Jews.

How This Book Is Organized

All but one of the chapter titles of this book come from the text of the Haggadah. They are given both in English, for the resonant power of these well-known key phrases, and in a transliteration of the Hebrew, for the musical qualities of our ancient tongue, as well as for that combination of the familiar and unfamiliar that Freud calls the uncanny, *unheimlich*.

The thirteen chapters of this book parallel the song "Echad Mi Yode'a," or "Who Knows One." In this children's counting song (the penultimate tune of the Passover seder), we are asked to supply something from Jewish tradition to associate with each of the numbers one through thirteen, one for the one God and thirteen for the classical number of *middot* (divine qualities). Hebrew letters all have a numerical value, and the letters of *echad* (one) add up to thirteen. The linear counting from one to thirteen is transformed into a circular movement from the One, to the One that is contained in the thirteen:

> *A flight of the Alone to the Alone.*
> —Plotinus

We will try to parallel that in our movement through a shifting variety of sedarim, from the simple and unitary to the most multi-layered matzo baker's dozen.

Biblical verses and quotations from many writers are scattered throughout this book, just as they are in the Haggadah itself. They function as proof texts to the main body of the work, just as the Haggadah's midrash on Deuteronomy 26:5–8 (beginning "Go and learn what Laban the Aramean intended") uses seemingly unconnected biblical verses to prove and explain that capsule summary of the Exodus story. The striking together of my flinty thoughts with the steel of great writers will, hopefully, produce some sparks of illumination.

Chapter One

Dayyenu:
It Would Have Been Sufficient

How We "Keep" Passover

Special among these grand gatherings . . . was the annual celebration of the Passover, a very ancient and remarkable feast which Jews still hold every year in the month Nisan, in eternal remembrance of their deliverance from Egyptian captivity.

—from Heinrich Heine, *The Rabbi of Bacharach*

To some, the Passover seder, that ancient and remarkable feast that we Jews still hold every year, must be the most scrupulous and complete recital of the text of the Haggadah, closing with a reading of Shir ha-Shirim (the Song of Songs), where only those foods that are allowed by halakhah (law) are served. To others, it can be simply getting together with other Jews on the most convenient night of Passover for a meal, which usually includes some dishes remembered from childhood: chicken soup with *knaydlach* (matzo balls), gefilte fish with beet horseradish, sponge cake, matzo.

I have learned over the years that the most rigid performance of the seder is not always the best way to teach or to generate fond memories. On the other hand, if all we do is get together as Jews for a meal, what makes this night different from all other nights?

Sometimes people know what they should do, but no longer care. They are tired of should and should not, kosher and *terefah, Pesachdikhe* and *chametzdikhe.* Other people just don't know. A friend of mine once went to a seder where a delicious, homemade apple pie was served. Only my friend knew that the flour crust was *chametz*—not kosher for Passover.

The essence of Passover is the celebration of freedom. Far too often, however, it has become a negative set of proscriptions whose performance is still observed even though their meaning has long been lost. Many of us are inclined to reject the whole thing, throwing out Moses with his basket. We unburden ourselves from what have become the smothering rules of this holiday dedicated to freedom. Ironically, our initial sense of freedom masks our loss of ritual, poetry, and connection through family and tribe with the past. The false sense of freedom that comes from dropping all the encumbrances of the holiday is no freedom when we forbid ourselves engagement in meaningful actions. That is just another kind of unfreedom.

I agree with Mordechai Kaplan, the founder of Reconstructionist Judaism, that we can reconstruct from tradition what we need to live in the modern world; but tradition fails when it acts as a rock drowning us in a sea of irrelevancy. Tradition should be heavy, but like the ballast that keeps a ship steady in an ocean of constant stormy change and the mundane flotsam and jetsam of our daily lives.

A Remembrance of Passovers Past

Passover, the ancient Jewish Festival of Unleavened Bread, the Season of our Freedom, and the oldest continuously performed ceremony in the world, has always been my favorite holiday. I loved getting together with extended family and the occasional stranger, the disruption of the quotidian, the change from our boring regular dishes to the quaint but motley assortment of glass and china we used for eight days a year. A story went with each dish and cup, whose kitchen it had come from and how we came to have it.

I loved the unique foods, especially apple and nut *charoset,* candy fruit slices, white, unsalted whipped butter we only had once a year, weird-flavored kosher chocolate, lemony sponge cakes, oddly labeled cans and jars, *matzo brei* and matzo meal pancakes with fruit preserves. My parents sold Passover foods in our grocery store in Toledo, Ohio, and often recalled that the holiday had gotten them through their first year in business. I can remember my father using a piece of taut string to cut individual portions for customers from industrial-size slabs of Pesachdikhe cream cheese.

We belonged to an Orthodox shul (synagogue), where I attended junior congregation services every Shabbos (Sabbath) and on *yontif* (holidays); four afternoons a week I went to *cheder* (Hebrew school); and on Sunday mornings I went to Sunday school. I was bar mitzvah at thirteen, graduated from Hebrew school after seven years, and confirmed after ten years of Sunday school. Most of the other kids who had the same experience and background as mine probably paid less attention to what was going on; but for me, in a world starved of intellectual nourishment, this became a kind of classical education where I devoured the Bible, prayer book, midrash, the little bit of Talmud we were given, Jewish history, law, customs, legend, and so on. Although I clowned around a lot, I loved this esoteric lore; and despite a variety of fairly radical changes in my lifestyle over the years, I still do to this day.

I grew up with a totally traditional seder and Haggadah— Stern's blue hardback from Hebrew Publishing, out of print, but still on the box of Streit's matzo. At first we had seders in my cousin's huge basement with our whole family, but when these became too cumbersome we broke up into smaller groups. I was always proud that it was my learned grandfather who had led the large seders, and even though we no longer met in an enormous group, our part of the family still had the leader, the *ba'al ha-seder.*

Grampa saw himself as our agent in accomplishing the task of completely reciting the Haggadah at our two sedarim every year. He felt that if we would only leave him alone, he would get us through the whole Haggadah as quickly and painlessly as possible. Instead of addressing the ceremony to anyone present, or to any human presence, he chanted his way through every Hebrew word of the text, including the Hebrew instructions, at a fairly good clip. It took some knowledge of Hebrew and the traditional melodies to understand his idiosyncratic accent and singing. The performance of the deed was its own *raison d'être.* The essence of the seder leaked into us by osmosis along with the food, the table talk, the symbols, and the rituals.

This led to perennial arguments with my grandmother, who wanted him to read, or apportion readings, in English from those parts of the Haggadah that were most memorable, and to allow the kids to get in on some of the most familiar songs. I would sit reading the Haggadah silently in Hebrew along with Grampa or else in English to myself, occasionally disrupting the proceedings with a joke. By the time we sat down for our family seder, we had already studied the Haggadah in Hebrew and English at cheder, had learned the songs, and had participated in model sedarim both there and at Sunday school. I ended up with a pretty good grasp of what was supposed to be done, why we did it, and the traditional tunes that we sang.

In 1967, when I left my home town to go away to college in Iowa, I gave up Passover and most of my Jewish practice. There seemed little point in doing it apart from the family context. Besides, I certainly could not begin to compete with my grandfather in leading a seder, or my grandmother in preparing the foods. I still retained an interest in Hebrew calligraphy and illuminated manuscripts, Jewish music, literature, and art, ritual objects, and Jewish history and languages, but I did not know how to connect any of this to practice. I managed to pursue my interest in kabbalah, Jewish mysticism, by studying with the only two professors at the University of Iowa School of Religion who knew anything about it. Even though this was the Sixties and everyone was chasing after gurus, swamis, and shamans, few seemed to notice that Jews were multicultural and had their own esoteric teachings.

Things went on like this until 1978, when my son was born. Questions about the *bris* (circumcision) and *pidyon ha-ben* (redemption of the firstborn) made me reconsider the necessity of ritual and ceremony: How else can we pass on being Jewish without some form of Jewish practice? If we only read books about it, then the Jewish people might just as well shuffle off the stage of human history as inconspicuously as possible.

I had moved to Berkeley, California, in 1972, and in 1976 I came to work for Pat and Fred Cody at their unique bookstore, Cody's. They had the revolutionary idea of allowing their employees to take responsibility for those sections of the store that were of most interest to them. This had positive and creative anarchistic results. It encouraged us to learn about our areas of expertise and about our customers' interests in those areas and so increase sales. If "a whaleship was . . . Yale College and . . . Harvard" to Herman Melville, then mine was a bookstore. I became Cody's Judaica buyer.

My biggest annual project has been the Passover sale every spring. When I started selling Haggadot, my idea was to provide a representative sampling of them to a Jewish community that seemed to have no center. My customers included students away from their family seder for the first time; professors and other émigrés from more well-defined Jewish communities; nonaffiliated Jews who did not fall into obvious sectarian categories; families who were tired of the same old Haggadah every year and those who were looking for the cherished old Haggadah of their childhood; even hippie Jews who mixed New Age ideas with kabbalah to create a post-Sixties kind of Judaism out of elements of tradition, Eastern mysticism, ecology, and feminism.

Berkeley was a tough audience: eclectic, politically correct, and anti-authoritarian; yet I was surprised then—and have been every year since—to see the kind of interest we have generated. What started as a few books on the corner of a table has grown to over two hundred different Haggadot, the world's largest selection, plus hundreds of other children's books, cookbooks, audio and video tapes, as well as cards, software, tchotchkes, *afikoman* prizes, and any number of other specialty items, such as a perennially popular matzo beach ball. Not only did everyone in town appreciate our selection, but we started getting noticed by newspapers, magazines, the Voice of America, and National Public Radio.

Almost everyone I spoke with wanted to participate in the ancient festival of freedom, but they were often confused as to what they needed to make a seder and what Haggadah would be most appropriate for the kind of seder they wanted to have. The questions people asked me year after year suggested that many did not know where to begin: What are the traditional foods and how do you make them? What is the correct arrangement of the seder plate? Where do you get horseradish root, a lamb's shankbone, and *shemurah* matzo? How do you learn the songs? What Haggadah would work for a group made up of an orthodox *bubbeh* with a *sheytel,* a disaffiliated vegetarian lesbian, a young couple with three kids under the age of twelve—the husband is a *shaygets* but loves Jewish holidays, an *apikoros* uncle who argues about everything, and a Reform family with a sullen teenager who keeps asking what this service means to us?

The Concept of This Book

I am an ecumenical person. I mean, I am not in the business of telling people they are wrong or right in how they do things. But I do feel that with just a little knowledge, time, and attention, both traditional and secular Jews can make their sedarim more meaningful. This book brings together all I have learned from the public about what they want to know and need to know to have a successful Passover seder: how to conduct the seder and why we do it, how to choose a Haggadah, what dishes to serve and how to prepare them, how to learn the songs.

It constitutes a primer on how to achieve the seder that is most appropriate to your specific needs. It addresses itself to all of the Children of Israel—the wise, the wicked, the simple, and the ones who do not know what to ask. I hope, like my grandfather, to get you through the seder as painlessly as possible. If all you want to do is read the reviews of a few Haggadot or compare my matzo ball recipe with yours, you can jump right to those sections. This book is meant to be inclusive, not exclusive; a movement away from "Thou shalt" and toward "Thou may."

Just getting together with family and friends to eat unleavened bread is like the simple melody of a song, and that might be sufficient for some groups. As we add on to the melody of our seder, layer by layer and year by year, we create chords and give harmony to that melody. If a simple meal with matzo suits you, that does not make you inadequate or less Jewish than the person who has an elaborate and strictly observed seder. On the other hand, expanding whatever seder you already perform need not be intimidating, embarrassing, or frightening.

Likewise, if you are traditionally inclined, you need not feel you have failed if you achieve anything less than absolute scrupulousness in your performance of the seder:

> *since feeling is first*
> *whoever pays any attention*
> *to the syntax of things*
> *will never wholly kiss you*
> —e. e. cummings

We say God and the imagination are one   —*Wallace Stevens*

Many Jews today are uncomfortable keeping Passover because they do not feel, or are bothered by, the concepts usually assumed to be religious. These "cultural Jews" do not identify with a particular organized wing of Judaism—Orthodox, Conservative, Reform, or Reconstructionist—but have racial, ethnic, and historic feelings about being Jewish, growing up Jewish in a Jewish family, knowing and being members of a unique and multiform tribe, Jewish education, attitudes toward books, politics, food, Israel, the Holocaust, Yiddish, and so on. None of this requires a set of beliefs. Indeed, Jews have no specific dogma, only a set of customs. Being Jewish, wanting to participate in the ritual of the seder, does not necessarily require any kind of religious belief. In fact, the word "Jewish," descended from Jacob's son Judah, or "Children of Israel," refers to our common ancestry and not to our beliefs. Yet a lack of conventional religious beliefs should neither limit the range of thoughts and feelings elicited by the unusual procedures of the seder, nor forbid us from choosing to participate in any arcane ancient practices and customs.

Those who are happily Jewish but feel an antipathy to what they perceive as Jewish law make a false dichotomy between law and custom: They are not two things, but one. We can feel as comfortable not eating bread at Passover as we are not eating a steak at Thanksgiving. There is no law that we must eat turkey at Thanksgiving, for example, it is only a custom; but most of us enjoy it and no one objects. Many post-Sixties Jews perceive themselves as non-practicing. They refuse to be bound by what they have allowed someone else to label as "law," and now they live in a world devoid of custom and ritual.

People often ask me, "Is there a Haggadah that does not mention God, the Jewish people, and Israel?" This is like asking to be shown a play in which there is no playwright, actor, or stage. In our ritual drama, the land of Israel is the universe or nature, the stage on which the Jewish people act out their relationship with God. That I and Thou relationship, in Martin Buber's terms, between God and the Jews, is our special story, but it is also a way that we can identify with the bondage and oppression of others. The Torah tells us to love the stranger, for once we were strangers in a strange land ourselves. For all those who can identify with our story, whether African-American slaves who sang "Go Down, Moses," or the Founding Fathers, who called George III "Pharaoh," the Atlantic Ocean "the Red Sea," and inscribed a bit of the Mosaic law on the Liberty Bell—"Proclaim liberty throughout all the land, unto all the inhabitants thereof" (Leviticus 25:10)—it is their story too:

> *Today I am as old in years as all the Jewish people. Now*
> *I seem to be a Jew. Here I plod through ancient Egypt.*
>
> —Yevgeny Yevtushenko

I understand why some Jews want to exclude these terms from their Haggadot. Some people find the story of the Jewish people, a Chosen People, exclusionary. Why our people, but no others? Some are opposed to the State of Israel for a variety of political and religious reasons. Some women feel excluded by the exclusively male ways of describing the divine—Father, Lord, and King. Some people are atheists and agnostics. The conventional conception of God, or any conception, makes them uncomfortable. Interestingly, many mystics and philosophers feel the same way. They take the ineffability of the holiest of God's names, YHVH, as an emblem for the divine. Just as it is unpronounceable, so God is unlimited, uncontained by definitions. They find any positive expression of God to be limiting and so avoid describing the divine. They too are uncomfortable separating God, Israel, and the Jewish people.

Holding these opinions does not make one less Jewish. Actually, this concern for exact expression reveals a passionate attachment to Judaism in spite of doctrinal differences. In fact, it is so important to some Jews that, rather than turn their backs on Jewishness, they will fight to the death about language. Something can be learned from all these positions, without letting words become intimidating bugaboos. We can be like Humpty Dumpty:

> *When I use a word . . . it means just what I choose*
> *it to mean. . . .*
> —Lewis Carroll

When some people say *God,* they imagine some kindly bearded figure watching over us from heaven; others think of an enormous ball of fire or the great and powerful Oz; someone else imagines all of Time and Space, the Source of all Existence, or the breakdown of the bicameral mind. None of these intellectual conceptions is that different from the others when judged against the awe we feel at the slightest touch of the infinite:

> *For Beauty's nothing but beginning of Terror we're still just*
> *able to bear, and why we adore it so is because it serenely*
> *disdains to destroy us.*
> —Rainer Maria Rilke

Words like God, Jewish, and Israel make some people uncomfortable, but they can be changed easily in the Haggadah into conceptions with which we are comfortable. Instead of letting them intimidate us and then becoming angry about that, we can fill them with the meanings that we think they should encompass:

I am large, I contain multitudes.
—Walt Whitman

These words can also be used as the vortices of discussion at the seder table, to bring out and resolve negative or ambiguous feelings we may have about them. In the meantime, remember: Although we cannot force our Passover story to be other than what it is, we can certainly find ways to extend its concepts of freedom into the present. Otherwise, how could there be so many different Haggadot?

That "Old Black Magic" That We Know So Well

We can understand the customs of the seder better if we see that they are rooted in folk magic. These practices were interpreted in a variety of ways by both kabbalists and halakhists (legalists). In most cases they went along with these practices. The kabbalist was able to transmute the dross of popular belief into the gold of mysticism, not unlike the Chinese Taoist philosophers. The legalist, already obsessed with proper performance, was poised on the edge of magic.

Since emancipation (that is, since the French Revolution when Napoleon "freed" the Jews and began the painful process of assimilation), this folk magic of our people has been an embarrassment to Jews who want to be perceived as modern, educated, normal, and bourgeois. Their strategy has been to play down the multicultural, push for tolerance, and maintain a low profile. They want Jews to be seen as normal people who happen to have the religion "Judaism," a splinter of what being Jewish is all about. They find much of Jewish practice and custom to be superstitious, aberrant, ignorant, and old-fashioned. Some of it is, and we should salute our enlightened coreligionists who helped to bring our people out of the Dark Ages. Most of us do not want to return to the exact way of life of the *shtetl*.

Many of these practices and customs are rooted in mythic ways of perceiving the world, in stories of our ancient and idiosyncratic tribe, and in symbolism. We do not want to lose these along with the paralyzing superstitions. We can enjoy all these wacky procedures for their very wackiness, like giving the Masonic grips and passwords. We are members of an exclusive club with elaborate rituals only we know. But the rituals have an element of the ridiculous:

> *The Secret is sacred but is always somewhat ridiculous.*
> —Jorge Luis Borges

Certainly, there is something silly about burning our bread crumbs, leaning to the left while eating and drinking, and removing drops of wine from our cups with our fingertips. Maybe it is all random and we can project meaning on to any string of images, symbols, ideas, words, numbers, and so on. Perhaps it is arbitrary, the result of a lot of strained invention. But what is not silly in ritual and belief?

> *It is believable since it is foolish.*
> —Tertullian

If the silliness of our customs is humbling to us, it is also humbling to the pomp and circumstance of the dominant culture around us, which generally chooses not to see that the emperor is stark naked. They are blind to it because there is nothing to place alongside of it for comparison. The variation on human behavior that the Jewish people perform calls into question the normality of what the majority do without thinking.

There is more to it than that, though. Unlike Freemasonry or other secret societies, where a minimal body of arbitrary custom was used as the underpinning to an enormous excrescence of fairly recent intellectual invention, the seder is the result of more than 3,300 years of human evolution in the creation of ritual. In spite of

certain Dadaist or enigmatic elements, completely appropriate on a
holiday devoted to freedom, the bulk of the seder ceremony represents an organic and consistent whole created not by a few brilliant
minds, but by the concerted actions of the Jewish people as a
whole. Though some of what we do may be silly, random, or arbitrary, most of it reflects the need we have to explain perplexing
aspects of the human condition to ourselves through the all-
embracing web of myth.

Today, when so many people, especially many young Jews, are
embracing Eastern religion or creating or recreating pagan, wiccan,
"Magickal," feminist, or men's movement rituals, it is ironic that
the pleasures, necessities, and ready-to-hand exoticism of the seder
ritual are often overlooked. Most newly created rituals, by their
very nature, will seem dated in just a few years. The seder will remain current well into the future, ceaselessly, almost imperceptibly,
adding new material about the Holocaust, Soviet Jews, or the State
of Israel as the need arises.

We run screaming from our own culture, from ourselves really; yet if anyone from India or Lapland or Japan allows us to
glimpse their customs, we are both flattered and charmed. If we
compare the seder to the Japanese tea ceremony, for instance, we
see that both are elaborate rituals that fully express the total cultures that generated them. Both are elaborations of the simple act
of getting together with people to eat and drink; both involve great
attention to the minutiae of preparation, presentation, and utensils; both allow for tremendous variations of practice, yet seem un-
changing in their overall performance. Is the tea ceremony a waste
of time; silly, old-fashioned, no longer pertinent to our lives; too
difficult, complicated, and painstaking; fenced around with too
much esoteric knowledge and detail? Its blend of aesthetics and
contemplativeness negates these criticisms. So why be embarrassed
about the same oddities and curiosities, now hoary with age, from

our own tribe? Enjoy them for their strangeness, their link to our ancestors, their aura of initiation and the inexplicable need we have to perform them:

> *Magic has power to experience and fathom things which*
> *are inaccessible to human reason. For magic is a great*
> *secret wisdom, just as reason is a great public folly.*
> —Paracelsus

Keeping Passover

Although the idea of "keeping Passover" has too often come to mean the strict observance of an unending string of ordinances, decrees, rules, regulations, testimonies, precepts, laws, and statutes, it can as well mean the safe*keeping* of something precious and worth preserving:

> *More than the Jews kept the Shabbos did the Shabbos*
> *keep the Jews.*
> —Achad ha-Am

We can say the same about our relationship with Pesach. Every spring for thousands of years now the Jewish people have had their spiritual batteries recharged during this remarkable holiday. We clean our homes and our psyches, deflate our bread and our egos, reconnect with our people and the rhythm of the seasons, celebrate life and freedom. There must always have been some who did it conscientiously, sloppily, rigidly, comfortably, scrupulously, casually, but still they did it:

> *Sometimes, because a person tries excessively hard to per-*
> *form a mitzvah in the very best way possible, he ends up*
> *not performing the mitzvah at all.*
> —Rabbi Nathan Sternhartz of Nemirov

A story is told of Rabbi Levi Yitzhak of Berdichev who performed a beautiful, devout, and holy seder, yet an inner voice told him that the seder of Chaim the water-carrier was more pleasing in the supernal world:

It seemed that Chaim had gotten drunk before Pesach, left his gathered chametz unburned, and awakened at the last moment on the evening of the seder. All he knew was that once we were slaves and God had redeemed us, and now we were slaves and God would redeem us again. At that point a miraculous table appeared, from which he ate and drank, toasted God, and said, "See, God, I drink this cup to you! And do you lean down to us and make us free!"

What was most pleasing in Chaim's seder was his direct comprehension of the meaning of the seder to him at that moment, and the intimate, immediate covenant relationship he had with his God.

What Chaim had achieved in his keeping of Passover had more vitality, meaning, joy, and holiness than any exact following of seder rules could have. That is what we all want to achieve. To do so, we need to give up the silly game of Jewish one-upsmanship—"My seder is purer than yours"—and realize that, *tuchis afn tish,* we are all Jews; and the fact that we all want to perform our ancient rituals in some fashion every spring is the tie that binds us together. When we embrace our past and our fellow Jews through enduring custom, it should be with the clasp of love and not the grip of rigor. After all, Ahavat Yisrael, love for our fellow Jews, is also a mitzvah (commandment). This book should help you to experience that attachment and love, to get the most out of whatever seder you have, and to expand your seder painlessly in whatever direction you choose to go. It should help you in keeping Passover.

Chapter Two

Shulchan Arukh:
The Prepared Table

A Festive Passover Meal

Shulchan Arukh, the prepared table, designates the meal in the middle of the seder, a break in the ritual when the Haggadot are set aside. For this simplest possible seder, we will set aside our Haggadot and deal only with the elaborate preparations—or as many of them as you choose to perform—that are necessary to set the Passover table.

In this chapter we limit the concept of the seder to a festive Jewish meal with family and friends. Even without ritual and text, you can still come together to relive the original seder, to celebrate the origins of the Jewish people and our freedom from slavery, to identify with our tribe and our history, and to do some psychic spring cleaning. If you find it is not enough, you can add more next year. If it is too much, scale it back next time:

> *Less is more.*
> —Robert Browning

For now, we will bring to the table everything necessary for a complete seder, but no ritual actions or text will be discussed. If you are a first-time celebrant or host, this should help you through the fairly complicated and painstaking task of setting—preparing—the table. The symbols will be explained when they make their appearance, but only to a point. So this chapter describes the bare minimum necessary for a seder: what you will need to allow people to come together for a festive and symbolic holiday meal. For some groups, *Dayyenu,* that might be enough.

It's a *Braw Brecht Moonlech Necht:* When to Have Your Seder

The first question is when to have your seder. In the Diaspora (that is, for Jews who live outside of Israel), Passover is eight days long; for Reform Jews and in Israel, it is seven days long. Traditionally we are to perform the seder on the first two nights of the holiday (for Reform Jews and in Israel, only on the first night).

The first night of Pesach falls on the fifteenth of the Jewish month of Nisan. Since the Jewish calendar is lunar, the first day of every month is the new moon, the first evening when we see the tiniest sliver of the moon, the merest grin of the Cheshire Cat. The fifteenth is the full moon. So, if we follow tradition, the first seder takes place on a bright, moonlit night.

Americans are used to having their holidays shifted around for the sake of mercantilism, convenience, and three-day weekends. We have gone for movable feasts in a big way. FDR started it by playing around with Thanksgiving. Now even the presidents' birthdays are not sacrosanct. We have come a long way from the days when people protested the change from the Julian calendar to the Gregorian calendar, demanding eleven days of their lives back. We have lost our awe of time since then.

The Jewish calendar, on the other hand, which moves in tandem with the moon, reminds us to look up at the sky, to notice its changes and our smallness. Since the Jewish lunar year is about 354 days long, eleven days shorter than the solar year, it must be adjusted on a regular basis to stay in alignment with the solar year. Otherwise Passover would sometimes be in the wrong season. This adjustment is done by intercalating a leap month on a regular basis. This constant shifting of the fifteenth of Nisan in relation to the solar year means that Passover can begin at any time from March 26 through April 23. Obviously, it neither falls on the same day of the week every year, nor even at the exact same time of the solar year. It will often fall on an inconvenient day, maybe the middle of the week instead of Saturday night or the day you are supposed to meet with your accountant to file your taxes.

Some people find that having a seder on a Wednesday, for instance, is difficult. They postpone their seder until the closest weekend evening or the night when everyone can most easily get together. They find it arduous to do all the elaborate things necessary to have a seder—shopping, cleaning, cooking, table preparation—in the middle of a work week. If that is true for you, it is better to have a seder on the wrong night than to have no seder at all.

The book of moonlight is not written yet.   —*Wallace Stevens*

We say we observe, rather than celebrate, our holidays, and in terms of the moon, that is true. We observe the phases of the moon in order to have our festivals on the right day. Our lunar, changeable, feminine calendar is a sacred cycle of days that pierces or intersects with the profane, rigid, male solar line of days:

> *We Jews fix our years by the moon, other nations by the sun.*
> *Those who depend on the sun are strong and fight for their*
> *survival and existence as long as fortune shines on them,*
> *but as soon as their sun sets, they vanish from the pages of*
> *history. Not so the People of Israel who live on and shine*
> *during the darkest stretches of the night, just like the moon,*
> *that sends forth its light in night's darkest hours.*

—Aryeh Leib, the second Gerrer Rebbe

Of course, we invent the structuring of time, but the solar calendar is the epitome of convenience for the sake of work, mammon, and the machine, while the Jewish lunar calendar goes against the grain of that efficient, streamlined sense of time. It was the Jewish calendar that first introduced the day of rest into the week. The pagans thought the ancient Jews were lazy in refusing to work one out of seven days.

The Jewish calendar imposes a kind of time that is in step with nature, the agricultural year, heavenly bodies, and human rhythms. Even the beginning and ending of the day is fluxional. Every new day begins at the actual moment of the sun's going down. By putting ourselves in tune with the ancient Jewish sense of time, we break the solar calendar's monopoly on time: "Sorry, I can't work Tuesday. It's Passover." We free ourselves from the slavery of repeating another tedious week, from rolling the rock of Sisyphus up that same hill again.

From the magical point of view, our ceremony is done at the right astronomical moment. Our being in tune with the universe means performing our human rituals in congruity with the operations of the rest of the universe. The arrival of, first, spring, the vernal equinox, and then the first full moon after that, is the time of Aries, the ram, and so our ancestors sacrificed their spring lamb, their *pesach,* at this time. In every generation we have added on to the meanings of the day, giving it renewed religious, political, cultural, even military content. On the fifteenth of Nisan in 73 C.E., the defenders of Masada committed suicide rather than submit to Rome. Almost two millennia later, the Battle of the Warsaw Ghetto began on the night of the first seder of 1943. Even if we reject magic and tradition, we might consider keeping faith at our sedarim with those Freedom Fighters by observing the night on which they chose to rise up against a twentieth-century Pharaoh.

So there is something to be said for observing Passover at the correct time. For a few moments, we can live in an entirely other time, a cyclical time that begins for us when we open our Haggadot, our once-upon-a-time story that is our passport to mythic time and our 4,000 years of history. We touch immortality:

> *Hold infinity in the palm of your hand and eternity in*
> *an hour.*
> —William Blake

It Happens Every Spring: Who to Invite

If this is the first time you have ever put on a seder, just getting everything to the table will seem a fairly daunting task. Before you even begin to set the table, you should decide how many people are coming and who they will be.

For the novice seder host, it is best to start with small groups and work up to larger parties. As with any gathering, the number of guests should not tax your ability to enjoy yourself. Last-minute changes of plans; unexpected arrivals of out-of-towners; nodding acquaintances who have the chutzpa (nerve) to invite themselves over; someone's new lover; strangers with nowhere to go—can all swell the proportions of the table. Be aware of your own limits: How many people can you feed and entertain?

As important as it is to have no more guests than you can handle, no guests at all makes for an empty celebration. We want to share our *simchah* (joy) beyond our own household. Having people over, giving of our largesse, confers speciality on the day. It is part of what makes a *yom tov* (holiday) memorable. We also want to hear how others celebrated the Passover in their homes, what they ate for the green vegetable, how they arranged the seder plate, and what melodies they sang. This enlarges the holiday beyond our little clan. The minimum necessary for a seder is three people, although even if you are alone, you should ask the four questions of yourself. When the rabbis met at Bene-Berak, they were only five. In the Israeli kibbutzim or a Miami hotel, hundreds may sit down together in a large hall with a public address system. Somewhere between these extremes, you will find the right size seder for your group.

Besides the number of guests, you might consider their compatibility. At the same time, you do not want to eliminate disagreement. There is a well-known Jewish saying that when you get two Jews together, you have three opinions. The freedom to disagree—grappling with tradition, wrestling, like Jacob, with the angel—should be the spice of your seder, furthering discussion and helping to frame thought.

Non-Jews at the Seder

A question frequently asked today is whether or not to invite gentiles. In the Jewish past, the seder was an oasis of freedom and safety for Jewish nomads wandering through a hostile world, "strangers in a strange land." No one would have thought to invite the oppressor into the home, nor would the non-Jew have been interested. Yet as early in this century as the Twenties, Rabbi Kook invited the British military governor of Palestine to his seder. I do not remember non-Jews at sedarim in the Fifties, but since the Sixties it has become quite common.

Still, the seder is an intimate event, reinforcing clan and tribal connections, and should be shared with those with whom you feel that kind of intimacy. Getting together with other Jews, both family and friends, who have shared similar seder experiences throughout their lives, will reinforce the *haimish* (homey) feeling that is our aim. If you have non-Jewish friends or family who are interested, comfortable, sympathetic, and respectful, by all means include them in. That does not mean we have to perform for anyone. The seder allows for drama, but frees us from exhibitionism. One of the nice parts of getting together with fellow Jews is that we can share moments of not being "the other," the outsider, someone else's symbol. We were all in bondage in Egypt, and we were all freed at the first Pesach.

Boredom Among the Guests

The presence of gentiles may actually enhance your seder. Non-Jews often take on the role of the child who does not know what to ask. In explaining everything to them, we become focused and tell ourselves aloud why it is we are drawn back year after year to this millennia-old ritual.

Surprisingly, it is often the Jewish guests who first become impatient or bored at a seder. Within a few moments of beginning, they are thrown back in time to unpleasant memories of childhood sedarim, scoldings for lack of attention and being disruptive, itchy wool pants, or stiff layers of crinoline, and waiting too long to eat. Now, as adults, they immediately regress to those childhood memories and have trouble sitting still through a ceremony that is certainly less painful than a bad movie. How we deal with the bad child within ourselves is one of the most difficult tasks for any seder celebrant. I can remember joking around with my cousins during sedarim, and how patient my grandfather was. He just kept plugging away at the text, ignoring our high jinks, occasionally rolling his eyes at my grandmother. We need to keep both perspectives in mind—the child's and the leader's—and have sympathy for both at all times.

Beating the Bounds: Children at the Seder

The Passover celebration is aimed at the child in all of us, allowing us to open our imaginations to rediscovering the lost elements of wonder, pleasure, and hilarity that are enclosed in this event. Having children at the seder can help make this happen.

If you have children of your own, you might want to have other children at your seder. This may help keep your own kids happy, interested, and occupied, while associating the holiday with visits from friends who share festive meals, join in holiday songs, and help search for the *afikoman*. (For more information on the role of children at the seder, see chapter 10.)

If we make our children unhappy, they will remember Passover, but not fondly. In the British Isles, there is a custom of taking sons out every year to "beat the bounds." Today they use the stick on the boundary markers, but they used to beat the boys at the site of those markers to ensure that they would remember the limits of ancestral property. Beating our ancient heritage into our children's psyches may make them remember, but is probably the reason so many people remember ritual and ceremony as intrinsically unpleasant. To encourage their enjoyment, try to begin early enough so that children do not get too hungry or sleepy or bored. The Talmud tells us that Rabbi Akiba distributed nuts and other snacks to his children so that they would be awake to ask the four questions. A late-afternoon meal will help to assuage hunger. Remember that the reason we do all of this is because of the biblical injunction:

> *And you shall tell your child on that day: "This is on account of what the Lord did for me when I came out of Egypt."*
> —Exodus 13:8

The Groaning Board: Keeping the Seder Under Control

One way to keep control of this complicated event is, paradoxically, to give up control. You do not have to take responsibility for every part of the seder. You might want to host the meal, but put someone else in charge of leading the ceremony. Or you may want to put a different person in charge of each section of the seder. Since there are fifteen sections to the seder (more on that in chapter 3), you can make each guest responsible for one or more of these parts. When it comes time to eat the *karpas* (the green vegetable), for example, one of the guests can make sure everyone has the parsley and saltwater. He or she might also want to explain the significance of that portion of the rite. This would allow each participant to really delve deeply into one particular part of the ceremony, more so than if only one person were leading the seder. As always, though, there should be a coordinator who makes sure that you are not unleashing fifteen anarchic mini-sedarim.

Likewise, you might turn the dinner into a potluck with one *baleboosteh* (chief cook and bottle washer) who makes sure dinner does not become six sponge cakes. If *kashrut* (strictness of observing food laws) is a concern, be sure that everyone agrees to the same rules beforehand. If there is going to be a vegetable dish, and some guests follow the strict Ashkenazic Passover prohibition of legumes, which are *kitniyot* (foods, other than grains, that can become leavened), be sure that string beans are not the vegetable dish. On the other hand, if no one observes the rule forbidding legumes, then by all means serve *haricots verts*—the Sephardim do.

The Invited: Seder Etiquette

What if you are just a guest? No one need be "just" a guest at a seder. Minimally, you are a celebrant, both performer and audience for the ritual drama. You participate in the ceremony and join with the other celebrants in creating a holy convocation, a group that exists somewhere between family, clan, and tribe. Being part of a seder confers a specialness on you. You bring off the mysteries with your seder group. Possibly you will meet with them for many other sedarim, enlarging the meaning of your belonging to that seder group. Perhaps you will go to other sedarim and bring your memories of seder thoughts, feelings, rituals, foods, songs, jokes, and stories to them. Either way, those who go to a seder attach themselves to the Jewish people:

> *You are assisting at a celebration.*
> —Stéphane Mallarmé

Offer to bring a dish, but be careful not to violate anyone's food restrictions. Just because something is Jewish or kosher does not make it kosher for Pesach (see chapter 9 for more details on kosher foods). Do not bring chametz like kasha (buckwheat groats) or a loaf of challah (Sabbath egg bread) to a seder. Check with the seder-givers on the parameters of food strictness. You might want to offer to bring one or more of the ceremonial foods: shelled hard-boiled eggs, individual portions of a green vegetable like parsley or a bitter herb like romaine, a fresh horseradish root, homemade beet horseradish, an unusual *charoset* preparation, or a box of matzo—especially one from Israel, or better still, Bene-Berak.

A bottle of kosher wine, either a sweet or a dry red wine, makes a nice contribution. (See chapter 9 for some suggestions on finding a good kosher wine). Offer to bring extra soup bowls, serving bowls and spoons, wine glasses, and so on, or cloths and napkins for the matzo and afikoman. If you own a beautiful seder plate, matzo cover, or Elijah's cup, volunteer them. Flowers (if no one has hay fever), besides being beautiful and fragrant, make a good spring symbol. A beautiful or unusual Haggadah makes an appropriate present, as does a box of *Pesachdikhe* candy—the more retro and nostalgic, the better.

Be prepared to help with setting the table, clearing the table, and washing the dishes, but take your lead from the seder-givers. They may not want everyone in the kitchen at the same time, if at all, and they may have their own timetable, based on the exigencies of the ceremony. To accommodate cleanup, some families take a longer break than others between the pre- and postprandial parts of the seder. One group may want to eat, quickly clear the table, and finish the ceremony, while another may eat, do the dishes, *shmoos* (talk) over tea and coffee, sponge cake, and afikoman, and then finish the ceremony. This may depend on how abridged or participatory the seder proper is and on whether children are present.

Do not just observe during the seder. Put in your two cents worth. Tell a story, volunteer a memory or a recipe, sing the songs. You do not have to be the life of the party or a mavin (authority), and you certainly do not want to monopolize the conversation, but you have a role to play in the drama of the seder. Pay attention to where you are in the proceedings, but do not feel bad if you occasionally read ahead or become absorbed in your own thoughts and feelings.

If you have never been to a seder or have not been to one in a long time, you may want to ask your host which Haggadah is going to be used so that you can get a copy of it to read ahead of time. (See chapter 5 for a list of Haggadot.) You may also want to get a tape of the songs that will be sung so you can join in (see the list in chapter 7 for some suggestions). No one cares how well you sing. Enthusiasm is a good substitute for talent.

Making a List, Checking It Twice: Symbols on the Table

Once you know you are going to have a seder and who is coming, you can clean the house, shop, cook, and set the table. In this chapter that is all we are going to do. Make a timetable for cleaning, shopping, and cooking that will allow you to satisfy your needs and still enjoy the seder. Get as much done on evenings and weekends before the seder as possible. You may want to prepare some dishes ahead, like soup stock or sponge cake, and freeze them until needed.

Setting the table is more important on Passover than on any other night of the year. Doing it so that everything is to hand when it is needed during the seder can mean the difference between a long, boring, drawn-out, bumbled-through seder and a naturally flowing, fresh, compact banquet. Make a checklist to keep from forgetting to put out any of the following items, and give yourself at least a full hour to arrange them on the table.

The Three Matzot (in a Napkin or Cloth Cover)

Matzo is the single most important symbol of the whole evening. We might dispense with everything else, but we would still need matzo to have a seder. Strictly speaking, only the first night of the holiday is Passover, but all eight days are Chag ha-Matzot, the Feast of Unleavened Bread.

It is customary to cover the matzot and to separate them from one another. You can do this with a large napkin, or you can use one of the commercially made three-pocketed matzo holders. You may also want to get a separate bag to hold the afikoman, the larger part of the broken middle matzo, which is reserved so there will be some matzo available as the last thing we eat at the seder.

We eat matzo because our ancestors ate it in the land of Egypt. But what is the symbolism? First, we eat matzo to give thanks for a successful winter wheat crop, just as the paschal lamb is our thanks for an abundance of spring lambs. Second, in a direct way, we are reminding ourselves that no matter how rich, famous, knowledge-able, or powerful we are today, we were once slaves in the land of Egypt. This reaffirmation of our common origin heightens the de-mocratic feeling at the seder table and within the Jewish commu-nity. When we become puffed up with the yeast of pride, our flat, simple matzo should remind us of our origins and help us to iden-tify with others who are enslaved, homeless, and hungry:

> *All of us are equal, and though you are poor you will not feel*
> *estranged at my table, for all of us were impoverished in*
> *Egyptian bondage.*
> —Don Isaac Abrabanel

When the Jews were expelled from Spain in 1492, Don Isaac, their leader, was exempted from that expulsion, but chose to join his people in exile. There is a pathetic irony, a sense of previousness in his words that points up our constant exile and the constant and recurring relevance of the seder ceremony.

Why three matzot? Because the Israelites who wandered in the wilderness for forty years received a double portion of manna be-fore the Sabbath, it is traditional to have two loaves of challah on Shabbat and festivals. Since matzo, the only form of wheat we can eat during Pesach substitutes for bread, we need two pieces. We also need a piece between these two pieces that can be broken in half for the afikoman, the hidden matzo. The small, broken piece represents matzo as the bread of affliction, the poor bread. Paradoxically, matzo is both a symbol of our slavery, and of the sudden freedom that rushed us out of Egypt without enough time to let our dough rise.

The three matzot, from top to bottom, also stand for the three surviving Jewish tribes: Kohen, Levi, and Yisrael. Other interpretations refer to the three Patriarchs, Abraham, Isaac, and Jacob; the three cakes of unleavened bread that Sarah made for the three angelic visitors who informed her of the future birth of her son Isaac; or the three portions of flour offered in thanksgiving by a freed prisoner, certainly an appropriate metaphor for our release from slavery.

Even though you will want to eat from the three matzot to fulfill the various seder requirements, you will also want to have plates full of extra matzo available as well.

You can use any kosher-for-Passover matzo for your seder, but the handmade *shemurah* (watched or guarded) matzo has a unique flavor, though it is occasionally on the stale or burnt side. In addition, shemurah matzot, which are round, asymmetrical, warped, and often slightly charred, reinforce the concept of the circularity of the year and the return of spring (see chapter 13 for a discussion of the Jewish holiday cycle); give the seder a taste of antiquity, as if you are eating the matzo of the first seder; and invite questions.

The wheat used in shemurah matzot is watched from the time of harvest until water is added to the flour. The water for all matzo must be drawn at night from a well, from the earth, as it were, and then allowed to "rest" until morning. The sun cannot shine on this water, even though the baking is in the daytime, so the rooms where matzo is made are shielded from sunlight. Only eighteen minutes, a significant number (as explained in chapter 6), can elapse once the water is added to the flour before the baked matzo is removed from an oven whose temperature may reach 2,500 degrees Fahrenheit.

Incidentally, matzot have not always been thin. During the Middle Ages, they were at least an inch thick.

The Seder Plate

The seder plate, or k'areh, holds six (sometimes five) of the primary symbols of the meal: zero'a, betzah, maror, charoset, karpas, and chazeret. There are many arrangements for the k'areh, according to which of a diverse group of authorities you choose to follow. Many fancy seder plates sold commercially have decorations, illustrations, and symmetrical or geometrical arrangements that ignore the various rabbinical patterns. You may also choose not to arrange the items, allowing the jumbled montage on the plate to display the symbols powerfully enough.

The most popular arrangement is that of the sixteenth-century Rabbi Isaac Luria, the Ari (Lion), who lived in the spiritual community of Safed in the Galilee along with fellow mystics Solomon Alkabetz, Moses Cordovero, and Joseph Caro. Coincidentally, this chapter's title, *Shulchan Arukh,* is also the name of Rabbi Caro's definitive compilation of *The Code of Jewish Law,* still the basis for Jewish practice today. The teachings of the Safed mystics transformed the kabbalistic or mystical conception of the Judaism of that time, and they are still dominant as we approach the end of the twentieth century. After we look at the individual symbols, we will see why the Ari's kabbalistic arrangement of the seder plate remains compelling to this day.

Most families today consider the seder plate's token amounts of ritual foods as strictly a set of symbols, and do not actually eat them during the seder. If you would like to get closer to the concept of that first seder in Egypt, use the seder plate as a shared

The arrangement of the k'areh according to the
sixteenth-century Rabbi Isaac Luria, the Ari of Safed

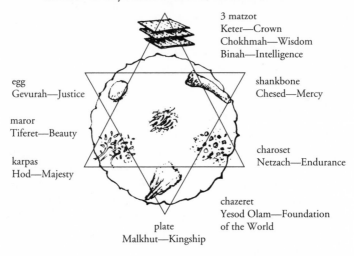

3 matzot
Keter—Crown
Chokhmah—Wisdom
Binah—Intelligence

egg
Gevurah—Justice

shankbone
Chesed—Mercy

maror
Tiferet—Beauty

karpas
Hod—Majesty

charoset
Netzach—Endurance

chazeret
Yesod Olam—Foundation
of the World

plate
Malkhut—Kingship

source for the symbolic foods. Put large enough portions of the six
symbolic foods on the k'areh so that everyone can help themselves
from the communal seder plate. Alternatively, you might make up
small individual seder plates so that everyone has their own personal set of symbols, or at least those that are eaten, in front of
them.

Zero'a, a Roasted Lamb Shankbone

The ancient Israelites came to the Temple in Jerusalem to sacrifice
on three occasions: Pesach (Passover), Shavuot (Weeks), and Sukkot
(Booths). The special Passover sacrifice was the spring lamb, the
paschal offering. Agriculturally, it represented the successful birth
of new lambs in the flock. One was offered to God in thanks. Historically, it represented the lamb whose blood was smeared on the
doorposts and lintels of the homes of the Israelites in Egypt. (The
mezuzot we affix to our doorposts today are a variation of that

The k'areh according to the Rema, Rabbi Moses Isserles

The k'areh according to the Gaon of Vilna

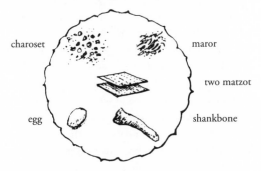

The k'areh according to other authorities

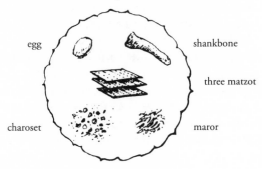

protective lamb's blood.) God "passed over" the homes of the Israelites on the night of the first seder, sparing our firstborn but
killing the firstborn of Egypt. Safe in their homes, but with their
loins girded, their shoes on their feet, and their staffs in their hands,
the Israelites ate the meat of that roasted lamb, in haste and without
breaking its bones.

Today, when there is no Temple, we cannot sacrifice, and so
Ashkenazic Jews avoid roast lamb at the seder (though Sephardim
serve lamb to remember the first seder meal). The lamb is present
by proxy in the form of the roasted shankbone. Zero'a means fore-
arm, and is suggestive of the "outstretched arm" of God, which delivered us from the house of bondage. If you are unable to get a
lamb shankbone, you may use a *gorgle* (chicken neckbone), or any
roasted bone from a kosher animal. Perhaps the gorgle suggests
that God stuck his neck out for the Israelites.

It is traditional to eat the roasted lamb shankbone for lunch on
the second day of Pesach, but if you want to eat the zero'a at the
seder, you can boil it instead of roasting it. You will then have to boil
another if you are having a second seder. The lamb shankbones that
kosher butchers give away have been stripped of all their meat; so if
you intend to get any nourishment from the zero'a, you might pay a
few dollars for a bit of shankbone from the end of a leg of lamb. It
will look better on the plate than the free, symbolic splinter. If you
are a vegetarian, the Talmud allows you to substitute a roasted beet.

There is still one Jewish community that does sacrifice lambs
every year. These are the few hundred remaining Samaritans in
Israel, the last remaining descendants of the people brought in
by the Assyrians in 722 B.C.E. to replace the exiled Jews. They
adopted Jewish ways, although they were rejected by the returning
exiles later. (The New Testament mentions them in the story of the
Good Samaritan.) At Passover, they camp out at the foot of Mount
Gerizim, where each family sacrifices and spit-roasts its lamb just as
the ancient Israelites did in the time of the Temple.

Betzah, a Roasted Egg

The roasted egg stands for the roasted Chagigah (pilgrimage) offering that each Israelite brought to the Temple on all three of the pilgrimage festivals. Since new life comes from the egg, it makes a good symbol for spring, a time of rebirth. Because the egg is round, it stands for the end of the old year and the beginning of the new, a never-ending circle. In the same way, it symbolizes the wheel of fortune. Though the Jewish people have experienced many tragic moments, the wheel can turn and bring us good fortune again. Jews eat hard-boiled eggs when they return from a burial, so it is also a symbol of mourning for the destroyed Temple.

Like all of the symbols at the table, it is ambiguous, paradoxical, and contradictory, actually empty and waiting to be filled with meaning by us. Magically speaking, by beginning the meal with the egg, we convince the demons that we are mourning, not celebrating, so they leave us alone. As you will see, the seder is packed with such anti-demonics, ways of averting the evil eye and warding off bad luck.

It is interesting to note that Christians have borrowed this symbol of the egg as the Easter egg, just as they have interpreted the symbol of the paschal Lamb as Jesus, the matzo and wine as his body and blood, and the seder itself as his last supper. In the Gospel of John in the New Testament, we find two interesting echoes of Passover. When Jesus is about to die, "They filled a sponge with vinegar, and they put it upon hyssop, and put it to his mouth" (John 19:29). A few moments later, the soldiers break the legs of the two thieves on either side of Jesus. "But when they came to Jesus, and saw that he was dead already, they brake not his legs" (19:33). The Israelites had been commanded to smear the lamb's blood on their doorposts with hyssop, and they were forbidden to break any bones of the paschal sacrifice. Was this coincidence, "the historical consciousness of the myth's biological necessity," or clever addition of detail to the story to match the expectations of the original Judean audience? Like all great myths, the Passover story resonates with the unconscious because its details continually repeat in all our lives and in every generation.

To prepare the egg, first hard-boil it to keep it from exploding when you actually roast it. Some add the outer skin of an onion to the water to brown it, or you could start with a brown egg. Once it's hard-boiled, you can either hold it over a flame for a while, put it in a 400 degree Fahrenheit oven for about half an hour along with the shank bone, or put it under the broiler until brown. This gives it a nice cracked and speckled look—even the simplest tasks have their aesthetic.

The self-revelation we achieve in discovering our own taste in these things is part of reclaiming Passover for ourselves, making it enjoyable and not merely obligatory. The kabbalists say that the Torah has 600,000 faces, one for each of the Children of Israel who took part in the Exodus. Not only does this mean that we all receive a unique and personal message from the Torah, but we each have a unique understanding to share with others:

> *To none other than he . . . will it be given to understand*
> *it in this special and individual way that is reserved to him.*
> —Moses Cordovero

Some Sephardim have the custom of the firstborn child concluding the meal by eating the roasted egg while concealed behind a door, linking the redemption of the firstborn with a Temple sacrifice and doorways. Alternatively, the *ba'al he-seder* or an unmarried woman may eat it.

Karpas, a Green Vegetable

Karpas literally means parsley, but in my family, and many others, karpas was a peeled boiled potato. Eating the boiled potato dipped in saltwater was always one of my favorite parts of our family sedarim, but I could not understand how the potato could be considered green.

The answer is that the Eastern European Jews had few green vegetables, but many root crops, so the familiar potato had to take the place of something green. By metonymy, its green shoots conferred greenness on the whole plant. Since the karpas is an appetizer and we do not eat again for a while, the somewhat filling potato works well at this point in the seder. Other vegetables, like celery, cucumber, onion, and radishes, can also be used. Parsley is traditional and truly green.

Have a bowl of whatever you are using for karpas on the table as well as on the seder plate. If you use potatoes, you can skip salting the cooking water since the karpas will be dipped in saltwater just before it is eaten.

Some traditions identify the karpas dipped in saltwater with the Israelites purified by passing through the salty Red Sea. Symbolically, the Red Sea is the narrow birth canal of the Jewish people, our exit out of Mitzrayim (Egypt), the dark womb of our incubation. Mitzrayim is formed from the same Hebrew root as limitation, and Passover can be seen as the dark rite of passage from the limitation of winter to the birth of the new year, a time fraught with both danger and possibility. Others see the parsley as the green hyssop dipped in lamb's blood used to mark the Israelite doorposts, a protective device as we pass through the two-faced, Janus-headed doorway of one year and into the next.

As green vegetable, karpas is another spring symbol. Passover, which falls on the full moon of the month of Nisan, the first month of the Jewish year, marks both Aviv (spring) and New Year. (There is more than one Jewish New Year. Rosh Hashanah in the fall and Tu bi-Shevat, the New Year of the Trees, in late January or early February are other Jewish New Years.)

Maror, a Bitter Herb

We eat maror, a bitter herb, to remember that the Egyptians made our lives in exile bitter with bondage:

> *Forgetfulness leads to exile, while remembrance is the secret of redemption.*
> —Ba'al Shem Tov

It was only in the late sixteenth century that freshly sliced or grated raw horseradish (*chrain*) became the most common choice for maror. For centuries romaine lettuce was the preferred bitter herb, and the Jews of Yemen still frame or circumscribe the whole table with a protective ring of romaine. The rabbis were obsessive in their instructions on cleaning it to avoid worms and other bugs that clung to the stalks. The somewhat exotic romaine was often difficult to get in Eastern Europe, and its rarity led to the triumph of horseradish, a readily available root crop. Today we can get romaine easily and it is returning in popularity as maror.

Personally, I cannot imagine Passover without horseradish—not only for the intense pleasure/pain we get when we eat it ritually with matzo, but also, in prepared form, as a condiment for gefilte fish and brisket. Its flavor is an intrinsic part of the holiday, and its combination of pleasure and pain makes a good analog for the bittersweet nature of our memories at Passover: We remember good times with family and friends, often with those who are no longer with us or are far away, and we give our brief lives added dimension by linking them to the past of our people, the pain and triumph of Jewish history. As the Irish fiddler Seamus Connolly once said in the name of his mother, "We're never so happy as when we're crying." We never enjoy the horseradish so much as when it brings tears to our eyes.

Slice or grate the horseradish just before the holiday begins, and keep it covered in the refrigerator so it retains its pungency.

There is a wonderful custom that if you forget to grate the horse-radish until after the seder has begun, it is permissible to do it then as long as you turn the grater upside down. Beyond the obvious attempt to trick the devil, like walking through a doorway backwards, this emphasizes the topsy-turvy sense of the day and piques the children's curiosity. Be sure to have an extra bowl of horseradish for the table.

Charoset, the Mortar: Clay, Straw, and Blood

In Ashkenazic tradition charoset is usually chopped apples and nuts mixed with wine and cinnamon, though many combinations of fruits and nuts are used around the world. The apples and nuts represent the clay of the bricks the Israelites made in order to build Pharaoh his pleasure cities of Pithom and Ramses. The cinnamon stands for the straw in the mortar. The wine is the blood of our ancestors spilled in bondage, or the blood of the baby Hebrew boys thrown into the Nile. In Hebrew, wine is called "blood of the grape."

I want my charoset to be as much like my grandmother's as possible, but obviously there is a great deal of latitude available to the charoset maker. I use crisp apples, like Granny Smith or Jonathan, and leave the peel on them; other people peel the apples. I chop them finely with walnuts; others may grind the walnuts, or (based on verses in the Song of Songs) use almonds or filberts. I add powdered cinnamon and sweet kosher wine, while others shred stick cinnamon and fresh ginger so that the mixture has the look and texture of the mortar that the Israelites were forced to make.

The Sephardim are much more adventurous than the Ashkenazim in making their chutney-like charoset, and in chapter 8 we will explore the range of these more exotic concoctions. One of the most literal yet inventive representations of charoset was conceived during the American Civil War, when a group of Jewish Union soldiers made a seder for themselves in the wilderness of West Virginia.

They had none of the ingredients for traditional charoset handy, so they put a real brick in its place on the seder tray.

Children love making and eating charoset. After they have chopped and mixed all the ingredients, have them shape it into a pyramid for presentation. Besides being fun, this strengthens the symbolism of the charoset and helps them to realize what our ancient Israelite ancestors accomplished while in slavery:

> *Who built the seven gates of Thebes? In the books are listed the names of kings. Did the kings heave up the building blocks?*
>
> —Bertolt Brecht

Make sure you have plenty of extra charoset.

Chazeret, the Top and Green Sprouts of the Horseradish Root

Some arrangements of the seder plate overlook chazeret, the top and green sprouts of the horseradish root, because as another bitter herb, it is redundant. Perhaps in America we no longer feel we need to symbolize our suffering at double strength. Most seder plate diagrams include it, however, and it is necessary for our symbolic purposes.

I like to buy my horseradish early, cut off the top, and allow it to sprout luxuriantly in a bowl of water. It makes another good symbol for spring, and everyone marvels at it when they see it on the seder plate. Elaborations that are out of the ordinary generate the questions that are central to the seder experience.

When you buy the horseradish root, which can be difficult to find, be sure it is neither spongy nor moldy. It should be as firm or firmer than a carrot or parsnip. If you can't find horseradish root, you can use a sprouting carrot or radish top.

Some people use the chazeret as the bitter herb in the korekh or Hillel sandwich. They might use horseradish for the first bitter herb and romaine as the chazeret, although you can use the same herb for both chazeret and maror. Indeed, chazeret means lettuce. Some use sliced horseradish for the maror and grated horseradish for the chazeret. After Passover you can plant the horseradish top in your backyard, and in a couple of years you will have your own homegrown chrain.

Hard-Boiled Eggs

It is traditional to begin the actual meal with a hard-boiled egg either dipped into the saltwater, or mashed up in the saltwater as a kind of cold, salted hard-boiled-egg soup. To save time, make the eggs earlier in the day, then chill and shell them before the seder.

Why an egg? Well, it certainly reinforces all the meanings of the roasted egg, but my favorite interpretation is the one that says that the hard-boiled egg is like the Jewish people: The hotter you make it for them, the tougher they get.

Saltwater

The saltwater represents the tears and sweat of the Israelites in bondage. Both the karpas and the hard-boiled egg are dipped into the saltwater. Mix this up ahead of time in a large jar or pitcher to your own taste. Give everyone their own small bowl of saltwater. Cider vinegar is an acceptable substitute. Some families put a bowl of saltwater on the seder plate.

The water performs the same function as the *mikveh* (ritual bath) or the Israelites' passage through the Red Sea: purification through immersion. Salt, like bitter herbs, is another anti-demonic. In Jewish tradition it is used to purify meat by drawing blood out of it in the kashering process, just as the High Priest in the Temple service used salt on the sacrifice. The prophet Elisha used salt to purify the water of Jericho. Every new home must have salt and bread. Every table must have salt on it, and bread is normally dipped in salt. There are conflicting views as to whether matzo needs to be dipped in salt at the seder, but most do not salt.

Pillows or Cushions for Reclining

The rabbis added the act of reclining while eating during the seder in imitation of Greek and Roman styles of banqueting. They wanted us to eat in the manner of free people and not as slaves. The seder should be seen as a freewheeling Platonic symposium held together by the story of the Exodus. As in a Greco-Roman banquet, the seder has multiple hand washings, continuous wine-drinking, an elaborate sequence of courses beginning with an appetizer, and a wide range of talk and song, as well as reclining. You can either give everyone a pillow or just give one to the *ba'al ha-seder,* who represents the whole company.

Wine Glasses and Bottles of Wine

Everyone needs a wine glass in order to fulfill the commandment to drink the *arba kosot,* the four cups of wine. For those who cannot or do not drink wine, grape juice will do. Some of the children will prefer grape juice, although we kids always had a small shot glass of sweet wine for each of the four cups. If wine and grape juice are both unacceptable, you may substitute fruit juice, tea, or coffee.

Our ancestors knew that wine might lead to drunkenness and excess, as in the cases of Noah and Lot; but they also knew that in the proper sacramental context, it can be intoxicating in a positive way: It can be the doorway to the divine frenzy of the poet. It can certainly enhance a celebration. We do not want to become sloppily drunk, but we should aim for a certain exaltation. You might want to try some of the good dry kosher red wines that have become available from Israel, California, and Europe in the last few years. You will probably want to provide a few bottles of traditional, nostalgia-laden, sweet kosher red wine on the table as well.

Custom urges us to use red wine, which is considered superior, but white is acceptable too. During the worst periods of the blood libel, which began in England during the twelfth century, Jews were accused of using the blood of Christian children to make their Pesach wine. The rabbis encouraged the use of white wine to avoid this paranoid and unfounded allegation. Ironically, pagan opponents had hurled the same accusations at early Christians. Bernard Malamud's novel *The Fixer*, based on the early twentieth-century Beilis case in Russia, reminds us that this anti-Semitic slur has not disappeared even in our own "enlightened" time.

We drink four cups of wine because of the four types of redemption that God performed for the Israelites:

> *I shall* bring you out *from under the burdens of the Egyptians, and I shall* deliver you *from their bondage, and I shall* redeem you *with an outstretched arm, and with great judgments. And I shall* take you *to me for a people . . .*
> —Exodus 6:6–7

Four (and any other even number) is usually considered unlucky (see chapter 6 for a discussion of the meaning of numbers), but on this protected night we ignore that belief. We want to toast our deliverance and invite the deliverer to our table. Because the passage continues with "I shall *bring you in* unto the land," some authorities believe that a fifth cup is needed, especially since the creation of the state of Israel. In the past the cup of Elijah was that fifth cup, waiting for realization, the final redemption. It also provides a little bit of extra protection just in case four should turn out to be unlucky. Today the fifth cup is optional, and is usually added between the third and fourth cups. Others allow wine to be drunk throughout the seder except between the third and fourth cup.

The fact that you are to have four cups of wine should not restrict the method in which you have them. You can belt them down in four fell swoops, or sip your way from one to the next. You can also have more than four cups, since wine drunk during the meal is not counted. We drink to celebrate our freedom, and we are free to drink.

Cup of Elijah, or Kos Eliyahu

It is said that the Prophet Elijah is present at every *bris* and every seder. He wanders the globe in the guise of a beggar to see if the Jewish people continue to remember to be kind to the stranger, the poor, and the outcast. On some occasion it is presumed that he will herald the coming of the Messiah, an age of universal peace and freedom. Even more miraculously, he will reconcile parents and children. In the meantime we set a place for him at the seder table by filling a large cup with wine in his honor, just as we provide a chair for him at a bris.

Children often watch to see if the level of the wine decreases during the seder. It always seemed to me that it had slightly. The glass that my grandfather used for the cup of Elijah had a long, Mexican name etched on it. All of us grandchildren wondered who this man was, and in my imagination he became one of Elijah's pseudonyms, perhaps the name he used now that he had retired to Puerto Vallarta.

After the seder you can return the wine from Elijah's cup to the bottle, as the Lubavicher Chasidim do; or, if this seems sacrosanct, you can save it for Kiddush at the second seder. The wine from that night's cup of Elijah can be used for the next Shabbat Kiddush.

It is said that all unanswered questions will be answered by Elijah when he comes to herald the Messiah. The cup of Elijah thus represents the rabbis' way of resolving the question as to whether there should be four or five cups of wine. Some people have the *minhag* (custom) of sharing the wine in Elijah's cup among all the celebrants after the fourth cup. One Chasidic *tzaddik,* Rabbi Naphtali Tzevi Ropshitser, had the custom of filling Elijah's cup with a small portion from everyone's third cup to indicate the human contribution necessary to effect redemption. Some families have the cup of Elijah full throughout the seder, while others fill it between the third and fourth cups. Besides the fact that we open the door for Elijah after the third cup, we are also less likely to spill his cup if we fill it after the meal.

Saucers (Optional)

Saucers, often of broken crockery, are sometimes used to catch spilled drops of wine. If you do not perform the ceremony of removing drops of wine in token of the ten plagues inflicted on the Egyptians, you will not use the saucers.

Candles, Candlesticks, and Matches (Optional)

If you omit all ritual, you will not light candles to demarcate the boundary between the sacred and the profane and to usher in the holiday. There are a number of kinds of Jewish *licht* (lights): Chanukkah candles, which burn too briefly; Havdalah (separation of the sacred and profane) candles, which are unacceptable because the merging of two or more wicks forms a torch instead of a candle; *yahrzeit* (memorial) candles, which burn too long and are inappropriate since they commemorate the anniversary of someone's death; and candles for Shabbat and festivals. These are usually white, burn about four hours, and contain no chametz or *trayf* (unkosher) materials. White candles are traditional, though not mandatory, and match the white clothing and tablecloths of the evening.

Pitcher of Warm Water, Bowl, and Towel (Optional)

If you perform the ritual hand washing that occurs twice during the seder, you will need a pitcher of warm water, bowl, and towel.

Again, if the complexity of your seder does not go beyond this first chapter, you can skip these items.

Yarmulkes

You may want to provide yarmulkes, *kippot,* or skullcaps, for those who want to wear them. I feel naked saying Hebrew with my head uncovered, yet other people feel silly wearing a skullcap or kippah. For me, putting on a yarmulke is one more action that separates the ceremonial world from the mundane. A nice-fitting, large, heavy, black satin yarmulke has a cozy feeling. For most of us, it is our last remaining vestige of Jewish costume, another link to our ancient Near Eastern origins. In the West we put on shoes and un-cover our heads to show respect. In the East we remove shoes and cover our heads to do the same.

I dislike those little knitted *kippot,* or the polyester ones that slip off your head, but that is a matter of personal taste. If you are com-fortable with a kippah, however, wearing it can aid in the transfor-mation from the profane to the sacred. You can also choose from the colorful hats of the Jews of Bokhara, Chasidic *spodiks* and *shtraymels,* even a baseball cap, a ten-gallon John B. Stetson, or a Sherlock Holmes-style deerstalker. Our grandfathers *davened* (prayed) like jazz musicians at a jam session, and they covered their heads with whatever hat they normally wore. Sometime after World War II, we stopped wearing those hats. The yarmulke is merely a convenience; anything that covers the head is acceptable.

Some go further than just covering their heads and wear a white garment called a *kittel,* indicative of purity. A *gartel,* a cloth belt, is tied around the waist so that we have our loins girded, as did our ancestors at the first seder. If this seems too formal or you feel foolish in an ecclesiastical garment, consider wearing white clothing and a white yarmulke. The Sephardim and the Lubavicher Chasidim, as a matter of fact, do not wear a kittel at the seder. For those who wear it, the kittel recalls the garments worn by the

Kohanim (priests) in the Temple service. It is also worn at Yom Kippur services, by the groom at a wedding, and as a shroud. To the twentieth-century mind, this seems morbid; but it is common for people to mitigate their happiness at festivals with some show of the awareness of our inevitable end—witness the Mexican Day of the Dead. We give the devil his due so that he does not come to take it. Much Jewish magic is concerned with propitiating malevolent forces. An occasional reminder to make us aware of our common finale is a philosophical way of doing this:

> *There are events of such overbearing magnitude that one ought not to remember them all the time, but one must not forget them either.*

—Rabbi Israel Spira of Bluzhov

Haggadot (Optional)

If you use any text, you will need some form of haggadah. This will be discussed in detail in chapter 5.

Symbola Aureæ Mensæ: From Symbol to Meaning

I do not want to limit the meanings of symbols to what others have said or what I might say. The proper performance of a seder, no matter how limited or extended that seder might be, occurs when the participants experience the meaning through their actions. Ritual, like poetry or Torah, is an empty vessel that we must fill with meaning:

> *I placed a jar in Tennessee, and round it was, upon a hill.*
> *It made the slovenly wilderness surround that hill.*

—Wallace Stevens

As Jews today, we have left Egypt but have yet to cross over Jordan. We wander through the desert and need the seder ritual to bring that wilderness into some kind of order. The fact that charoset represents the mortar of Egyptian bondage, or that the hard-boiled egg symbolizes mourning for the Temple, the curving-back-on-itself cycle of the year or the toughness in adversity of the Jewish people may be less important at some particular seder than the Proustian remembrances evoked by our first bite of matzo or some fresh perception that erupts from the table talk.

I remember one seder when we came to the passage from Psalm 113, the Hallelujah, where God "lifts the needy out of the *dunghill,*" I turned to my uncle and said "That's a *pile of crap.*" Almost wordlessly, and almost without laughing, we shared a particularly Jewish, intellectual appreciation of a good joke that I have never forgotten.

Ah, Sweet Mystery of Life at Last I've Found You: Jewish Mysticism

Why have we made these elaborate preparations? We understand the obvious concept: We do this because if God had not freed our people from bondage, we might still be slaves in Egypt. We can also understand how the individual symbols build on that theme, but what about their elaborate interconnection on the seder plate? Here we must learn at least a little kabbalah, Jewish mysticism.

Kabbalah is a unique form of mysticism because it represents the transcendental experiences of an unusual ethnic group, the Jews. Our mysticism is rooted in our intense relation to our sacred texts and their study and our history, a repetition of similar oppressions and partial redemptions for millennia.

At the same time, kabbalah also reveals a Jewish interest in the lost wisdom of ancient Gnosticism and neo-Platonism. Through Gnosticism, it infuses Judaism with the myth of the feminine aspect

of God—feminine sparks of the divine, our souls, for instance—
that shares our exile. As we are in exile from our promised land, the
feminine part of the divine is in exile from its masculine self.

From neo-Platonism came the idea of upper and lower worlds
that could be in or out of harmony, and of ideal archetypes, which
have their physical analogs in our world. These same ideas, the
wretched refuse of Greek philosophy and Near Eastern religion,
were also swept up by the Western occult tradition. This allows us
to make useful analogies between kabbalah and alchemy, ritual
magic, astrology, and secret societies:

> *. . . to divine secret and concealed things from unconsidered*
> *and unnoticed details, from the rubbish heap, as it were, of*
> *our observations.*
>
> —Sigmund Freud

These mystical perceptions of life raise the spiritual beyond
mere religion, cultic behavior, the warding off of evil by accepted
magical means; through mysticism we gain a sense of purpose behind the confusing events of our less-than-heroic lives. We feel a
connection to larger forces in the universe, whether we call them
God, Time and Space, or:

> *The force that through the green fuse drives the flower.*
>
> —Dylan Thomas

The complexities of the kabbalah are beyond the scope of this
book, but we can grasp certain key concepts. Like the medieval alchemists, the kabbalists believed that:

> *As above, so below.*
>
> —the Emerald Tablet

The two planes of reality (heavenly and earthly) operate together, whether we are aware of it or not. The universe obviously
touches and influences us; but our actions, those of the microcosm,
the human, little world, also have an impact on the macrocosm,

the universe, the big world. Finally, an elaborate table or network of correspondences describes the connections between the two planes of reality:

> *Nature is a temple, in which living pillars sometimes utter*
> *a babble of words; man traverses it through forests of symbols*
> *that watch him with familiar regard.*
> —Charles Baudelaire

The seder table recreates the Temple that was destroyed in Jerusalem, and so becomes our altar, an earthly version of the ideal Altar in the upper world. We hope that our actions at the seder, which parallel and reenact those of the Israelites in Egypt on a fifteenth of Nisan 3,300 years ago, will effect the same redemption for us that they did for our ancestors. Even at our most minimal seder, we are engaging in a display of symbols that works to heal the rift in creation. What we do at the seder affects the universe. Likewise, a deeper understanding of these symbols can tell us a lot about that which is beyond us and our brief lives. So we see that even in the simplest possible seder—one without ritual or liturgy, a mere prepared table—many of the key concepts of the Passover celebration can still be brought forth:

> *Truly, this table has such a likeness to that of the world*
> *above, that it is meet for us to dignify and crown it with*
> *the words of the Torah.*
> —*Zohar* II:157a

My Beloved Is Mine and I Am His   —*Song of Songs 2:16*

Kabbalah means "received tradition." One of the central problems for the kabbalists was the connection between our world of matter, imperfection, evil, and death, and the perfect world of pure spirit that is the Godhead. They solved this problem, and described the life of the divine, through the elaborate metaphor or paradigm of the *sefirot,* an algorithm of the flow of spiritual energy. In the kabbalah, there are ten sefirot (divine emanations). The three highest are

1. Keter, the crown
2. Chokhmah, wisdom, the right brain, the first male quality, the Father
3. Binah, intelligence, the left brain, the first female quality, the Mother of multiplicity

These upper three sefirot, symbolized on the seder table by the three matzot, represent the merciful but transcendent aspect of the divine, which is often out of touch with or removed from our world. When the ten sefirot are pictured as a human being, these three are the head.

The middle six sefirot are the six foods on the seder plate:

4. Chesed, divine love, is the shankbone, obviously male, the patriarch Abraham, the outstretched arm of the Exodus story, the right arm on the body.
5. Gevurah, divine judgment and power, is the egg, obviously female, the patriarch Isaac, the left arm.
6. Tiferet, divine beauty, is the bitter herb, the patriarch Jacob, the heart, which balances and reconciles mercy and judgment.
7. Netzach, divine endurance, is the charoset, Moses, the right thigh.
8. Hod, divine majesty, opposite endurance, is the karpas, Moses' brother Aaron, the left thigh.
9. Yesod Olam, the foundation of the world, is the chazeret, Joseph or David, and by implication the Messiah, the receiver of the totality of the divine flow from the previous eight sefirot, the circumcised male sexual organ in the body. Remember, Joseph resisted Potiphar's wife. He maintained the purity of his circumcised member.

Likewise, among males, only those who were circumcised were allowed to take part in the seder. The sprouting top of the horseradish root seems particularly appropriate here.

The kabbalah, like alchemy, is rampant with erotic symbolism to describe the inner workings of divine process, but it is not a sniggering, vulgar, cheap kind of sexual innuendo. Using the same metaphors as the Song of Songs, which some read at the end of the seder, the kabbalah treats sex as a divine mystery:

> *All the writings are holy, but the Song of Songs is the Holy of Holies.*
> —Rabbi Akiba

Physical love becomes a holy act because it parallels the divine process. Eros is one of the clues to the workings of the universe, a gift from the divine, a hint:

> *The God at Delphi neither tells nor conceals but gives a sign.*
> —Heraclitus

These middle six emanations together form the wrathful, dark side of the divine, the unmerciful, judgmental side. Our specific task as Jews is to synchronize the merciful and wrathful aspects of God. We want the angry, lower six sefirot to look up toward the merciful, upper three sefirot and stop tossing thunderbolts down on us. We do this through Jewish practice. Specifically, performing the ritual of the seder will ensure a good crop of wheat and barley, fertility in our flocks, rain and dew in their season, freedom for us as a people, and ultimately redemption.

Working on our side is the bit of the divine that shares our Exile with us. The concept of exile is more than our dispersion outside of Eretz Yisrael, the physical Holy Land. This recurring motif in our history is an external symbol of the human condition: our separation from the holy, from God. Yet we have been given a piece of the divine, the human soul, that can aid us in the return to the indivisible God.

The final sefirot is

10. Malkhut, the immanent, feminine presence of God, variously referred to as the Sabbath Bride, the beloved of the Song of Songs, Rachel weeping for her lost children, the kingdom, the divine spark within our world of matter, or the Shekhinah.

The lower six sefirot are like the six profane days of the week, whose effect is softened by the seventh day, the Sabbath Bride, the Shekhinah. On Passover this is represented by the round seder plate itself. When we place the objects upon the plate in the position of the lower six sefirot, we are mimicking the symbolic sexual conjunction we wish to take place within the divine. That is how we make the angry side of God look up toward the merciful side. Like the Neolithic hunters of the Salisbury Plain who built Stonehenge, we show the heavens a sign that we grasp and wish to be in tune with some part of their complex workings. Our human actions are necessary to the proper functioning of the universe. This is why we exist, to fulfill or carry out God's role in history and on earth, to complete and give closure to the original creative act:

> *Like the creation of the world, the creation of the people contains the final goal, the final purpose for which it was effected.*

—Franz Rosenzweig

Plus Ça Change

Although the seder ceremony has been performed continuously for over 3,000 years, there is a great deal of variation in the choice of foods for the seder, the way they are prepared, and their arrange-ment. Many of what we think of as the most familiar customs of the seder are fairly recent additions: removing drops of wine (thirteenth century), eating hard-boiled eggs (sixteenth century), ransoming the afikoman (seventeenth century), and the cup of Elijah (late sev-enteenth century). Clearly, the way in which we celebrate the Exo-dus from Egypt has changed and evolved over the last 3,300 years.

A wonderful, paradigmatic story has been told by many Jew-ish authors and repeated by many others and in many Haggadot. I first saw it in Gershom Scholem's *Major Trends in Jewish Mysticism,* where he tells it in the name of the Nobel laureate S. Y. Agnon:

> When the Ba'al Shem had a difficult task before him, he would go to a certain place in the woods, light a fire, and meditate in prayer—and what he had set out to per-form was done. When a generation later the Maggid of Mezhirech was faced with the same task, he would go to the same place in the woods and say: We can no longer light the fire, but we can still speak the prayers—and what he wanted done became reality. Again a generation later Rabbi Moshe Leib of Sasov had to perform this task. And he too went into the woods and said: We can no longer light a fire, nor do we know the secret medita-tions belonging to the prayer, but we do know the place in the woods to which it all belongs—and that must be sufficient; and sufficient it was. But when another gener-ation had passed and Rabbi Israel of Ruzhin was called upon to perform the task, he sat down on his golden chair in his castle and said: We cannot light the fire, we cannot speak the prayers, we do not know the place, but we can tell the story of how it was done. And, the story-teller adds, the story which he told had the same effect as the actions of the other three.

On the surface, this story is about how the Chasidic movement changed over four generations, but it also tells us about how Judaism itself has changed over four millennia. In the days of the Temple, they knew how to light the sacrificial fires and they did it in the correct place, the Temple Mount. After the Temple was destroyed, the prophet Hosea said, "Instead of bulls we will pay the offering of our lips" (Hosea 14:3). Today, we cannot light the fire, nor do we know the place or the mystical meditations, but our telling of the story of the Exodus must be sufficient—*Dayyenu*—to accomplish the same task as our ancestors. And, I would add, it is sufficient.

Our task is not to match our sedarim to some arbitrarily defined correct way to do them, but to reachieve the affect of the historical seder. Like Jorge Luis Borges's fictional character Pierre Menard, we "have taken on the mysterious duty of reconstructing literally" this "spontaneous work." In doing that—in reconstructing literally the paschal sacrifices that preceded the Exodus, the first seder in Egypt, the Temple pilgrimages, the two thousand years of Diaspora sedarim—we find we have changed them without even attempting to do so. Even if we change nothing, the seder is changed by the flow of events. The history of the seder during the Bar Kokhba revolt of 135 C.E. and the Warsaw ghetto revolt in 1943, in sixteenth-century Safed and in secret Marrano cellars, alters the meaning of the words and the actions we say and do.

Conversely, the mere fact of our having the seder changes the past and its meaning. Our contemporary changes and additions are part of that evolutionary process of recreating ourselves anew in each generation. When we perform our own sedarim, we become like Stephen Daedalus:

> *I go to encounter for the millionth time the reality of experience and to forge in the smithy of my soul the uncreated conscience of my race.*
>
> —James Joyce, *Portrait of the Artist as a Young Man*

This is a serious responsibility. We decide what Judaism is now and give shape to what it will be in the future. This is how we affect history, how we are history, every single individual, every separate seder on every successive Pesach. It is in that sense that Elijah does indeed visit each one of our sedarim. This is also the challenge given to us at every seder by the last great twentieth-century kabbalist:

> *The old may become new and the new may become holy.*
> —Rabbi Abraham Isaac Kook

Chapter Three

Mutus Liber:
The Mute Book

Ritual Actions of the Seder

In the last chapter we created an elaborate table of food and beverage, at once symbolic and to be consumed, but we did not discuss how, when, and in what order we would eat and drink them. In this chapter we will add the ritual actions to the prepared table, and we will also discuss the traditional order—the "seder"—of the Pesach meal.

Blessed rage for order   —*Wallace Stevens*

I would imagine that what makes most people uncomfortable at a seder is the recitation of what seems like hours of unintelligible Hebrew. Here and there certain inexplicable ceremonial procedures are performed, and the whole evening is, happily, punctuated by periods of intense eating. Perhaps the text, which we will begin to look at in chapter 4, is actually getting in the way of our seeing the process as a whole. Let us get up from the table and see what the seder looks like from a slight remove.

Without text, we observe a set of silent ritual actions similar to the late-seventeenth-century alchemical *Mutus Liber*, or Mute Book. In this silent book the whole process of alchemical transmutation, the Magnum Opus or Great Work, is explained solely through a set of fifteen wordless copperplate engravings that show a husband and wife engaged in a series of laboratory procedures. These plates are reminiscent of the woodcuts and copperplate engravings used in early printed Haggadot showing, oddly enough, the fifteen stages of the seder.

Dumb Show: A Sequence of Actions

The following is the commonly agreed upon sequence of obligatory actions necessary for a seder. The Roman numerals refer to the fifteen prescribed steps of the seder, which are explained at the end of this chapter. The Arabic numbers enumerate the separate ritual actions of our mute book. If you are wary of biting off more bitter herb than you can chew at your first seder, consider this the bare minimum. You can add on to it as you become more familiar with the Haggadah. You need do no more of these rituals than you wish.

Before the Seder

Ritual action 1: On the night before the seder, we search the house for any crumbs of *chametz,* leavened food, that might have escaped our attention in the rush to shop, clean, cook, and prepare for *yontif.* This final search lets us focus on the simple, tiny thing for which we are looking. The search is conducted by candlelight, and any crumbs that are found are swept up with a feather on to a wooden spoon. So as to have a reason for performing this mitzvah, ten bits of bread or crumbs are put out ahead of time. We already know that ten symbolizes the ten *sefirot* (aspects of God) in the kabbalah, so as we find and eliminate the chametz, the yeast of puffed up pride, and the physical manifestation of the ten impure, unholy, or evil sefirot, we ascend the ladder of the holy sefirot and come closer to God.

The fact that we search down to the last crumb and with such painstaking tools indicates how seriously we take the injunction to rid ourselves of all leaven. At the same time, in this first ritual action, we see the elements of enigma, ludicrousness, and inversion of the normal that help to catch the interest of children. We should not be too quick to think we have understood the meaning of our actions. God willing, we have a lifetime of sedarim in which to reflect on these strange customs, which combine humor, intellectual provocation, and magic in a uniquely Jewish way. Already we have a good beginning for our mute book.

Ritual action 2: The next morning we burn all the chametz we found the night before.

Ritual action 3: That evening we begin the festival with the lighting of candles.

The Fifteen Steps of the Seder

Looking at the seder ritual without text, we can see its structural elements in high contrast.

Step I. Kadesh

Ritual action 4: The seder begins when the first cup of wine is poured, lifted, and drunk, leaning to the left. Throughout the ceremony, whenever we lift the wine cup or drink the wine, the matzot are covered. The matzot are slightly uncovered the rest of the time.

Step II. Urchatz

Ritual action 5: The hands are washed by pouring water from a pitcher over them.

Step III. Karpas

Ritual action 6: A green vegetable is dipped in saltwater and eaten, either leaning to the left or sitting upright.

Step IV. Yachatz

Ritual action 7: The middle matzo of three is broken in half. One half, the *afikoman,* is wrapped up. It is then either stolen from the *ba'al ha-seder* by the children, or hidden from the children by the leader.

Step V. Maggid

Ritual action 8: The seder plate and matzot are lifted up and displayed.

Alternatively, the seder plate is removed or put at the opposite end of the table temporarily, and the remaining two and a half matzot are lifted up and displayed. Some remove only the shankbone and egg during the display of the matzot, especially if the matzot are on or within the seder plate. Other alternatives are to lift only the seder plate or only the matzot.

Ritual action 9: The second cup of wine is poured.

Ritual action 10: The wine cup is raised, then put down.

Ritual action 11: Three drops of wine are removed drop by drop from the cup, then ten, then three more.

Ritual action 12: The leader lifts up or points to the matzot.

Ritual action 13: The leader lifts up or points to the *maror.*

Ritual action 14: The wine cup is again raised and put down.

Ritual action 15: The wine cup is raised and the wine is drunk while leaning to the left.

Step VI. Rachtzah

Ritual action 16: The hands are washed again.

Step VII. Motzi

Ritual action 17: The matzot are held.

Step VIII. Matzo

Ritual action 18: The upper matzo and the remainder of the middle matzo are held.

Ritual action 19: Matzo from the upper two matzot is eaten while leaning to the left.

Step IX. Maror

Ritual action 20: Bitter herb is eaten after being dipped in *charoset.*

Step X. Korekh

Ritual action 21: A sandwich of bitter herb between pieces of the bottom matzo is eaten while leaning to the left.

Step XI. Shulchan Arukh

Ritual action 22: A hard-boiled egg is eaten, usually dipped or mixed in the saltwater, while leaning to the left. At this point an elaborate meal of traditional foods can be eaten, although the hard-boiled egg stands for the whole meal.

Step XII. Tzafun

Ritual action 23: The sequestered piece of the middle matzo— either hidden and found, or stolen and now ransomed—is eaten while leaning to the left. Nothing more may be eaten for the rest of the night.

Step XIII. Barekh

Ritual action 24: The third cup of wine is poured. Wine is drunk while leaning to the left.

Ritual action 25: The door is opened for the prophet Elijah, for whom a cup of wine has been poured.

Ritual action 26: The door is closed.

Step XIV. Hallel

Ritual action 27: The fourth and final glass of wine is poured and drunk while leaning to the left.

Step XV. Nirtzah

This is the concluding, acceptance part of the seder, for which there are no ritual actions.

These simple actions—wacky, archaic, talismanic, tribal, mnemonic, at once allegorical and symbolic—constitute the bare bones of our seder. For some, *Dayyenu,* this might be a sufficient seder, this mute set of actions that point to and hint at the meanings of the Passover symbols. Most of us are going to want more; but no matter how much more we want or add, that more is going to be rooted in these brief, evocative actions.

Before the Seder Begins

For many of our grandparents and great-grandparents, Passover in the Old Country was not just eight days. The whole year revolved around this day, from the growing of wheat and the baking of matzot, to the making of wine and beet borscht (soup) to the accumulation of schmaltz (chicken fat) for months ahead of time. The fires of the matzo ovens were started with willows saved from the *lulav* shaken during the preceding Sukkot. Today, all of this is done for us commercially and we take it for granted; but in the world of the *shtetl* (Jewish villages of Eastern Europe), the connection between daily work and the cycle of the holidays was unbroken.

Every creature shall be purified   *—Christopher Marlowe*

Before the holiday could begin, everything in the house had to be cleaned and all leaven removed. Crumbs were shaken out of books, dishes changed. Everyone got new clothes. All of this cleaning and purification took a full month, from the day after Purim—Jewish carnival, with its costumes, wine-drinking, and Purim-*shpils* (plays on the theme of the Book of Esther, the Purim story)—until the night before the seder, the fourteenth of Nisan, when we are instructed to rid our homes of leaven. For some time before Passover, certainly from the day before, no matzo was eaten, so that the taste at the seder would be a fresh experience. The morning after the search for chametz, bonfires signaled the reduction of all leaven to ashes and dust. Just as the earth was renewing itself, so were the people. (As we have seen before, a Jewish motif—in this case Purim, excess, followed by Passover, selective restriction—was copied in the Christian carnival/Lent cycle.)

Not only was the house purified, but men purified themselves by going to the *mikveh* in the daytime before the seder. Firstborn sons were obligated to fast or complete a tractate of the Talmud by going to the synagogue, where a section of Talmud was conveniently concluded. On the Shabbat ha-Gadol (the Great Sabbath) before the seder, special prophetic portions about Elijah that hinted at a future redemption in the month of Nisan were read and sermons about the holiday delivered. By the time the seder actually arrived, people were already in a state of heightened awareness, anticipation, and preparation.

Ritual Action 1: Search the house for chametz. We may no longer go through all the elaborate preparations and rites of purification that our ancestors went through, but cleaning the house, buying new clothes, acquiring good food and wine, and the bedikat chametz can still be part of the holiday. The ritual search for chametz was fading during my childhood, but seems to be enjoying a comeback today. This ancient ritual, which involves children in a hide-and-seek or treasure hunt game, acts as a *forshpeis* (appetizer) to the elaborate rituals and games of the following night, screwing us up to the proper tension and whetting our appetites in anticipation of the following night's banquet of curios and food.

Ritual Action 2: Burn the chametz. If the seder falls on a Saturday night, the search for chametz is carried out on Thursday night and the burning on Friday morning since, traditionally, we do not make a fire on the Sabbath. The usual method of burning the chametz is a bonfire, which children love; but you can burn it in your hibachi if that feels safer and simpler.

Ritual Action 3: Light the candles. On the evening of the first night, we immediately perform certain actions that alter the normal sense of the day. First, candles are lit, usually by a woman (though a man may light the candles if preferred or necessary). This is traditionally done eighteen minutes before sundown, so as not to kindle a flame after the festival or Sabbath has begun. (For a Saturday night seder, we wait until Shabbat is over before lighting the candles.) Eighteen, a recurring number in Jewish custom, has the same numerical value as Chai (life). As in the *Mutus Liber,* it takes both the female and male working in conjunction to complete the transmutative or transforming operations.

This holiday, like all other major Jewish festivals, is ushered in by a woman lighting candles. She stands at the gateway between the profane, secular time and the sacred time of the holiday. It is through the woman that the Shekhinah (feminine presence of God) enters the home via the light of the candles. This most important ceremony of the year takes place in the feminine home as opposed to the masculine synagogue. As the light of the male sun dwindles and the light of the female moon comes up, the *soror mystica* kindles a light in the darkness. She mimics the original act of creation, "Let there be Light."

Not only do we take the unusual step of lighting candles before we begin, but we light them in an unusual way. After lighting at least two candles, the person who does *bentsh licht* (makes the benediction over light) draws the light toward herself three times, like drawing water from a pool, covers her eyes on the third drawing of the hands toward her, then uncovers them:

> *Shut your eyes and see.*
> —James Joyce

(The halakhah or legal reason for this has to do with the bene-diction and will be explained in the next chapter.) Some families light one candle for each child or for each family member.

The light is being drawn inward. With the eyes closed, we provide the inner darkness and silence in which the inner light and voice can be seen and heard:

> *Blessed is the match consumed in kindling flame.*
> *Blessed is the flame that burns in the secret fastness*
> *of the heart.*
> *Blessed is the heart with strength to stop its beating*
> *for honor's sake.*
> *Blessed is the match consumed in kindling flame.*
>
> —Hannah Szenes

When we open our eyes again, it is with a fresh perception of the external light. Either our actions changed reality or the break-ing of the routine heightened our senses. Hoodwinking ourselves, covering our eyes, also suggests the initiatory passage from dark-ness to light, from ignorance to knowledge.

The simple lighting of candles, which many of us have watched our mothers do from our earliest childhood, is one of the most evocative of all Jewish rituals. Men *daven* together for hours in the synagogue hoping to achieve the drama and transforming magic of the wave of a woman's hands. Unlike the elaborate archi-tectonic structures of synagogue service, it has the almost invisible quality one finds in worship to the gods and goddesses of stoves, hearths, thresholds, gateways, and crossroads. A similarly invisible, feminine act of worship is the taking of challah, the burning of a small part of the dough, when making either bread or matzo. This is in lieu of the priestly portion of Temple times. My mother al-ways lights the candles at the correct moment, usually without an-nouncement, but you manage to see it out of the corner of your eye. Her actions allow everything else to proceed. Though not bound by time-related rules, woman establishes time, creating the time in which the sacred can occur.

The Seder

Following these preliminary actions, the seder proper can begin.

Step I. Kadesh

Ritual action 4: Pour the first cup of wine, lift the cup, and drink.

Everyone pours a cup of wine, lifts the wine cup—holding it in the palm of the right hand, fingers upraised—and drinks the first of four cups of wine sitting down and leaning to the left:

> *This is the "cup of benediction" which has to be raised by five fingers and no more, after the model, of the lily, which rests on five strong leaves in the shape of five fingers.*
> —*Zohar* I:1a

At this point, if we were adding the text, we would say the Kiddush. Normally, before drinking wine, we would rise for the Kiddush, but not on Passover when we exult in our freedom (though some rise for the Kiddush and then sit to drink).

In order to emphasize this freedom, some have the custom of not pouring their own wine. We can carry this out in a democratic way by filling one another's cups. Just as lovers know that candles and wine create a certain mood, most Jewish holidays begin with candle lighting and wine. We say they hallow or sanctify the moment, that is, they create a sacred space, a protected circle, that is separate from the drab, everyday world of work and routine. Here we have added the further embellishment of lifting the cup in a salute to our deliverer and leaning to the left. We are changing our normal balance. At the same time, since we are celebrating our liberation, instead of rising for the opening toast, we recline in freedom.

During the seder, whenever we raise the wine cup, drink, or refer to the wine, we cover the matzot. We say that we do not want to insult, or shame, the bread by having it uncovered when we are ignoring it in favor of the wine. We treat the challah the same way on Shabbat and other festivals, but once we have made the benediction over the wine, the bread can be uncovered. Not on Passover. Throughout the seder we will constantly cover the matzot whenever the wine takes prominence in the ritual. The matzot should be slightly uncovered during the rest of the seder.

There must be some conflict between these two key elements in the seder, the bread in the form of matzo and the wine. Matzo—dry, cold, earthy, and fixed—is made of white, unfermented flour, while the wine—moist, hot, airy, and volatile—is preferably red and by definition fermented. (It is the one decayed substance we allow at the seder, although no yeast is added to the grapes in the making of Passover wine. Fermentation is allowed to occur naturally instead.) There are three matzot, a male number, and four cups of wine, a female number (see chapter 6 for more on numbers). Making matzo involves restrictions of ingredients and time. As alcohol, wine implies freedom, even license, unrestriction. The wine corresponds to the feminine egg, symbol of death and birth: the blood of our ancestors shed by Pharaoh and the Israelite baby boys drowned in the Nile; while the matzo parallels the white, masculine shankbone: the merciful "outstretched arm" of God, sparing our firstborn and giving us life while inflicting the ten plagues on the Egyptians.

This antithesis of:

wheat	grape
three	four
odd	even
dry	moist
cold	hot
bone	blood
fixed	volatile

earth	air
white	red
mercy	justice
control	abandon
masculine	feminine
patriarchs	matriarchs
Apollonian	Dionysian
unleavened	fermented

is reminiscent of the alchemists' symbol system, in which all opposites are described as either solar or lunar, gold or silver. Kabbalah reverses the alchemists' symbols though, since mercy, white, male, and silver are counter to judgment, red, female, and gold. Through the symbols of the seder table, the contradictory elements in our psyches and our society are transmuted and resolved. As we cover and uncover the matzot, moving back and forth between the poles of male and female, mercy and judgment, we allow ourselves to synthesize and balance these contradictory forces. We are the alchemical vessel in which the Great Work is accomplished. The sulfur, mercury, and salt used in our operations are both symbols and real foods that we consume sacramentally, raising the divine sparks within them up from their animal, vegetable, and mineral natures to the spiritual level:

> *Kabbalah is based on scientific fact, its laboratory the human organism.*
> —Rabbi Levi I. Krakovsky

Step II. Urchatz

Ritual action 5: Wash hands.

Next we perform a ritual ablution—we wash our hands in a particular way. This is another act of purification. The night before we searched for everything that was impure, and in the morning we used fire and burned what we had found. Now we further purify ourselves with water by washing our hands in a ritualistic way. Just as the Kohanim washed before performing the Temple service, so we wash, reminding ourselves that the table is our altar. We also want to make sure that no demons—none of the *klippot,* the shards of evil scattered through our material world, no negative forces—enter us with our food.

The traditional method of washing the hands is either to pour the water from the pitcher on to the right hand twice and then on to the left hand twice, or on the right then the left, then the right and then the left again. The fingers should be turned up and splayed so that water covers the whole surface of the hand.

The water should be comfortably warm. It should be a pleasant experience that helps to focus the attention on the moment. A nice way to do this, so that no one is merely the servant to everyone else, is to pour the water for one another in succession. In doing this we create a circle of purity around the table. Alternatively, the leader alone can wash and be the stand-in for everyone else, or everyone can retire to the kitchen and wash their own hands at the sink. We must wash our hands before coming to the table as the Kohanim did before coming to the Temple altar.

In Sephardic custom the youngest children walk around the table with bowl and pitcher to wash everyone's hands. These innocents, in circumambulating the table, help to create a purified, protected, holy circle.

Step III. Karpas

Ritual action 6: Eat the green vegetable dipped in saltwater.

Having made the moment special through purification and sanctification, we can now eat an hors d'oeuvre, the raw green vegetable. There are mixed opinions about leaning to the left during this step. Some do, some do not.

This is both the first food of the evening, as well as the simplest and least altered. As the symbol of spring, the simple *karpas* is the foundation of the whole ritual. Although, as we saw in the last chapter, we can allegorize it, we do not have to do that in order to realize its fundamental meaning. Unlike the other symbols, which relate to the remembrance of the Exodus or to the ancient shepherd's and farmer's holidays of lambs and wheat, the greens can refer simply to spring and be sufficient unto themselves. The fear and excitement that are awakened each spring as we "pass over" winter and enter a new year were the primal elements of the holiday we now celebrate:

> *April is the cruellest month, breeding*
> *Lilacs out of the dead land, mixing*
> *Memory and desire, stirring*
> *Dull roots with spring rain.*
> *Winter kept us warm, covering*
> *Earth in forgetful snow, feeding*
> *A little life with dried tubers.*
> —T. S. Eliot

When we eat the greens (which can be a tuber, like the potato), we still act in a way that is out of the ordinary. We eat only a small, sacramental amount of the vegetable, which we dip into saltwater. Both the water and salt are purifying, as mentioned earlier. Then, having stimulated both our appetites and our curiosity, we eat nothing else for quite a while. Getting to the meal is going to involve knowing the passwords and having the keys at a lot of doorways, just as the ancient Israelites had to obtain the lamb's blood clavicles for their own portals.

Step IV. Yachatz

Ritual action 7: Break the middle matzo and set aside the afikoman.

We remove the middle matzo from the group of three, break it in half, and return the smaller half to its middle position. Then we either set aside the larger half, the afikoman, and wait for the children to steal it, or else we hide it from the children. This is based on a Talmudic passage that tells us to anticipate or grab the matzo.

The large half of the middle matzo is reserved so that we have some matzo at the end of the seder to fulfill the obligation to end the meal with the taste of matzo in our mouths. At the same time, from this step on, our matzot are incomplete. Part of the process of the seder is to achieve closure, completion, but throughout we are made aware of our distance from perfection by the broken matzo. Like the Jewish people or the Shekhinah, the afikoman is in exile during the seder. Although we have literally broken bread, we do not yet eat any of the matzo.

When we break the seder apart into symbol, ritual, text, and music, we lose sight of those moments, rare in Judaism, that are surrounded by silence, that call out for explanation. The first washing of the hands without a benediction, the eating of the greens with the simplest of blessings, and the breaking of the middle matzo, all coming at the beginning of the seder, are calculated to pique our curiosity, to make us ask questions, since no answers are forthcoming.

Non-Ashkenazim do not steal or hide the afikoman. They have their own unusual customs associated with it though. Some put it under the tablecloth, while others place the afikoman on their shoulder and walk around with it in memory of our ancestors who left Egypt:

> . . . *with kneading troughs bound up in their clothes upon their shoulders.*
> —Exodus 12:34

They ask and answer each other: "Who are you?" "I am a Jew." "Where do you come from?" "Egypt!" "Where are you going?" "Jerusalem!" "Do you have food for the trip?" They point to the broken matzo on their shoulder. This poor bread has sustained us for thousands of years in the wilderness between slavery and redemption.

Step V. Maggid

Ritual action 8: Display the matzot and the seder plate.

We next display the remainder of our matzot (the two whole pieces with the small broken piece between them) along with the symbolic six foods of the seder plate. At this point there is a lot of variation in procedure, but the crucial element is the display of the matzot. One custom that strengthens the bond of the seder circle is for everyone at the table, or at least those who can reach it, to assist in lifting the seder plate. In some Sephardic families they pass the seder plate over the heads of everyone around the table, or the hostess holds the matzo above everyone's head.

The importance of wheat in its most basic form, with only water and fire added to make it edible after milling, suggests that this wheat has a large role in the proceedings. In the Temple service, the day after the paschal sacrifice, a sheaf of barley, the omer, was waved, displayed, to ensure a good harvest. Part of the omer was burnt, sacrificed, and part was eaten, as unleavened barley matzo, by the Kohen, the high priest. This was repeated through forty-nine days until Shavuot, the commemoration of the receiving of the Torah at Mt. Sinai, arrived and the barley harvest came in. The eating of unleavened bread for eight days at the beginning of the barley harvest suggests the hushed silence and walking on tip-toes of people who do not want to jinx their good luck. Although we are no longer barley farmers, we still nominally count the omer for forty-nine days after the first day of Passover.

This Temple service, with its prominent display of the sheaf of grain, is reminiscent of certain suggestions about the mysteries that took place outside of Athens in the little town of Eleusis. In these celebrations of the return of fertility in spring, symbolized by Demeter's daughter Persephone's return from the underworld, people from all over the Mediterranean came to be initiated into the mysteries of Eleusis. They first came to Athens, which had appro-

priated the cult of suburban Eleusis. There they performed ablu-
tions in the sea, sacrificed a pig, and then made a pilgrimage, which
included crossing a bridge—in other words, crossing water—to
nearby Eleusis to witness the dramatic performance of the mystery,
whose content is unknown for certain to this day.

One clue to the dramatic revelation in the mystery is the
prevalence of motifs having to do with ears of corn, that is, sheaves
of wheat, in both the art and the legends of Eleusis. Demeter is, of
course, the same as the Roman Ceres, the goddess of cereals, grains.
Some scholars believe that at the critical moment of the drama or
ritual reenactment, in the Telesterion, the subterranean vault where
the mystery took place, a trapdoor was opened and a beam of light
shot down upon a displayed sheaf of wheat. This would symbolize
the return of Persephone, the rebirth of the decayed seed that had
been buried in the dead winter, and the promise of our own rebirth
since we too are buried after death. In a similar fashion, at Passover
we remove everything from our homes that has to do with the fermented, decayed grain of wheat, a symbol of death. Only matzo
which has never undergone fermentation is acceptable.

The argument against the wheat as the displayed object at
Eleusis is that it is shown in the Eleusinian art and is obvious from
the story, so how can it be a mystery? However, it is not the specific
content of the display that is the secret, but what is inferred and realized from the performance. The initiate left Eleusis, not merely
with the secret of the displayed grain, but with the realized knowledge, the gnosis, of what it meant. The mystery could not be revealed. It could only be known. It could be publicly displayed
without fear of revelation because to the initiate, once initiated,
everything pointed to and hinted at the mystery:

> . . . *it is understood that all words name it or, rather,
> inevitably allude to it . . .*
> —Jorge Luis Borges

Analogously, although there were some specifically esoteric mystical practices, the majority of Jewish mystics appropriated normative Judaism as their mystical method. They merely did what everyone else did, both at home and in the synagogue. There was nothing to be hidden. It was their understanding of these practices that made them mystical:

> *A secret is something you say in such a way that everyone can hear it, and yet no one who is not supposed to know can know it.*
>
> —Rabbi Simchah Bunem of Przysucha

So when we display the matzo, we express the inner contradiction of the seder. We are not only simultaneously holding up the symbol of our affliction and our freedom, but also of death and rebirth. The mystery, ambiguity, and paradox of the historical symbol is paralleled in a similar confusion in the agricultural symbol. That confusion is resolved at the same moment, in spring: when new life erupts from decayed seeds; and on the anniversary of our redemption, when a despised *lumpen,* a "mixed rabble," were born as a people.

Mal Occhio: Anti-Demonics in the Seder

The following sequence of actions is intended to protect us from any malevolent spirits that might want to join our seder.

Ritual action 9: Pour the second cup of wine.

Ritual action 10: Raise and lower the wine cup.

Ritual action 11: Remove three, ten, and three drops of wine from the cup.

Ritual action 12: Point to the matzo.

Ritual action 13: Point to the maror.

Ritual action 14: Raise and lower the wine cup again.

Ritual action 15: Raise the wine cup and drink the wine.

Wine is poured, there is a toast, but no wine is drunk. Instead, drops of wine, first three, then ten, then three more, are removed from the glass. Then the leader points to the matzo, followed by the maror. (In some medieval manuscript Haggadot, when the moment of pointing to the bitter herb arrives, the male chauvinist leader points to his wife.) There is a further toast without drinking, and then finally the second cup of wine is drunk leaning to the left. It would seem that a certain amount of preparatory action must take place before we can have this second cup of wine: propitiatory toastings, displays of unleavened bread and bitter herbs—talismanic foods, sacramental foods, out of the ordinary foods, oxymoronic foods, foods that are their own negation—bread that does not rise like bread and vegetables that we say are unpleasant, but which we enjoy.

Then there is the removal of the drops of wine, a reduction of our cup of joy. We say that we do it in sympathy for the Egyptians who suffered from the ten plagues, which are conceived of in sets of three, ten, and three. The numbers three, ten, and three in connection with the drops of wine, suggests, from a kabbalistic point of view, a bracketing of the totality of the ten sefirot within the three upper, merciful sefirot. Three is traditionally the most powerful of all magical numbers and would be the most able to contain any negative energy still inhering in the names of the ten plagues. Not only do we worry about uttering these ten *makkot* (strokes), but we further avoid saying them outright by compressing them into an acronymic mnemonic: the second set of three drops refers to three words formed from the first letters of each of the ten plagues. These are magical words, words that contain some of the power of the plagues they denote. Their initials alone are powerful.

We mention the passage in the Talmud where God reproaches the angels for singing hymns at the Red Sea, "The works of my hands are drowning in the sea and you offer songs of praise." This is the reason we only sing the half Hallel in the synagogue on the last six days of Passover. We want to avoid gloating over our enemy's defeat.

We also do not want to let the Devil see us looking too happy, so there are mixed opinions on whether we top off our cups after removing the token drops. Those who refill are clearly not diminishing their joy. Their ten drops are like the scapegoat sent into the wilderness at Yom Kippur for Azazel. The ten drops then are a removal of our sins. Often, the dishes that are used to catch the drops are broken crockery. These shards are analogous to the klippot, the shards of negativity scattered throughout our world of imperfection. According to the kabbalah, they are the remnants of earlier worlds that God made with too much Gevurah, Justice or Rigor, and so they shattered.

This custom is also reminiscent of the ancient Egyptian practice of writing spells on incantation bowls and then breaking them. If you cannot unbreak the bowl, you cannot break the spell or reverse the incantation. So as we protect ourselves from the evil eye, we also throw whatever negative forces are in those drops of wine upon our enemy. Just as some add three drops of water, signifying mercy, to the first cup of wine, so the removal of drops of wine signifies the infliction of divine justice:

> *And at each pest shake off the drop with the vindictive zest.*
> —Abraham Moses Klein

We even retain this symbology in America when we sing, "He is trampling out the vintage where the grapes of wrath are stored."

The broken crockery to catch the drops of wine also reminds us of the breaking of a wineglass at a wedding, another anti-demonic. Beyond all the allegorical meanings, however, it is a way of scaring off demons, most active during periods of transition like changes of season or the passage from slavery to freedom. The devil hates loud crashing noises and jagged edges.

Now, finally, we can drink the second cup of wine.

The Left Hand of God

Why do we lean to the left for our four cups of wine and most of our foods? The obvious answer is that we are leaning to express our freedom, our ease, in the manner of the Greeks and Romans at their symposia. We lean to the left because we eat with our right hands. We should always begin with the obvious answer and see how far we can go with it. What if we are left-handed? We are still supposed to lean to the left. So the obvious answer is insufficient here, especially when we know that other activities, like putting on tefillin (phylacteries), are done in reverse by southpaws.

In the kabbalah, as we have seen, the left side is the judgmental, female side of God. The left is literally sinister. This is the shadow side of the divine, the source of death and evil and creativity. It can be dangerous, seductive, and inspiring. It is certainly ambiguous. Throughout the seder we flirt with this side; we open ourselves up to it, yet protect ourselves from it. For this reason our seder ritual is full of many of what I have called anti-demonic features. We wish to avert the evil eye by appearing unhappy, even though we are celebrating. At the same time, we celebrate the Passover while acknowledging that "Now we are slaves." We have left Egypt, but have yet to reach the Promised Land. We understand our precarious fiddler-on-the-roof position in the world and still we celebrate. We perform many protective rituals and have many protective foods, yet we also thumb our nose at the devil and enjoy ourselves. Even though we are slaves all year long, at the seder we are free.

Superstitious as much of this seems, weren't our medieval forebears reinvesting the seder night with some of the same ominous qualities that the first seder in Egypt had? Wasn't that seder "a night of watching," marked by the protective charm of the lamb's blood smeared on the doorposts? The ancient Israelites had as much to fear on that night as so many other Jews on so many other seder nights: those Jews who feared the blood libel of the Middle Ages every Passover for over 800 years, right on down to the Beilis case in twentieth-century Russia; the Marranos, the secret Jews of Spain, who risked their lives to have the seder and matzo; Soviet Jews who did the same until the breakup of the Soviet Union; the inmates of the death camps who explained to God why they ate bread instead of matzo and were themselves to bake in the ovens, themselves to be the paschal lambs, the holocaust or "wholly burned" sacrifice; and the partisans of the Warsaw Ghetto who understood why their uprising needed to begin on the night of the first seder, the night of our original deliverance:

> *But no more will the Jews to the slaughter be led.*
> *The truculent jibes of the Nazis are past.*
> *And the lintels and doorposts tonight will be red*
> *with the blood of free Jews who will fight to the last.*
> —Bunim Heller, Warsaw, April 19, 1943

And what of the five rabbis of the Haggadah, Akiba, Tarfon, and their compatriots, who met for seder at Bene-Berak around 132 C.E.? They took so long to elaborate on the Exodus that they were still going on when their students told them it was time for the morning prayers. Were they oblivious to the rising sun, or were they hiding in a cave from the Roman oppressors, plotting the ill-fated revolt led by Bar Kokhba? They understood that the words Pharaoh and Egypt did not refer to just one person in one time and place. Akiba and Tarfon were martyred. They too gave up their lives for freedom:

> *Since the Exodus, freedom has always spoken with a Hebrew accent.*
> —Heinrich Heine

So if we accept all this magic in that spirit, we see that our seder is a special moment of protection in a dangerous and frightening world. It is also a time to make peace with the danger. When we lean to the left, we incline toward the shadow side, the feminine, the creative. We are not paying homage to the devil or propitiating malevolent spirits, though. We are attempting to balance the two sides of human nature by overcompensating for spending so much of our lives in the mundane, ordinary, normal, logical, regular, daylight, orderly, male world. The dark night of Passover is an enchanted evening in which we come together within the protective circle of the seder to drink deeply from the four cups of myth, magic, miracle, and mystery.

Step VI. Rachtzah

Ritual action 16: Wash hands again.

At this point we wash our hands again. (The difference between this hand washing and the first one is that we now say the *berakhah* (benediction), which we omitted the first time. More on that in chapter 4.) We must be doubly purified on this night. Both hand washings are immediately preceded by the drinking of wine. Sanctification is followed by purification. Actually, the wine represents purification from the left, feminine, judgmental side, while the water, like dew and rain, represents purification from the right, masculine, merciful side. Some have the custom of adding three drops of water, symbolic of the upper three merciful sefirot, to the first cup of wine, tempering justice with mercy. The original meaning of temperance, as evidenced by the Tarot card showing a woman adding water to wine, was not abstinence, but dilution of strong wine with water.

Step VII. Motzi

Ritual action 17: Hold the matzot.

Now that we have washed (and said the berakhah), we can eat more than a token amount of food. We display the two and a half matzot again. Clearly, we are building up to eating it. By holding all the matzot, minus the afikoman, we emphasize the mood of celebration.

Step VIII. Matzo

Ritual action 18: Hold the upper and middle matzot.

We display the upper and broken matzot, distinguishing between the meaning of all the matzot and part of the matzot. By holding only part of the matzot, we emphasize the element of affliction and incompletion.

Ritual action 19: Eat from the upper and middle matzot.

All of the matzot are bread, but we eat the upper two because we have designated them as the unleavened bread of our seder. We finally get to eat the matzo, from the upper and middle matzot, and we do so *heseba,* leaning to the left. We are eating the matzo as the bread of affliction here. Notice that we completed our first two cups of wine before we ate the matzo. There will be no more wine ritually until after we have eaten all the matzo we are going to have. Some authorities make a point of rinsing the wine glasses after the meal to remove any matzo crumbs that may have fallen into them. The Jews of Morocco have a custom, which they begin to carry out at this point in the ceremony, of kissing the matzo, then the maror, and at the end of the meal, the afikoman. As they thank God by kissing the symbols of our release from Egyptian bondage, they also express a fervent eagerness to accept the yoke of the mitzvot.

Step IX. Maror

Ritual action 20: Eat the bitter herb and charoset.

Next we eat the bitter herb dipped into the charoset. This is our second dipping. We do not lean, because the bitter herb represents bondage, not freedom.

There are differences of opinion as to whether we eat the charoset with the bitter herb or merely dip it in the sweet charoset, which is then shaken off. Those who shake it off let the children eat it for dessert. I would feel disappointed if I were denied charoset at this point. Perhaps we can compromise here by eating a bite of maror dipped and shaken so that we realize that quality of bitterness slightly mitigated by sweet, and then follow that up with a free mixing of our bitter herb and charoset.

The original symbolism may have been intended to suggest a bitterness only slightly mitigated by the sweet things in life. Today, especially for those of us living in the United States, our desire to eat a good share of charoset with our maror may suggest that we feel that we can have a full share of sweet with the bitter. The Sephardim, whose customs are generally more easygoing than those of the Ashkenazim, eat copious amounts of charoset with matzo following the ritually obligatory eating of the dipped maror.

Step X. Korekh

Ritual action 21: Eat the Hillel sandwich.

We do lean when we combine the matzo and bitter herb in remembrance of Hillel, who did this in the time of the Second Temple. It is said that Hillel invented the sandwich by wrapping his paschal lamb up with romaine lettuce, chazeret, in between matzot. Our matzo does double symbolic duty here as both itself and a symbol of the paschal lamb. This is carried through later when the afikoman stands in for the paschal lamb. Considering that our matzo is probably more stringently made than Hillel's, what he most likely invented was spit-roasted lamb in pittah with romaine and fruit chutney. His intention was the same as ours, though: to wrap together the symbols of bondage, freedom, and redemption—all of whose symbols are food—into one object/action.

Again, there is some conflict here between common practice and halakhah (rabbinic law). We are told to eat bitter herb between matzot, but almost everyone adds charoset. Even the rabbis argued about this. Eating a Hillel sandwich with just bitter herb first and then eating it again with charoset is one way to solve this problem.

Step XI. Shulchan Arukh

Ritual action 22: Eat the egg.

These actions, full of anti-demonics, reach their conclusion when we eat the hard-boiled egg, a symbol of mourning, dipped in saltwater. The Sephardim understand that this is a mourning custom and many do not do this at their less melancholy sedarim.

We have now carried out the dangerous portion of the seder. From this point on we are truly free. Having carried through the charade of mourning with the egg and the anti-demonic saltwater, we can thoroughly enjoy our meal of chicken soup with *knaydlach,* gefilte fish with beet horseradish, chopped liver, matzo meal sponge cake, and whatever else we want.

Step XII. Tzafun

Ritual action 23: Eat the afikoman.

When the meal is over, we want to finish with the taste of matzo, symbolizing the paschal lamb, on our tongues. We have saved our afikoman for this occasion. It will be the last thing we eat during the seder. Just as we searched for leavened bread on the previous night, on the night of the seder we search for unleavened bread. Just as we broke it in silence at the very beginning of the seder, so we now eat it in silence at the end of the meal. As we will find out in a later chapter, there is no text attached to either of these actions. Paradoxically, that indicates the important role these actions play. Unspoken verses, unconsumed wine, and unexplained actions, all point to one of the goals of the evening: to bring redemption, to bring the Messiah, to repair the universe; not just to remember, but to experience freedom:

> *Heard melodies are sweet, but those unheard are sweeter.*
> —John Keats

We break the wholeness of the circle, the round matzo, hide the larger part—just as God, the greater part, hides or is hidden from us—and then find it and return it to wholeness by incorporating it into ourselves.

I Wish He Would Explain His Explanation   —*Lord Byron*

In an unfortunately complicated, but entirely consistent symbology, the kabbalists associate the letter *he* (ה) with matzo and *chet* (ח) with chametz. These two words, matzo and chametz, are composed of the same letters, except for the *he* and *chet*. When the middle matzo is broken, they see the *he* being broken into a small *dalet* (ד) and a large *vav* (ו), two other letters that together form the physical sign for *he*.

Moroccan Jews follow the same interpretation. When they split the matzo, they sing about the splitting of the Red Sea. Then they place the *dalet* and *vav* pieces of matzo over their eyes as they say *Ha lachma anya*, "This is the bread of affliction (or poor bread)." The word *ha* can be read as the letter *he*, implying that the matzo, the *he*, is now poor since it has become broken.

The numerical values of *dalet* and *vav* are four and six, respectively, which add up to the ten sefirot. Only when we find the afikoman can the matzo and the sefirot become whole again. The refinding of the hidden afikoman symbolizes the sexual conjunction of the Shekhinah with the lower six sefirot, which represent severity, and their further harmonization with the upper three sefirot, representing mercy. The middle and bottom matzo stand for the second and third sefirot, wisdom and understanding. The larger part of the second broken matzo is the *vav*, which stands for Da'at, knowledge, a kind of hidden eleventh sefirah, that links and harmonizes wisdom and understanding. This is not your average garden variety of knowledge. This is mystical knowledge, gnosis, the knowing:

> *Where do we come from? What are we? Where are we going?*
> —Paul Gauguin

It does not matter if you understand that last paragraph. The important fact to take away from it is that at the beginning of the seder, we hid this knowledge, the *vav*-shaped matzo. Now we have found it again. We take the knowledge into ourselves by eating it. This is not something we can know in the way that we know Cartesian geometry or how to tune an automobile engine. This is knowledge that must be experienced, ingested physically. Our actions hint and urge and persuade our redemption, but we keep silent so as not to put the whammy on our wish, just as we keep our wishes secret when we blow out the candles on a birthday cake.

The idea of either the children holding the stolen matzo for ransom or making a treasure hunt out of finding it is quite recent. When they find it, the children must be paid for its return. This keeps the children awake and attentive until after the meal. It involves them in the seder as "a night of watching." Many of our actions will make the children watch us closely and ask questions: candles, reclining, hand washing, dipping, odd foods, their display, unusual ways of eating the foods, removing drops of wine, opening doors, and so on.

The afikoman is also our final anti-demonic. Traditionally, it became a talismanic object, a piece of it being saved for the rest of the year for good luck. It could be carried as an amulet, nailed on the wall, or saved between the pages of the Haggadah, waiting to be shaken out the following spring to make way for next year's afikoman. The time from its removal during the search for the chametz the night before, until its replacement in the Haggadah at the end of the meal, was fraught with possible mishap. My grandfather told us to put it in a drawer until the following Pesach.

Beyond keeping the children interested throughout the seder, the ritual of the afikoman also fits in with the sequence of inversions that have characterized the night. Not only have we all come together as Jews, whether child or adult, woman or man, Kohen, Levi, or Yisrael, learned or *am ha-aretz* (people of the earth, ignorant), rich or poor, but we have ignored those distinctions at the table in favor of creating community.

We have made the evening child-centered in a variety of ways.

We share wine with the children, erasing boundaries of age. Many of our actions are aimed at arousing the curiosity of the children. We eat unusual foods in unusual ways. We sit down to eat and do not eat. We purge our homes of the most basic food, bread, the staff of life. Later we will see that two main parts of our Haggadah text, the *fier kashes* (four questions) and the parable of the four children, occur near the beginning of the seder. Without a child to ask the four questions, we could not even begin to explain why we do what we do. Further, no matter our age or level of learning, we are enjoined to put ourselves into the role of the child on this night. We are here to learn:

> . . . *and a little child shall lead them.*
> —Isaiah 11:6

The specific relationship that brings us together is that we are all the Children of Israel.

Now we go further. Not only are the children necessary to kick off the seder, but at this point we cannot continue without them. By whatever methods, either stealing or finding, they have possession of the one object we need to continue and they are holding it for ransom. One year my son felt the reward was inadequate to the value of the afikoman, and it took quite a bit of cajoling and intimidation to pry it loose from him. He was within his rights, actually. He knew that through the process of inversion he was in charge, however briefly. Indeed, without the transmission of our heritage to our children—not just our giving it, but their receiving it as well—not only the seder, but our very culture cannot continue.

Step XIII. Barekh

Ritual action 24: Pour the third cup of wine, lift the cup, and drink.

Having finished the meal, we cap it off with a third glass of wine.

Ritual action 25: Pour the wine for Elijah and open the door for him.

We are so confident now that we pour a cup of wine and open the door for the prophet Elijah—or are we checking for eavesdroppers, informers, calumniators, and Cossacks? Perhaps for a moment we can expand our protected circle to include all the Jewish people who are, in a manner of speaking, simultaneously opening their doors to the common visitor at every seder, Elijah. The honor of opening the door is usually given to a child. It is through our children that we receive our future. This custom of opening the door may go back to Temple times. The historian Josephus mentions that the priests would open the Temple doors immediately after midnight on Pesach. Similarly, we must finish our afikoman by midnight, and shortly thereafter we open our doors.

Ritual action 26: Close the door.

Step XIV. Hallel

Ritual action 27: Pour the fourth cup of wine, lift the cup, and drink.

Following this adventurous opening of ourselves up to chance, we close the door, have a final glass of wine, and are finished. There is more to the seder, but nothing more of a ritual nature.

XV. Nirtzah

And so the seder is concluded.

The Rite of Strict Observance

This is a good place to discuss what I consider overly scrupulous Passover and seder practices:

- Since we are told we are going to dip twice, some people object to dipping their egg into saltwater because it constitutes a third dipping. That explains the hard-boiled-egg soup mystery. Those who mash or slice up their egg in the saltwater ahead of time are obviously avoiding a third dipping. It is possible, though, that egg dipping developed as a way of avoiding the unlucky aspects of double-dipping.

- One Passover accessory that is available to the most neurotically observant is a laminated sheet showing how quickly and how many *ka-zayit* (ounces) of the matzo, afikoman, and bitter herbs should be eaten during different parts of the ritual.

- No further back than the nineteenth century, some Chasidim decided that it was improper to make any dish in which liquid was added to matzo since fermentation might occur. Those who observe this rule do not eat any *gebroks* (broken and moistened matzo): no matzo balls, matzo meal pancakes, *matzo brei,* or almost anything else that reveals the ingenuity of the Jewish people and lends distinctiveness to the holiday cuisine can be eaten except on the last day, the eighth day added to the festival by the rabbis.

Strict adherence to these rules suggests an intensification of the pain of the *galut* (exile) and a feverish drive to hasten the coming of the Messiah by ever more rigorous ritual practices:

> *The Messiah will come only when he is no longer necessary; he will come only on the day after his arrival; he will come, not on the last day, but on the very last.*
>
> —Franz Kafka

Be that as it may, these are the kinds of practices that turn many people away from Jewish practice. They reflect an unmitigated theurgical approach to Judaism in which our lives are not only congruent with the divine plan, but in which we can even exercise power over God and force the divine hand.

It is ironic that the most strictly observant Jewish group today is the Chasidim since they were reviled by their original opponents, the Mitnaggedim, for laxness of observance. It would take an enormous volume unto itself just to tell all the Chasidic anecdotes that emphasize the importance of heartfelt emotion over correct performance. So just this one: The Ba'al Shem Tov, the founder of Chasidism, told a disciple the *kavvanot* (mystical intentions) that should be in his mind as he pronounced the order of notes for the blowing of the shofar (ram's horn) on Yom Kippur (Day of Atonement). The disciple wrote them down, but then lost the slip of paper. When it came time to announce the notes in their proper sequence, he could only state them simply while weeping over his loss. Later the Ba'al Shem indicated to him that his feelings had been more effective in performing the rite than all the kavvanot because God loves a broken heart.

Most of us fall somewhere between ultra-orthodox performance of Jewish ritual and a complete turning away from Jewish practice. Our task is to decide what is the right way, the natural way, the comfortable way for us to be Jewish. We want to find our own proper balance of freedom and discipline so that we can release those profound feelings that are enfolded in the seder performance.

Again, with just the prepared table plus the addition of this mute book, symbol and ritual alone with no liturgy or song, we have been able to convey a great deal of the content of the traditional seder. This might be enough for some celebrants, this:

> . . . *foster-child of silence and slow time* . . .
> —John Keats

In the next chapter, we will slowly begin to add texts to our minimalist ceremony, or wordless happening, in order to strengthen our mute book with words and music.

Kadesh Urchatz: Fifteen Steps to the Temple

Now that we know what is brought to the table and how and when we use it, we should note that the seder itself recognizes its own order. Indeed, seder means order, just as *siddur* (the prayer book), refers to the order of prayer, *sidre* refers to the six orders of the

Mishnah, and *sidrah* (the weekly Torah portion), refers to the order in which the portions are arranged. This order of the seder not only gives order to our ritual meal, but brings us into order with the world. It aligns us in time and space every spring.

After the candles are lit and before the Kiddush, we chant Kadesh Urchatz, the mnemonic poem or table of contents that tells us what we must do to complete the performance of the seder. There are fifteen elements that comprise the totality of what we need to accomplish on the night of the fifteenth of Nisan, just as there were fifteen semicircular steps in the Temple:

I.	Kadesh:	*Sanctify* the evening with wine.
II.	Urchatz:	*Wash* the hands.
III.	Karpas:	*Green vegetable* is eaten dipped in saltwater.
IV.	Yachatz:	*Divide* the middle matzo, reserving half for the afikoman.
V.	Maggid:	*Tell* the story of the Exodus.
VI.	Rachtzah:	*Wash* the hands for the meal.
VII.	Motzi:	*Blessing* is said and . . .
VIII.	Matzo:	. . . *Matzo* is eaten.
IX.	Maror:	*Bitter herb* is eaten dipped in charoset.
X.	Korekh:	*Sandwich* bitter herbs between matzot and eat them.
XI.	Shulchan Arukh:	*Prepared Table,* eat the meal.
XII.	Tzafun:	*Hidden matzo,* the afikoman, is eaten.
XIII.	Barekh:	*Blessings* in thanks for the meal are said.

xiv. Hallel: *Praise* songs are chanted.

xv. Nirtzah: *Acceptance* of our seder is
                            beseeched.

When we compare our symbolic and ritual seder with the
complete one, we find that we are only missing four of the fifteen
requisite parts of a traditional Passover service: the four sections
where text is intrinsic to the fulfillment of the directive. For some,
this might be enough. When we start to add the text in the next
chapter, we will begin to glimpse a further layer of complexity.

Chapter Four

Barukh Attah:
Blessed Art Thou

The Benedictions

Now we are ready to add our first texts, the simplest *berakhot* (benedictions), to the prepared table and the mute book. Their language and form date back to the biblical period. Jews love to come up with occasions, both unusual and common, on which to utter these one-line appreciations: from seeing rainbows or the Northern Lights to eating a loquat. The seder is crammed full of them: candle lighting; six in conjunction with the wine plus the Kiddush; the She-Hecheyanu, twice at the first seder; the green vegetable; hand washing; two over the matzo; the bitter herb; four within the Birkat (Grace after Meals); the counting of the omer at the second seder; and two for Havdalah when the seder is on Saturday night.

These Are the Words of the Lord: Hebrew or English?

If you dislike reading an unintelligible foreign language, by all means read the berakhot in English. It is not only permissible to recite the Haggadah in the vernacular, it is incumbent upon us to be sure that everyone understands why we are performing the ceremony. The English language—if used as a way of telling the story, explaining the symbols, and shaping the seder—is essential for most of us.

If words like bless, Lord, God, King, sanctify, and command-ments make you uncomfortable, however, be aware of two consid-erations. First, the English words only approximate the meaning of their Hebrew counterparts. Even if we cannot understand the He-brew, at least we are freed from listening to the mediocre language that usually passes for translations of Hebrew. Too often these translations, in an effort to achieve the majestic, have substituted dead, sanctimonious, oily, lethargical/liturgical words in place of either the original or a living, heartfelt English:

> It frequently happens that where the second line is sublime,
> the third, in which he meant to rise still higher, is perfect
> bombast.

—Longinus

We can enjoy the music of the ancient tongue, its unique throat clearings and glottal stops, its incantatory quality, its rhyth-mic repetitions of phrases all fitted to the natural human breath. Breath in Hebrew is *ruach,* but it is also wind, spirit, the Spirit of God that hovered over the Deep to create the world, and one of the five human souls.

Once we begin to learn the Hebrew, we find that these words are a code for describing a feeling of awe before the universe that is not open to simple word-by-word translation. For example, mitz-vah, sometimes translated as commandment and at other times as good deed, implies a uniquely Jewish attitude toward social and spiritual obligation that is merely hinted at in the English. Many of the other words from Jewish sacred texts are best understood in their relationship to the ten *sefirot.* All of the names we give to God and all of the descriptive adjectives about God can only be under-stood as they are connected to God's various emanations and to our role in the process of helping to make the divine energy flow properly from one sefirah to the next.

Only when we hear the words of the Haggadah in Hebrew, or at least certain key words, can we begin to hear the repetition of sounds, word roots, and references to the emanations of the God-head, to the situation of the Jewish people throughout history, to the specifics of the story of the departure from Egypt, to the symbols on the table. All these words echo back and forth throughout the ceremony, vibrating different chords of meaning for each seder celebrant.

In English we hear too much of the Egypt and Pharaoh of the past; but in Hebrew the scene shifts to Mitzrayim, which not only means Egypt but also means borders, limits, the narrow place, straitened circumstances. The forty years in the wilderness is Be-Midbar, the Hebrew name for the fourth book of the Torah, Numbers. It is also the word for speech, and the Israelites heard God's speech at Sinai, in Midbar. More than just the Sinai Peninsula 3,000 years ago, it is the metaphorical place between confinement and freedom. And it is also the Sinai Peninsula today, where history continues to repeat itself. In English it is a Sunday school lesson. In Hebrew it is the rubbing together of an incredible range of ideas, feelings, memories, sensations, jokes. They come from psychology, history, literature, childhood, meals, school, headlines, gossip, common knowledge, from undesignated places; and through the focusing and arranging of the seder, they are put into an order whose whole is greater than the sum of its parts:

> *The ordinary man's experience is chaotic, irregular, fragmentary. The latter falls in love, or reads Spinoza, and these two experiences have nothing to do with each other, or with the noise of the typewriter or the smell of cooking; in the mind of the poet these experiences are always forming new wholes.*

—T. S. Eliot

Participating in the seder lets us bring order out of the chaos. We reconnect the fragments—of our scattered thoughts, of the divided matzo, of our wandering people, of the sparks in exile. The use of even minimal amounts of Hebrew strengthens our ability to connect with these mythic and poetic modes of thought through both compression of meaning and a combination of the familiar and unfamiliar. Once this starts to happen, we can begin to return real value to the English words, bringing them to life again. Suddenly we wonder about the actual meaning of bless, Lord, God, King, sanctify, and commandments.

The second consideration is that you might freshly translate the Hebrew if you have the language skills, or retranslate the translations into meaningful English for yourself. If you are a feminist and want to say, "O Shekhinah our Goddess Queen of the Universe," mixing politics and kabbalah, that is fine, though you can probably do better than my glib inversion. Really understanding these words by our own lights will require many thoughtful sedarim. The following translations will stay close to the familiar, but feel free to change them to suit yourself.

Poetry is what is lost in translation   —*Robert Frost*

So we see that Hebrew is a poetic, magical, poignant medium apart from what it denotes. The kabbalah provides us with the concept of *kavvanot,* intentionality. Every symbol, action, and word should assist us in getting focused, concentrated, on the events of the seder. That is why the appearance, ingredients, and flavor of everything matters, why we decide how to lean as we eat, how to wash our hands and hold our cup of wine. It is why we attach an importance to the language in which we communicate with the divine. If we merely do these things in an automatic way, then our culture has degenerated into a set of superstitious, apotropaic (warding off evil) customs.

All religions have that element in them, and it is not necessarily bad. At least everyone in the culture shares the same sanctions and taboos. Today we all have to start from scratch and make up our own individual magic, a mixture of respect for the devil and ways to trick him. We can achieve magic in a higher sense, however, not by performing arcane rites, but by engaging in the same customs as the rest of our community. Magic need not be esoteric, secret, in order to be soteric, redeeming. In fact, the more common the custom is, the better for our purposes. Length of time, well over three millennia in fact, and a people as numerous "as the sand which is upon the seashore" (Genesis 22:13), have polished the rough edges off these stones of custom until they have been ground as brilliant and hard as adamantine.

We have to invest these actions with power not through rigorous performance of magical rites, but through *kavvanot*, intentionality: paying attention, noticing, raising our actions beyond the mundane, separating the sacred from the profane. This process of separation is the same as that of the alchemist or spagyrist (from the Greek for "to separate and reassemble") who raises our dull, heavy, leaden self into spiritual gold. The use of Hebrew can assist us in separating the sparks of the holy from the profane matrix of our world in which they have become embedded.

Most religions generate the holy through the creation of enormous spaces devoted solely to the community's worship of God. Jewish practice, though, avoids the monumental in favor of the trivial, which literally means "the place where three roads meet, a crossroads, that which is common":

> *It is manifest to all men, the poor have more of it than the rich. The good part of it people discard, and the bad part they retain. It is visible and invisible, children play with it in the lane.*
>
> —Paracelsus

Perhaps because we were wanderers without a homeland, there was little point in erecting vast edifices to our God—buildings that we might have to leave behind quickly, fleeing persecution with our kneading troughs on our shoulders. What's more, those among whom we lived often forbade us to build large structures that might vie with their own. In Prague the fourteenth-century Altneuschul, the oldest surviving European synagogue, could not be built taller than the lowest nearby churches, so the community scooped out the basement level to increase the interior height of the synagogue. Usually, however, instead of gigantic structures fixed in space, Jews created small portable ritual objects that were easily packed up if you had to move quickly, like *chanukkiyot* and Havdalah spice towers that referred to the Temple of the past and hoped-for future.

Not only were the objects themselves small, but they celebrated small moments, like lighting candles or smelling spices. Homemade wall hangings and challah and matzo covers literally weave the name of God into the fabric of everyday life. Jewish practice occurs in the everyday. It has to do with the human activities of eating food, drinking, walking through doorways, gathering bread crumbs or casting them away. A Chasidic story tells how Rabbi Leib, son of Sarah, the hidden *tzaddik,* asserted that he had not gone to his teacher, Dov Baer, the Maggid of Mezhirech, to hear Torah, "But to see how he unlaces his felt shoes and laces them up again." It is in the simplest actions that we can learn to sacralize the everyday, the trivial:

> *That's it, that's joy, it's always a recognition, the known*
> *appearing fully itself, and more itself than one knew.*
> —Denise Levertov

The kabbalists developed a variety of mystical intentions that were to be said and thought before performing any of the mitzvot. For instance, before reciting the Kiddush over the initial cup of wine, some have the custom of saying:

> Herewith I am prepared and arrayed to fulfill the command of the first of the four cups to the unification
> of the Holy One, blessed be He, and His Shekhinah,
> through Him, the Hidden One and the Secret One,
> in the name of all Israel.

Kavvanot were added on to Jewish practice when that practice had become formulaic. Unfortunately, the kavvanot can become just as much rote practice as the berakhot. You can add these statements of intention to your seder performance if you want to, or you can accomplish the same result through focused concentration on the berakhot themselves, especially if they are said in Hebrew. That does not mean that the use of English will act as a fiery, whirling sword barring our access to Paradise, but within the context of the seder, Hebrew has some strong advantages. You will have to make the final decision on what is a comfortable balance between Hebrew and English at your seder. On the side of English, there is familiarity and total comprehension. On the side of Hebrew, there is transforming power, aesthetic pleasure, the link to all the Jewish people and authenticity:

> *The authentic! It rolls just out of reach . . .*
> —Denise Levertov

Hebrew increases the potency of the rituals. Adding even a small amount of Hebrew to the seder will break the wall that separates our everyday speech from the poetic:

> *In modern prose all poetry seems drowned.*
> —Israel Zangwill

English will no longer be standing alone. Its monopoly on meaning will be shattered. It will be humbled, deflated. The Hebrew words will confer their meaning onto the English and it will begin to have meaning again: "This is the bread of affliction." If you add only a dozen one-line Hebrew berakhot to it, your seder will metamorphose through a Red "sea-change into something rich and strange." Hebrew has power for many reasons. It is one of the most ancient languages on earth. It is the language of creation and revelation. It does not just describe the world, it makes it. The actual Hebrew words of the Torah are assumed to be the words God used to create our world:

> *One little sound might destroy the Earth. One little sound might create a new universe.*
> —Hans Arp

Hebrew is also resonant with our whole, heartbreaking history. It is our memory. We have heard it and not quite understood it all our lives. It partakes, then, of what Freud calls *unheimlich*, the uncanny, something totally strange and yet completely familiar, *haimish*. It is our double; ourselves and not ourselves. Through the use of Hebrew, we attach our seder not just to history, but to myth as well:

> *A myth is as good as a smile.*
> —James Joyce

These simple, terse utterances create an envelope or frame for our actions. It is the frame that helps us to give meaning to the seder:

> *Rite words in rote order.*
> —James Joyce

The most stringently made shemurah matzo only becomes acceptable for ritual use if the baker recited the appropriate benediction before making it. Although we may not know any Hebrew, we can learn to say the berakhot through transliteration and by listening to tapes. Though the bulk of our Haggadah may have to be said in English, just peppering that recitation with the Hebrew berakhot will give it real Jewish *ta'am* (flavor).

Blessings without Number

It is traditional to try to say 100 benedictions a day, and the seder gives us a good start with at least nineteen on the first night. Berakhot begin with the word *Barukh*, usually translated as "blessed," which comes from a root meaning "to bend the knee." So when we make a berakhah, we are bending the knee to the source from which all blessings flow. The standard opening is:

Barukh Attah Adonai Elohenu Melakh ha-Olam . . .

Blessed are You, O Lord our God King of the
Universe . . .

The word Adonai, one of the many names of God, is substituted vocally for the visual sign made up of the four Hebrew letters
Yod He Vav He, or YHVH, the unpronounceable Tetragrammaton.
We know this in English as Jehovah, a word you get when you add
the vowels of Adonai to the four Hebrew letters YHVH. Jews know
of no such being as Jehovah, but since we always say Adonai when
the Tetragrammaton appears, Christians merged the vowels of the
spoken substitute name onto the consonants of the unpronounceable name and came up with a new name of God.

The Tetragrammaton, a variant of the Hebrew verb "to be"—
as in Ehyeh Asher Ehyeh, "I am that I am," another of God's
names—was pronounced only once a year, by only one person, and
in only one place. That was when the High Priest uttered it on Yom
Kippur in the Holy of Holies of the Temple as part of the process
of receiving atonement for the Children of Israel. Possible permu-
tations and combinations of ways of saying YHVH were utilized by
ecstatic mystics like Abraham Abulafia as part of their contempla-
tive practice. Today, however, no one knows how to say it and for
millennia we have substituted the word Adonai wherever the Tetragrammaton is written.

The fact that there are two names for God in this one sentence, the Tetragrammaton and Elohenu, suggests an attempt to
make God and his name one, as it says in the Alenu prayer at the
close of every prayer service. That is, our usually limited, fragmen-
tary perception of the divine will become equivalent with the actu-
ality of the divine. This is one of the goals of the Jewish mystic. We
express the same desire when we recite the paramount statement of
faith, the Shema:

Shema Yisrael Adonai Elohenu Adonai Echad.

Hear, O Israel, the Lord Our God, the Lord Is One.

Adonai is a euphemism for the Tetragrammaton here as it is in the berakhot. In both cases, the masculine Tetragrammaton is linked to the feminine Elohenu, the Shekhinah; the transcendent aspects of God are linked to the immanent aspects; the singular and unitary is linked to the plural and multiplicity. Our opening benedictory phrase is completed with the expression "King of the World" or "universe." So each time we say a berakhah we are trying to unite the separated parts of God, the heavenly male part and the female part that shares our exile. As we are in exile from Israel, so is part of God in exile from itself.

After that opening phrase, our berakhah can go in two directions. Either we have a simple prayer of thanks specifying bread, fruit, wine, vegetables, and so on, or if we are fulfilling a commandment, we add the phrase:

> . . . *Asher kiddeshanu be-mitzvotav ve-tzivvanu* . . .
>
> . . . Who has sanctified us with Your commandments and commanded us to . . .

Either way, the specific reason for the benediction comes at the end. We bless God for divine blessings and we are made holy by performing God's commandments. The berakhot give us a way to become focused on our actions by telling ourselves what we are doing and why we are performing the rituals and so heightening our awareness of our actions. As a title can provide an entrance to an abstract painting, the berakhot give us a handle for entry into the amorphous actions we are performing. By uttering benedictions, the simple acts of eating certain foods, lighting candles, or washing the hands, are changed into magical or transforming rites.

They are an especially good way for us to begin to add text to our mute book because of their terseness and simplicity.

Two Boxcars of Seder Benedictions

We will use the same system of headings and numerals as in chapter 3 so that you will know exactly where to insert the berakhot into the seder. A few other passages in the Haggadah can be considered benedictions, but the following are certainly the most prominent and relevant to our prepared table and mute book. You can do all of these, or just pick and choose the ones that fit with your own feelings and into your own seder.

Ritual action 1: Search the house for chametz. Before searching for the chametz on the night preceding the seder:

> *Barukh Attah Adonai Elohenu Melekh ha-Olam asher kiddeshanu be-mitzvotav ve-tzivvanu al biur chametz.*
>
> Blessed are You, O Lord our God King of the Universe, who has sanctified us with Your commandments and commanded us concerning the removal of leaven.

Ritual action 2: Burn the chametz. No benediction.

Ritual action 3: Light the candles. The phrase in parentheses is added on Friday nights:

> *Barukh Attah Adonai Elohenu Melekh ha-Olam asher kiddeshanu be-mitzvotav ve-tzivvanu le-hadlikh ner shel (Shabbat ve-shel) Yom Tov.*
>
> Blessed are You, O Lord our God King of the Universe, who has sanctified us with Your commandments and commanded us to kindle the (Sabbath and) festival lights.

Benedictions are almost invariably said before performing the mitzvah or eating the food, but lighting candles poses an unusual problem. Once we say the berakhah, we may not make fire on the Sabbath; but if we light the candles first, then the berakhah becomes an afterthought. There could have been many answers to this problem, but the traditional solution allows for one of the most beautiful moments in all of Jewish ceremony. We light the candles, then cover our eyes while saying the blessing. When we open our eyes again, there is a sense of surprised delight at the festival *licht*. They sneak up on us. "Boo!" they say. Oddly, just watching someone else go through this beautiful, yet evanescent, performance achieves the same effect. Even though the custom began for Shabbat, it has been extended to the holidays by most people.

The She-Hecheyanu blessing that follows immediately after is to be said for something new: new clothes, first peach or pomegranate of the year, or as in this case, reaching the milestone of the beginning of a festival. It has a beautiful melody (see chapter 7 for recordings), dreamy and hypnotic, entrancing us from the profane through the entrance to the sacred, and makes a good warm-up for the group singing to come. Most people do not say it on the second night:

> *Barukh Attah Adonai Elohenu Melekh ha-Olam she-hecheyanu ve-keyamanu ve-hegeyanu lazman hazeh.*
>
> Blessed are You, O Lord our God King of the Universe, who has kept us alive and sustained us and enabled us to reach this season.

At this point it is traditional to bless the children. This priestly benediction, from Numbers 6:24–26, carries out one of the seder motifs because it consists of fifteen words. If you want to add this to your seder, place your hands on your children's (or even your guests') heads and say:

Yavorechachah Adonai ve-yishmorechah. Ya-air Adonai
pahnav ehlechah vichunachah. Yisah Adonai pahnav
ehlechah, ve-yahsame lecha shalom.

May the Lord bless you and protect you. May the Lord
make His face to shine upon you and be gracious to you.
May the Lord favor you and grant you peace.

Step I. Kadesh

Ritual action 4: Pour the first cup of wine, lift the cup, and drink.
Kiddush, the sanctification over the wine, is one of the fifteen prescribed parts of the seder, the Kadesh. It is ascribed to the Men of
the Keneset ha-Gedolah (the Great Assembly), who were active in
the early period of the Second Temple (sixth century B.C.E.). If the
holiday begins on a Friday night, you say Genesis 1:31 and 2:1–3
as a preamble. The initial letters of the last two words of 1:31 and
the first two of 2:1 spell the Tetragrammaton, YHVH. The second
sentence connects the original creation and God's rest with the regular recurrence of the day of rest. At this point the Sephardim
shout, "*L'chayim!*" "To Life!" You then continue with:

> *Barukh Attah Adonai Elohenu Melekh ha-Olam borey peri*
> *ha-gefen.*

> Blessed are You, O Lord our God King of the Universe,
> who creates the fruit of the vine.

> *Barukh Attah Adonai Elohenu Melekh ha-Olam asher*
> *bachar banu micahl-ahm ve-romamanu mikol-lahshon ve-*
> *kiddeshanu be-mitzvitahv. Vahtitan-lanu Adonai Elohenu*
> *be-ahavah (Shabatot limnuchah u-) moahdim le-simcha*
> *chagim u-zemanim le-sahsone et-Yom (ha-Shabbat hazeh*
> *ve-et-Yom) Chag ha-Matzot hazeh zeman chayrusaynu*

(be-ahavah) mikrah-kodash zaychehr litziyot Mitzrayim.
Ki vanu vachartah ve-osanu kiddashtah mikol-ha-amim
(ve-Shabbat) u-moahday kadshecha (be-ahavah u-veratzon)
be-simcha u-vesahson hinchaltanu. Barukh Attah Adonai
me-kadesh (ha-Shabbat ve-) Yisrael ve-ha-zemanim.

Blessed are You, O Lord our God King of the Universe,
who chose us from among all the peoples and exalted us
from among every tongue and sanctified us with Your
commandments. With love, O Lord our God, You have
given us holidays for gladness (the Sabbath for rest),
festivals and seasons for rejoicing, this (Sabbath and
this) day of the Festival of Unleavened Bread, the season
of our deliverance (with love), a holy convocation in
remembrance of the departure from Egypt. For You have
chosen us and You have sanctified us from among all the
peoples (and the Sabbath) and the holy days of Your
sanctification (with love and favor) You have given us, to
inherit with joy and gladness. Blessed are You, O Lord,
who sanctifies (the Sabbath and) Israel and the seasons.

This long paragraph is a berakhah itself. The portions in
parentheses are read on Friday nights. The melody is exalted and
beautiful. Even in the Kiddush for festivals (as well as the Shabbat
Kiddush) we make mention of the departure from Egypt.

If Passover begins on Saturday night, you can say two further
benedictions for the Havdalah, the separation of the holy from the
profane, another creation of the Men of the Great Assembly. Since
we are moving from Sabbath to festival, though, we speak of dividing the holy from the holy. There are many magical customs associated with this demarcation of a fleeting moment. While saying the
benediction, it is customary to hold your fingers in front of the
flames to see the difference between shadow and light, as well as
the lunar crescents on the fingernails. During the first benediction

over fire, you look at your fingernails resting on your thumbs and then, during the second benediction, extending the fingers, look at the backs of your hands.

We enter Shabbat and the holidays with gesture and leave the Shabbat with a parallel set of hand gestures. Usually we smell spices to revive our fading spirits at the loss of the Shabbat and our extra Sabbath soul, our link to the Shekhinah, but that is omitted tonight because we remain in the realm of hallowed time and space. One of the paradoxes of a Saturday night seder is the fact that we light candles and say Kiddush over the wine to usher in the festival and immediately make benedictions over the same candles and the same wine ushering out the Shabbat.

> *Barukh Attah Adonai Elohenu Melekh ha-Olam borey me'orey ha-esh.*
>
> Blessed are You, O Lord our God King of the Universe, who creates the light of the fire.

Since my intention is to add terse Hebrew passages, I will give only the English for the second Havdalah benediction:

> Blessed are You, O Lord our God King of the Universe, who divides the holy from the profane, light from darkness, Israel from the nations, the seventh day from the six days of work. You have divided the sanctity of the Sabbath from the sanctity of the holiday and have sanctified the seventh day above the six days of work. You have set apart and hallowed Your people Israel with Your sanctity. Blessed are You, O Lord, who divides the holy from the holy.

This is spagyric—to separate and recombine, to transmute. We do this not for the purpose of making one set of things unholy, but to assist us in constantly rescuing the sparks of the holy, changing unholy, profane, secular actions like eating, drinking, and hand washing, into heightened moments of awareness. Following that remarkable passage giving definition to an intangible moment of transition through time, the Kiddush closes with a repetition of the same She-Hecheyanu berakhah we said after lighting the candles. Some have the custom of only saying the She-Hecheyanu once, but common practice is for the woman, or candle lighter, to say it over the candles and the man, or Kiddush maker, over the wine. Again, most do not say the She-Hecheyanu at the second seder. Immediately, with just the recitation of these few benedictions, we have heightened the feeling of creating a protected, holy circle at the seder table.

Since this sequence of five berakhot can become confusing, a mnemonic phrase was used to remember the order in which to say them. Using the first Hebrew letters of the words *yayin* (wine), Kiddush (sanctification), *nehr* (light), Havdalah (separation), and *zeman* (season or time, referring to a key word in the She-Hecheyanu), the phrase *yaknehaz* was created. The Yiddish writer Shalom Aleichem set some of his stories in a town with this name, while another Yiddish writer, Isaiah-Nissan Hakohen Goldberg, took the mnemonic as his pen name. To the Yiddish or German speaker, yaknehaz sounds like *Jag' den Has* or Hunt the Hare. Many old Haggadot simply show a hare hunt at this point, without bothering to mention the *aide mémoire*.

Since Jewish tradition frowns on hunting, and certainly for the non-kosher bunny, why this illustration? Art historian Marc Epstein has analyzed this motif brilliantly and arrived at the conclusion that the hare represents the Jewish people. In Jewish illustration and midrash, we find that Esau, the father of the Edomites, Rome, and Christianity, made a savory rabbit stew for his father, Isaac. Not only was this not kosher, which reflects badly on Esau, but it signals his antipathy for his brother Jacob, or Israel. Medieval Christians associated the unclean hare with the Jews, and we in turn adopted and inverted this badge, interpreting it positively. In other words, Jews do not identify with the hunters, but with the hunted who constantly elude their foes. In some Haggadot the hares do escape from their pursuers.

Step II. Urchatz

Ritual action 5: Wash hands. No benediction.

Step III. Karpas

Ritual action 6: Eat the green vegetable dipped in saltwater. The green vegetable is the first food of the evening and merits its own blessing, which also covers the bitter herbs eaten later in the ceremony:

> *Barukh Attah Adonai Elohenu Melekh ha-Olam borey peri ha-adamah.*
>
> Blessed are You, O Lord our God King of the Universe, who creates the fruit of the earth.

Step IV. Yachatz

Ritual action 7: Break the middle matzo and set aside the afikoman. No benediction.

Step V. Maggid

Ritual actions 8 through 14: No benediction.

Ritual action 15: Raise the wine cup and drink the wine. The second cup of wine is drunk, while leaning to the left, just before the meal. The usual berakhah is preceded by a benedictory paragraph given here in English. This passage reminds us that the actual Temple service was a bloody sacrificial cult involving up to 250,000 lambs at a Passover. Although these were all eaten, the actual ritual slaughtering involved an enormous amount of lamb's blood being dashed against the sides of the altar. Judaism, since the destruction of the Temple, has spiritualized the Temple cult into prayer and the sanctification of the trivial; the altar, with its sacrificial fire and table of showbread, into the dinner table with candles, bread, wine, and salt; and animal sacrifice into the ritual method of slaughtering kosher animals for human consumption.

Whenever the *shochet* (ritual slaughterer) kills an animal today, it is done in the same way that the Kohanim (priests) did it ritually in the Temple service. Our usual modern way of killing animals is far more brutal than Jewish ritual methods, which have the intention, usually forgotten today, of making us aware of the animal life we are taking in order to sustain ourselves. This is similar to what Native Americans and other traditional people do when they appropriate something from nature for human use. They do not want to deaden themselves to the sacrifice of life that is necessary to support human life.

As we move toward the meal, we also mention the matzo and bitter herbs we are just about to eat. The following passage is ascribed, at least in part, to Rabbi Akiba.

> Blessed are You, O Lord our God King of the Universe, who redeemed us and who redeemed our ancestors from Egypt and who has brought us to this night to eat matzo and bitter herbs. So, O Lord our God and God of our fathers and mothers, bring us to other festivals and holy days that come toward us, in peace, happy in the building of Your city and joyous in Your service. And there may we eat of the sacrifices and the paschal offerings whose blood will be sprinkled on the walls of Your altar for acceptance. Then we will give thanks to You with a new song, for our redemption and the liberation of our soul. Blessed are You, O Lord, Redeemer of Israel.

> *Barukh Attah Adonai Elohenu Melekh ha-Olam borey peri ha-gefen.*

Blessed are You, O Lord our God King of the Universe, who creates the fruit of the vine.

Step VI. Rachtzah

Ritual action 16: Wash hands. The hands are washed a second time, but with the addition of the benediction. We move from a simple to a complex level of purity. The first hand washing was based on the old custom that one washed before eating any food dipped in a liquid. Now that we are actually going to eat a true meal, we increase the level of intention we accord to the washing of the hands. The word for washing, *netilat,* also means to lift up and some lift the hands after pouring water on them. Through our actions, benedictions, and intentions, we lift the sparks of the holy that have become mired in matter.

> *Barukh Attah Adonai Elohenu Melekh ha-Olam asher kiddeshanu be-mitzvotav ve-tzivvanu al netilat yadayim.*

Blessed are You, O Lord our God King of the Universe, who has sanctified us with Your commandments and commanded us concerning the washing of the hands.

Step VII. Motzi

Ritual action 17: Hold the matzot.

The Motzi is said over the two whole matzot and the half piece in their simple role as bread:

> *Barukh Attah Adonai Elohenu Melekh ha-Olam ha-Motzi lechem min ha-aretz.*

Blessed are You, O Lord our God King of the Universe, who brings forth bread from the earth.

Step VIII. Matzo

Ritual action 18: Hold the upper and middle matzot. The specific benediction over matzo as unleavened bread is said over the upper Kohen matzo and the broken half of the Levi:

> *Barukh Attah Adonai Elohenu Melekh ha-Olam asher kiddeshanu be-mitzvotav ve-tzivvanu al akelat matzo.*
>
> Blessed are You, O Lord our God King of the Universe, who has sanctified us with Your commandments and commanded us concerning the eating of unleavened bread.

Ritual action 19: After berakhot, eat matzo.

Step IX. Maror

Ritual action 20: Eat the bitter herb and *charoset*.

The bitter herbs are eaten. We only need one blessing for the mitzvah of eating the bitter herbs, since the blessing over the green vegetable covers our eating the maror. The following blessing also covers our eating of the Hillel sandwich, the *korekh*.

> *Barukh Attah Adonai Elohenu Melekh ha-Olam asher kiddeshanu be-mitzvotav ve-tzivvanu al akelat maror.*
>
> Blessed are You, O Lord our God King of the Universe, who has sanctified us with Your commandments and commanded us concerning the eating of bitter herbs.

Step X. Korekh

Ritual action 21: No benediction.

Step XI. Shulchan Arukh

Ritual action 22: No benediction.

Step XII. Tzafun

Ritual action 23: No benediction.

Step XIII. Barekh

Ritual action 24: Pour the third cup of wine, lift the cup, and drink. Grace is said concluding with the berakhah over the third cup of wine, usually voluntary with the Grace, but at the seder, mandatory. Birkat ha-Mazon, the Grace after Meals, is considered to be four benedictions, although some of them do not conform to the usual pattern. The following is a transliteration of the first paragraph and the four benedictions of the Grace after Meals in English followed by the standard blessing over wine.

> *Barukh Attah Adonai Elohenu Melekh ha-Olam hazan*
> *et ha-olam kulo be-tuvo be-chain be-chesed uv-rachamim.*
> *Hu nosain lechem le-chal basawr ki le-olam chasdo. Uv-*
> *tuvo ha-gadol tamid lo chasar lanu ve-al yachsar lanu*
> *mazon le-olam vaed ba-avur shmo ha-gadol. Ki hu el zawn*
> *u-mfarnase la-kol u-mativ la-kol u-machin mazon le-chol*
> *be-riotav asher bara. Barukh Attah Adonai hazon et ha-kol.*

Blessed are You, O Lord our God King of the Universe, who sustains the whole world with goodness, kindness, and mercy. . . . Blessed are You, O Lord, who sustains all.

We thank You, O Lord our God, for having given a pleasant, goodly, and broad land to our ancestors as a heritage; for having taken us out, O Lord our God, from the land of Egypt and freed us from the house of bondage; for Your covenant which You sealed in our flesh; for Your Torah which You have taught us; for the life, grace, and kindness You have bestowed on us; and

for the sustenance You grant us continuously. . . .
Blessed are You, O Lord, for the land and for the
sustenance.

Have mercy, O Lord our God, on Israel Your people,
on Jerusalem Your city, on Zion the abode of Your glory,
on the royal house of David Your chosen one, and on
the great and holy Temple that bears Your name. . . .
Blessed are You, O Lord, merciful Restorer of Jerusalem.
Amen.

Blessed are You, O Lord our God King of the
Universe. O God You are our Parent, our King, our
Creator, our Redeemer, the Holy One of Jacob, the
Shepherd of Israel, the good King who does good to all.

May the Compassionate One send us Elijah the
prophet, may his memory be for good, to bring us good
tidings, deliverance and comfort.

*Barukh Attah Adonai Elohenu Melekh ha-Olam borey peri
ha-gefen.*

Blessed are You, O Lord our God King of the Universe,
who creates the fruit of the vine.

The four benedictions of the Grace are said to have been composed by Moses, Joshua, Kings David and Solomon, and the last
by the talmudic sages around the time of the Bar Kokhba revolt.
Almost every important aspect of being Jewish is named in just the
short extract given here: the covenant of circumcision, the deliverance from Egypt, the Torah, the Promised Land, the Temple in a
restored Jerusalem, and the Messiah son of David, along with the
obvious thanks for sustenance. Grabbing a bite is no small accomplishment. Our brief lives are viewed within giant vistas. Notice
that the third benedictory paragraph concludes with the word

Amen. Usually, if we say a berakhah, we do not say Amen. Those who listen without reciting the words of the benediction along with us do say Amen. This portion of the Grace is the exception to that rule, and everyone says Amen.

A wonderful call and response *zimmun* (invitation) that precedes the actual Birkat can be recited whenever three or more people eat together. Further words can be added if you have a minyan (a quorum of ten).

Ritual action 25: No benediction.
Ritual action 26: No benediction.

Step XIV. Hallel

Ritual action 27: Pour the fourth cup of wine, lift the cup, and drink. Along with steps I (Kadesh), III (Karpas), VI (Rachtzah), VII (Motzi), VIII (Matzo), IX (Maror), and XIII (Barekh), Hallel is the last of eight out of the fifteen prescribed parts of the seder that requires a benediction. We said the Kiddush over the first cup of wine, the Maggid over the second cup, and the Grace after Meals over the third. Now we have said Hallel and other songs of praise over the fourth. If we look back over our benedictions, we can see that each of the four cups of wine was drunk with both the usual berakhah over wine as well as with a special set of benedictions particular to itself. Here is the final blessing over the wine, followed by the first and last lines in English of the special benediction said after the fourth cup:

> *Barukh Attah Adonai Elohenu Melekh ha-Olam borey peri ha-gefen.*

> Blessed are You, O Lord our God King of the Universe, Who creates the fruit of the vine.

> Blessed are You, O Lord our God King of the Universe, for the vine and for the fruit of the vine, for

the produce of the field, and for the land, pleasant,
goodly, and broad, which You favored and gave as an
inheritance to our ancestors, to eat of its fruit and to be
satisfied with its goodness. . . . Blessed are You, O Lord,
for the land and for the fruit of the vine.

Step XV. Nirtzah

On the second night of Passover, having completed our obligatory
recounting (*sapehr*) of the Exodus, we begin the counting (sefirah)
of the omer after the formal service has ended by saying the following berakhah:

> *Barukh Attah Adonai Elohenu Melekh ha-Olam asher*
> *kiddeshanu be-mitzvotav ve-tzivvonu al sefirat ha-omer.*
>
> Blessed are You, O Lord our God King of the Universe,
> who has sanctified us with Your commandments and
> commanded us concerning the counting of the omer.

We conclude with the formal statement that "Today is the first
day of the counting of the omer." This is repeated every day for
forty-eight more days until Shavuot, both the barley harvest and
the anniversary of the giving of the Torah at Mount Sinai.

Wheat is associated with our origins and redemption, while the
later barley harvest is associated with revelation. The forty-nine-day
period between the two pilgrimage festivals is considered an ominous time, lightened only on the thirty-third day, Lag Ba-Omer.
Through the counting and anticipation of the *sefirat ha-omer,* we
forge a link between these two pilgrimage festivals, between freedom and revelation. The same root is the source of the Hebrew
words for telling the story of the Exodus, counting the omer, and
the ten sefirot. We can understand the act of counting seven weeks
of seven days as another bringing of order or bringing into conjunc-

tion of the Shekhinah and the other six lower sefirot. Each week and each day is assigned to one of the sefirot, beginning with Chesed, continuing through Gevurah, Tiferet, Netzach, Hod, Yesod, and ending with Malkhut. The first day of counting becomes Chesed within Chesed and the last day is Malkhut within Malkhut. Lag Ba-Omer would then be Hod within Hod, majesty within majesty. For a fuller explanation of the ten sefirot, see chapter 2.

By adding these few familiar, easily learned, spoken, and understood passages, we have added a sparse liturgy to our prepared table and mute book. The symbols and rituals are now held together by a frame of intentions. That framework is resonant with the power of the Hebrew berakhot: magical, stirring, polyvalent, and nostalgic. At the same time, their minimal content manages to convey a good deal of information not only about Passover, but about a particular Jewish view of life. We have learned that this simple seder can be looked at from a variety of perspectives that go a long way toward making our actions meaningful and self-revelatory. For some, this might be a sufficient amount of text for their seder. If you agree, you can stop here. *Dayyenu.* But if you need to know more about why this night is different from all other nights, you will have to continue.

Chapter Five

Mah Nishtannah Ha-Layla Hazeh: Why Is This Night Different?

The Texts of the Haggadah

Now that we have brought everything to the prepared table, performed the rituals of the mute book, and learned to say the simple words *Barukh Attah,* we need to answer the question as to why we are differentiating this night from all other nights. We do this by adding the sometimes sung, sometimes recited, highly evocative poetic texts of the Haggadah to our seder.

The Haggadah

What could be more Jewish than a meal that cannot be eaten without a book? Perhaps this is just a clever way to get to read at the dinner table. The Haggadah is the book containing all the texts and ritual directions for the Passover seder. Pieced together with bits of Tanakh, *siddur,* Mishnah, Talmud, midrash, medieval *piyyutim* (liturgical poems), and folk song, it is a collage of 4,000 years of Jewish life, thought, and literature. It is our ancient *grimoire,* a grammar of the seder's magical rites, casting spells, enchanting, and calling down curses. Yet it goes beyond the magic of revenge, desire, and prophylaxis. It is through this variegated text that the protective magic of the mute book is elevated to a higher level of personal and communal transformation.

If the parts of the Haggadah seem disconnected from one another, it may be because this book is actually the surviving fragments of an anthology on the subject of Passover chosen over the last 3,300 years. The originals may have made more sense, but our people culled out of them whatever was not poetry. The dull prose that made it all cohere was jettisoned along the way. Only those bits and pieces that were green and alive, that spoke to the heart, were kept in the final work, which is never truly finished. This assemblage quality is part of its charm. If we had been obligated to spend the evening reading every relevant passage in the Bible, the Talmud tractate Pesachim, the festival prayers for Passover, plus relevant materials from the *Shulchan Arukh* and midrashic texts, that boring seder would long ago have disappeared from Jewish life.

Instead we get just a taste of all the ways that we can think about Pesach. We become exposed to a variety of intrinsically Jewish modes of thought. We hear the phrasing of the Psalms and the storytelling of the Torah. From later times comes the laconic utterances of the Mishnah, the argument and hermeneutical dexterity of the talmudic rabbis, the pleonastic praises of the siddur, and constant cataloguing, listing, and enumeration. We have all had the traditional forms of Jewish thought inculcated in us at the seder table.

And yet there is a sense to it after all. The whole performance is a memory theater that evokes its referents through a dense network of associations: some on the table, some in our actions, and some in the text. The use of juxtaposition highlights each piece, raises it in relief, and increases its power to make the spark of connection when rubbed against another touchstone of text, bringing things (to paraphrase Thomas Paine) "to light, which might otherwise have lain forever undiscovered." As we make our peripatetic way through the Haggadah, over and over, year after year, our steps, as John Locke said, "by often treading, are worn into a smooth path, and the motion in it becomes easy, and as it were natural." At the end of this section, we will see that, in spite of abrupt transitions and elaborate tracery, we can still find some patterns in our text.

Simple benedictions; hymns of praise, love, and awe for God and God's universe; magical incantations full of divine names; the chants of the angels around the heavenly throne; complicated analyses of biblical verses—all this and more have gone into the Haggadah. Even some of the rabbis' ancient jokes are embedded in it. Stories and legends stretching from the time of the patriarchs and matriarchs, the Exodus from Egypt, the Temple, the Babylonian exile, the *tannaim* and *amoraim,* bump up against the modern bondage of the Holocaust and our most recent miraculous deliverance, the creation of the State of Israel:

> *At this table the father of the family sits among relations and friends, and reads to them from a very curious book called the Haggadah, whose contents are a strange mixture of legends of their forefathers, wondrous tales of Egypt, remarkable stories, questions of theology, prayers and festival songs.*
> —Heinrich Heine, *The Rabbi of Bacharach*

Something in the material and arrangement of the traditional Haggadah has an effect on us that "can communicate before it is understood," as T. S. Eliot said of genuine poetry. We may love it, struggle with it, or change it, but we have to deal with it. The fact that it is cryptic or disjointed has little to do with its ability to work its magic on us. When we participate in the reading of the Haggadah, we become heir to this resonant, multilayered tradition of Jewish life and learning. As the sages said of the Torah, "Turn it and turn it again, for everything is in it."

The Structure of the Seder

Now we will go back over what we have already brought to the seder table and see how it meshes with the Haggadah text. The passages will be referred to by their Hebrew and Aramaic tag lines or with extracts in English. As with the *berakhot,* the more Hebrew you can comfortably add to the recitation, the more powerful are the tools you have at your disposal for breaking through to "what is this service to you," a heightened sense of the moment, the holy. At the end of this chapter you will find an annotated bibliography of Haggadot, which should help you to choose the appropriate one for your seder.

We will use the same system as we have in previous chapters, steps I through XV indicating the fifteen steps of the seder, and Arabic numerals 1 through 27 indicating the separate ritual actions. The words of the Haggadah have been broken down into twenty-six brief, manageable, interlocking pieces. We will designate these pieces of the text with the letters a through z. You can choose from this abecedary of textual fragments the elements you want to add to your seder. At this point, you might want to have a copy of the traditional Haggadah to hand so that you can read the passages in their entirety.

Ritual action 1: Search the house for chametz. This is a good place to mention that besides the berakhah said before the *bedikat chametz,* the following is said in Aramaic after the search:

> All leaven in my possession which I have not seen and
> have not removed and of which I am not aware is hereby
> nullified and ownerless as the dust of the earth.

Ritual action 2: Burn the chametz. By nine or ten o'clock on the morning before the seder, *erev* Pesach (the day preceding Passover), we should have eaten the last *chametzdikhe* food we had set aside. After that, we burn all the chametz turned up in our search the night before and say the following variation of the above statement:

> All leaven in my possession which I have seen or not seen, which I have removed or not removed, is hereby nullified and ownerless as the dust of the earth.

Martin Buber relates that when the Chasidic *tzaddik* Rabbi Baruch of Medzibezh burned his chametz, he spiritualized this Aramaic legal formula by explaining:

> "All leaven in my possession"—all that seethes—"which I have seen or not seen"—even though I believe I have looked into myself thoroughly, I have probably not looked thoroughly at all—"which I have removed or not removed"—the Evil Urge within me tries to convince me that I have removed everything, but not until now do I see that I have not removed it, and so I beg of You, God, "it is hereby nullified and ownerless as the dust of the earth."

Ritual action 3: Light the candles. Berakhot over the lighting of candles followed by the blessing of the children. At this point we can add the table of contents to our seder, Kadesh Urchatz, the recitation or chanting of the fifteen prescribed steps of the ceremony, as listed at the end of chapter 3. Many mnemonic lists of the steps of the seder have been created. This simple rhyme, which has room for the tiny moments as well as the grand, has outlasted all others. It is sometimes attributed to the eleventh-century Rabbi Solomon ben Isaac, known as Rashi, among the greatest Torah and Talmud scholars of all time. Others ascribe it to the thirteenth-century scholar Samuel ben Solomon of Falaise.

Up to this point, all we have done is prelude or overture to the seder proper, which is now ready to begin.

Step I. Kadesh

Ritual action 4: Pour the first cup of wine. As we have seen, this Kadesh can involve up to five berakhot. Throughout the ceremony, whenever we lift the wine cup or drink the wine, the matzot are covered. The matzot are slightly uncovered the rest of the time.

Step II. Urchatz

Ritual action 5: Wash hands, Urchatz, by pouring water over them from a pitcher.

Step III. Karpas

Ritual action 6: Eat the green vegetable dipped in saltwater. Everyone dips the karpas and eats, either leaning to the left or sitting upright, after reciting the berakhot.

Step IV. Yachatz

Ritual action 7: Break the middle matzo and set aside the afikoman. The middle matzo of the three is divided, Yachatz, in half. One half is wrapped up either to be stolen from the leader of the seder by the children or hidden from the children by the leader. We have had wine, an appetizer, and broken our bread, but we do not eat. We have done quite a number of mystifying procedures and by now everyone should be eager to find out why.

Step V. Maggid

Ritual action 8: Display the matzo and the seder plate. The seder plate and matzot are lifted up and displayed. Alternatively, the seder plate is removed or put at the opposite end of the table temporarily, and the remaining two-and-a-half matzot are lifted up and displayed. Some remove only the shankbone and egg during the display of the matzot, especially if the matzot are on or within the seder plate. Other alternatives are to lift only the seder plate or only the matzot.

This Is the Bread of Affliction

Text a: We have finally come to our Haggadah text, the Maggid, the actual "Telling," from the same root as Haggadah. We explain what we are doing, why we display the matzot and seder plate symbols, with the Aramaic words, *Ha lachma anya.* These words refer to eating the Passover sacrifice as well as being in exile, inconsistencies that make it impossible to date this passage with certainty. Some people have the custom of opening the door while this is being said:

> This is the bread of affliction which our ancestors ate
>> in the land of Egypt.
> Let all who are hungry enter and eat, let all who are
>> needy enter to share our Passover.
> This year here, next year in Israel.
> This year as slaves, next year in freedom.

Notice the parallel construction of the sentences, common throughout Jewish literature, especially in the Bible. The sages of the Talmud made a pun out of the words *lechem oni,* "the bread of poverty," and read it as *onin,* making this key phrase mean "the bread over which many words are spoken."

Why Aramaic? A folk belief has it that demons can only understand Hebrew, so we avoid the possibility of inviting them by phrasing the invitation in Aramaic. Beyond that, Aramaic was the language of our exile in Babylonia in the sixth century B.C.E., and continued to be the Jewish vernacular until the ninth century C.E. Aramaic stands as the first lingua franca of the exilic world, the first attempt at a Yiddish or Ladino. That was our first reexperience of exile and the model for all future exiles. Aramaic is used to this day in some of the most familiar parts of the Jewish liturgy: Besides appearing in the Haggadah and the text for the search for chametz, it is the language of the Kaddish (prayer for the dead); Kol Nidre (annulment of all vows), which commences Yom Kippur; the

Akdamut (prefatory words) recited on Shavuot; of the Ketubbah (marriage document) and Get (divorce agreement); parts of the biblical books of Daniel and Ezra; most of the Talmud; and the *Zohar.*

In using it we remind ourselves of the repetition of our exile, the paradigm of Jewish experience. We also remind ourselves of key transitional moments in our lives: marriage, divorce, death, holidays, and bar mitzvah (*bar,* son, is Aramaic). We associate it with the important Jewish metaphysical activities of study, Talmud, and mysticism, *Zohar.* Aramaic was the language of the common people, of the poor, like the poor bread (ha-lachma anya) we display at this point. It was a language whose inviting words would have been understood by all. It reminds us that once we were all slaves.

> *By the rivers of Babylon, there we sat down, yea, we wept, when we remembered Zion. . . . For there they that carried us away captive required of us a song. . . . How shall we sing the Lord's song in a strange land?*

—Psalm 137:1, 3–4

Each successive year of exile has required that we answer that last question anew to our own satisfaction.

Aramaic represents a specific phase in the development of the Haggadah. As with the successive stages in the Neolithic building of Stonehenge, the seder and Haggadah passed through many different versions on the way to their present form. The oldest stratum would be the celebration of spring and the vernal equinox. Then comes the addition of the specific way of life of the people, either shepherds or farmers. The antipathy between the wandering and the settled mode of survival can be seen in the story of Cain and Abel. From the farmer comes the wheat, matzo; from the shepherd, the lamb, pesach. These symbols are merged into the spring holiday.

Only after these two stages exist can the historical phase of bondage in Egypt and redemption be added on. As we will see, the whole story of the Jewish people from Abraham on is encompassed in the Haggadah narrative. Following the forty years of wandering, entry into Canaan, and building of the Temple, we have the phase where we have been redeemed and we have our own land. Then the story leans more toward total joy, with only the slightest mingling of melancholy about our past and dread of the wild forces of the universe.

The catastrophe of the Babylonian captivity gives the Haggadah a whole new meaning. Now we had a ceremony and story ready-made to explain this crisis. Again, the exile ended and there was a re-turn to the Holy Land. A new Temple was built and sacrifices began again. Neither of these Temple periods was insignificant. Each went on about 500 years. That is roughly a millennia of Passovers reenact-ing the Exodus paschal sacrifice. Further catastrophes occurred, in-cluding the final destruction of the Temple and banishment from the Holy Land, and they were added on to the book and the ceremony, but always within the context of the Babylonian exile.

Ritual action 9: Pour the second cup of wine. During the breaking in half of the afikoman and the mentioning of the bread of affliction, the wine cup was empty. As we move toward our next toast, we refill the cup. It will take a long time until we drink this cup, but throughout this Maggid section the wine cup will have many featured moments. There is a certain comicality in our con-stant movement toward drinking the wine and the equally con-stant way that the Haggadah pulls the cup away from us. We recited the Kiddush over the first cup of wine. With the cup empty, we display the matzo, beginning the Maggid. Now we recite the rest of the Maggid over this second cup of wine.

Why Is This Night Different?

Text b: Following our argument or abstract, the invitation and gen-eral statement of what we are doing, comes the most famous text of the Haggadah, the *fier kashes* (four questions or perplexities), from which this chapter takes its title: *Mah Nishtannah Ha-layleh Hazeh mi-kol ha-laylot.* This is usually translated as "Why is this night different from all other nights?" or "What is different about this night from all other nights?" It could also be rendered, "How different this night is from all other nights!" Originally, the leader asked the questions, but since the later Middle Ages the youngest child has become the traditional catechist. Not only are the unusual actions of the evening being questioned, but also why this evening merits this distinction. It is through the questions of the youngest that the rest of us are instructed.

The questions, or amplification of the first question, continue with:

1. For on all other nights we eat leavened or unleavened bread, on this night only unleavened.
2. For on all other nights we eat all kinds of herbs, on this night only bitter.
3. For on all other nights we are not obligated to dip even one time, on this night we dip two times.
4. For on all other nights we eat either sitting up or reclining, on this night we all recline.

The Sephardim ask the questions in the order 3, 1, 2, 4. Note the repetition of the fact that all of this takes place at night. In the original Mishnaic passage, there are only three questions, and they refer to why we eat only unleavened bread, only roasted meat, and why there are two dippings instead of the usual one. As practices changed, so did the questions. After the Temple was destroyed and the Jews could no longer bring their sacrificial lamb to Jerusalem, the question about roasted meat was out. In fact, Ashkenazim specifically avoid roasted meat. When the ancient custom of dipping an hors d'oeuvre became passé, both dippings were questioned. That meant that the need for only bitter herbs had to be explained. As customs changed and reclining at meals became an oddity, the last question added had to do with that.

These questions were originally asked after the meal, when they would have made more sense. The questions and the Maggid were moved ahead of the meal so that the children would be awake to hear the story. When they were moved to the beginning of the seder, along with the rest of the Maggid, they became quizzical in themselves. Their function now is to generate the remainder of the Maggid section of the Haggadah. These specific questions are not needed to kick off the answers. Any question will do to generate the "Funny you should mention that" response. In fact, they are never directly answered in the Haggadah at all, although we can piece together the answers from the ensuing reply. They represent the types of questions that we might ask, or could ask, or should ask. They prime the question pump.

Once We Were Slaves

Text c: The general answer to all these questions and to everything else odd about tonight is that Avadim Hayinu, Once we were slaves:

> Once we were slaves to Pharaoh in Egypt, and the Lord our God brought us forth from there with a mighty hand and an outstretched arm. And if the Holy One had not brought our ancestors forth from Egypt, then we and our children and our children's children would still be slaves to Pharaoh in Egypt. And even if all of us were wise, all of us full of understanding, all of us elders, all of us full of knowledge of the Torah, we would still be obligated to perform the mitzvah of recounting the story of the departure from Egypt. And the more one elaborates upon the departure from Egypt, the more praiseworthy one is.

Here, in a passage usually read in unison by the whole company, we see some key themes developing. The Mishnah requires that the Haggadah begin in shame, our slavery, and end in glory, our redemption. Our liberation was not something done once and no longer relevant, but affects us to this day. No matter how old we are or how much we know, we must tell the story anew every year. Indeed, the more we tell, the better it is.

Rabbi Louis Finkelstein has used this and other passages in the Haggadah to build a case for a pre-Maccabean origin of parts of the text. He assumes that the downplaying of Egypt as an enemy, evidenced here by the expression "from there" instead of the biblical "from Egypt," indicates that this was written during the Hellenistic period when Seleucid Syria vied with Ptolemaic Egypt for control of Palestine. In his argument, "there" refers to Pharaoh's Egypt and not to any contemporary Egypt, so as not to offend the Ptolemies. His theory is fascinating and worth considering, but highly speculative:

> *What song the Sirens sang, or what name Achilles assumed when he hid himself among women, though puzzling questions, are not beyond all conjecture.*
>
> —Sir Thomas Browne

The opening sentence of this passage can be found in Deuteronomy 6:21 as the answer to be given by the parent when the child asks about the statutes and laws of the holiday. The phrase about "an outstretched arm," though, is an addition from the Septuagint, the translation of the Bible into Greek completed between the third and first centuries B.C.E. in Alexandria, Egypt. By this addition we bring the word *zero'a,* our seder plate shankbone, into the Haggadah text. Note in the catalog of virtues the pairing of wisdom and understanding. These are two of the ten sefirot, the second and third after Keter, the Crown. Even if our comprehension of the Exodus reached to Wisdom, Chokhmah, and Understanding, Binah, we would still be obligated to tell the tale. A few phrases later, a further kabbalistic term is implied when the text refers to those who are full of the knowledge of the Torah, *yodim.*

This word for knowledge comes from the same root as Da'at, the hidden sefirah that reconciles male wisdom and feminine understanding.

A Tale of Rabbi Eliezer

Text d: Abruptly, we jump into the story of the five rabbis, although the implication is that no one could have had more wisdom, understanding, and knowledge than these five sages:

> A tale of Rabbi Eliezer and Rabbi Joshua and Rabbi Eleazar ben Azariah and Rabbi Akiba and Rabbi Tarfon who reclined together at Bene-Berak. And they recounted the departure from Egypt all night until their students came to them and said, "Masters, the time has come to recite the morning Shema."
>
> Said Rabbi Eleazar ben Azariah, "I am like a seventy-year-old, yet I never found biblical proof as to why the Exodus from Egypt should be recited in the evening service until Ben Zoma explained the verse, 'so that you may remember the day of your departure from the land of Egypt all the days of your life' (Deuteronomy 16:3). 'The days of your life' implies the daytime, while 'all the days of your life' implies the nights." And the sages amplify this by saying, "'The days of your life' refers to this world; 'all the days of your life' to Messianic times as well."
>
> Blessed is the Place, blessed is God. Blessed is the giver of the Torah to God's chosen people Israel. Blessed is God.

The transition from the students rushing in to warn the rabbis that the time for the morning Shema has arrived to the statement by Eleazar ben Azariah that he had trouble finding a biblical passage to explain why we mention the Exodus at night seems like a non sequitur, but there is a connection.

More than the single statement of faith given in chapter 4, the Shema as part of the morning and evening prayers consists of three separate biblical extracts. The third of these paragraphs (Numbers 15:37–41, my bar mitzvah *maftir,* incidentally), which mentions the *tzitzit,* the fringes of the tallit (prayer shawl), makes sense in the morning when we are wearing the tallit; but why should we repeat this paragraph at night when we are not wearing the prayer shawl? That is what ben Azariah is asking. The answer can be found in the last sentence of the paragraph enjoining us to put fringes on our garments, "I the Lord am your God, who brought you out of the land of Egypt to be your God: I, the Lord your God" (Numbers 15:41). The announcement by the students following the rabbis' night-long discussion of the Exodus makes the connection for ben Azariah between the morning and evening Shema. We can imagine the five sages getting up from their reclining positions after a night of food, drink, and conversation. As they put on their *talaysim* to begin their morning prayers, Ben Azariah volunteers his insight, which expands from a simple reference to the evening prayer to include their whole night-long talk and future talk of the Exodus during the days of the Messiah.

This *derash* (interpretation) closes with the quadruplicate benedictory sentence. *Ha-Makom* (the Place, or Space) is one of God's names. We say that God is the place of the world, yet the world alone is not his place. The world is within God, but does not contain God. Judaism leans toward panentheism, not pantheism. Night represents the present as we sit at the seder table waiting for the future dawn of redemption. This emphasis on the night is repeated in the parable of the four children that follows.

As mentioned earlier, these rabbis may have been plotting the Bar Kokhba revolt of the second century C.E. in the vicinity of Akiba's academy at Bene-Berak. The story occurs only in the Haggadah, though a similar story is told of Rabban Gamaliel and another group of sages at Lydda. Eliezer ben Hyrcanus, Joshua ben Hananiah, Eleazar ben Azariah, and Tarfon were the teachers and contemporaries of Akiba, the greatest of all the Mishnaic tannaim. The story of these great sages spending all night discussing the Exodus should suggest to us that no one knows so much that they can exempt themselves from the fulfillment of this mitzvah, or that knowledge can substitute for practice. What we derive from the experience of the seder transcends mere information.

The benedictory passage that closes this section acts as a vest between the story of the rabbis and the following parable. It refers to the Jewish people as "chosen," a concept that has drawn the attention of both Jews and gentiles:

> *How odd of God to choose the Jews.*
> —William Norman Ewer

> *It's not so odd. The Jews chose God.*
> —Leon Roth

Just so, the choosing comes from both sides. Like calls to like. Far from implying superiority, it suggests responsibility accepted. Looking at our history, it is hard to believe we are not chosen, but the question becomes, "What have we been chosen for?" There are four blessings just as there are four children, but the key phrase thanks God for the Torah, which leads naturally into the next section.

The Torah Contrasts Four Children

Text e: One of the best-known parts of the Haggadah is the parable of the four children, based on the four times that we are instructed to tell our children about the Exodus in the Torah. We have just finished thanking God for the Torah. Now we give a concrete example of its wisdom. Not only does it tell us the story of our deliverance, it tells us that we must suit the telling to the capacity of the hearer. The Torah does not waste words, so if we are told to tell our children in four separate passages, then that must mean that there are four types of children. Just as there were four questions before, so there are four stated or implied questions here, only these questions have more to do with the inquirers than with the ceremony. The ceremony derives meaning from our questions.

> The Torah contrasts four children: one wise, and one wicked, and one simple, and one who does not know how to ask a question.
>
> What does the wise one say: "What mean the decrees, laws, and rules that the Lord our God has enjoined upon you?" (Deuteronomy 6:20). And you teach the laws of Passover saying, "You may not conclude the Passover by saying, 'Now to the entertainment.'"

In other words, you instruct the *chacham* (wise child) in the customs right through to this, the last statement of the Mishnah on Passover. The Mishnah uses the word afikoman to mean entertainment, though today we usually understand the word to mean dessert. The afikoman, the hidden matzo as dessert, is the last thing we are allowed to eat at the seder. In Mishnaic times, though, the afikoman meant the postprandial reveling, or *epikomion,* that was a part of the classical symposium. The rabbis are forbidding us to go seder-hopping, to look for further entertainment at successive sedarim. We are to remain attached to that group, now a holy convocation, with which we began the evening.

Don Isaac Abrabanel infers that the wise child is one who is a little too cocky and proud of mere intellectual abilities. The chacham believes that intellectual apprehension alone is sufficient to understand the performance of the seder. In spite of immense learning and respect, the wise child, like the wicked child, is distanced from the events of the Exodus by seeing the rules as applying to the parent, "enjoined upon you." The complex question demonstrates a desire to impress us with vast knowledge. We reply with an appropriately detailed answer that pushes knowledge to its limits:

> *If the fool would persist in his folly he would become wise.*
> —William Blake

What does the wicked one say: "What is this service to you?" (Exodus 12:26). To you and not to them. And since they remove themselves from the community and so deny God, you must set their teeth on edge and say, "It is because of that which the Lord did for me when I came forth from Egypt" (Exodus 13:8). For me and not for them. If they had been there, they would not have been redeemed.

The fact that the Haggadah deals with the wicked child in a passage that goes back to Mishnaic times indicates that there must always have been those who rejected being Jewish and the Jewish covenant with God. In fact, the text never mentions denial of God. It actually says that to remove oneself from the community is a denial of Jewish principle. Although denial of God, our deliverer, is implied, the literal offense is dissociation from the tribe. The wicked child is as intelligent as the wise child, perhaps more so, but is ruled by "the imp of the perverse." That is why we must set their teeth on edge, to wake them up to their connection with the group.

In some early illustrated Haggadot, the *rasha* (wicked child) is shown in armor, a soldier. Jewish experience of soldiers was negative. Under the guise of fighting for noble causes, the soldier passed through the Jewish community looting, pillaging, raping, and murdering. No one wanted to say, "My son, the mercenary."

Other illustrations of this type have shown an assimilated Jew with no link to traditional community. Obviously, Jewish self-hatred, seeing oneself through the eyes of the oppressor, is not a new phenomenon. Still, the group does not give up on the wicked children. They are included in the seder even if they try to exclude themselves. Most of us have gone through periods when our link to our people was weak, when we could not be bothered, when we mocked our traditions, when our limited personal experiences blinded us to the larger canvas of Jewish history. No matter. Yiddishkeit is always waiting both within us and without to welcome us back. Sometimes our rebelliousness, anger, and perversity lend strength and depth to our return.

> What does the simple child say: "What is this" (Exodus 13:14). And say to them, "With a strong hand the Lord brought us out from Egypt, from the house of bondage." (Exodus 13:14)

The *tam* (simple child) has no interest in the complexities of the seder, its manifold meanings. For the simple, the biblical promise of the Israelites to God is sufficient: *Na'ahseh ve-Nishma*— "We will do and we will hear." Without knowing or even being told, we will do; then we will hear the secondary what and why. The Vilna Gaon sees this child not as simple (tam) but as perfect, complete, sincere (*temim*). They humbly recognize their inability to understand God's ways, yet they accept those ways and the traditional wisdom that explains them.

> And with the one who does not know how to ask you must open the discussion and say, "And you shall tell your child in that day, saying: it is because of that which the Lord did for me when I came forth out of Egypt." (Exodus 13:8)

In another appropriate inversion, the Chasidic tzaddik Levi Yitzhak put himself in the role of the child who does not know how to ask:

> *"The one who knows not how to ask," that is myself, Levi Yitzhak of Berdichev. I do not know how to ask you . . . I do not beg you to reveal to me the secret of your ways—I could not bear it! But show me one thing; show it to me more*

> *clearly and more deeply: show me what this, which is hap-*
> *pening at this very moment means to me, what it demands*
> *of me, what you, Lord of the World, are telling me by way*
> *of it. Ah, it is not why I suffer, that I wish to know, but only*
> *whether I suffer for your sake.*
>
> —Levi Yitzhak of Berdichev

These contradictory interpretations of the four sons demonstrate the open-ended nature of the Haggadah. Nothing is obvious
or to be taken for granted. It repays the time we spend trying to understand it. The parable concludes with a short analysis of the last-
mentioned verse from Exodus explaining, again, why we have the
seder at night. We are all put in the position of the child at the seder:

> *Every single person may contain within himself all the four*
> *sons mentioned in the haggadah.*
>
> —Rabbi Israel Lipkin of Salant

At First Our Ancestors Worshiped Idols

Text f: Mitchilah Avdey Avodah Zarah, "At first our ancestors wor-
shiped idols, but now we have been brought near the service of the
Omnipresent." The word for worship here is actually *avodah,*
which also means "serve." Throughout the Haggadah there is a
constant interplay between the use of the word avodah to mean
slavery or the worship of idols and the same word being used to
refer to the service of God. We do not object to being owned by or
slaving for God, something larger than ourselves, as opposed to a
mortal king. *Kervanu,* the word used for "brought near," also constantly used in the Haggadah, is the same as the word *korban,* "sacrifice." When we could perform the sacrifices to God at the
Temple, we were near God. Now we pray to be brought near again.

This passage represents a second answering of the four questions. This is a bigger answer, not just why do we do such odd things tonight, but the whole immense backdrop to both what we do tonight and what we did 3,300 years ago tonight. This is the answer to the questions of all four types of children. It begins in the shame of idolatry and ends in the glory of the worship of the one true God. The answer comes from Joshua 24:2–4 followed by a benedictory verse, and more of our story outlining the divine intention in Jewish history and the promises God made to our ancestors from Genesis 15:13–14. The reason there are two passages beginning in shame has to do with a disagreement between the amoraim Rav and Samuel. For Rav, our spiritual shame was in having once been idolaters, as mentioned in this passage. Samuel is the source for the earlier passage Avadim Hayinu, "Once we were slaves," our physical shame. At the same time, the Haggadah wants to go back to God's promise to Abraham, since it includes the prediction that his descendants would be slaves in a foreign land. A larger perspective is encompassed in this passage. Our centuries in exile are part of a divine plan that includes not just Jacob and his children, but stretches backward to Abraham and forward to our final deliverance. Finkelstein sees this second passage beginning in shame as a muting of the first anti-Egyptian passage.

Ritual action 10: Raise and lower the wine cup.

And It Is This Promise Which Has Sustained

Text g: We toast God, but do not drink. When we come to the Hallel later, we will see that Psalm 116:13 says that we "will lift the cup of deliverance." Our repeated toastings are not only in praise to our deliverer, but in the manner of encouragement as well. We want God to deliver us again. That is our covenant with God and one of the reasons that every generation must see itself as having been brought forth from bondage. We urge and remind by saying Ve-Hi Shayamdah:

And it is this promise which has stood by our ancestors and us. For not one enemy alone has risen to destroy us. In every generation, there arise those who would destroy us. But the Holy One saves us from their hand.

Go and Learn What Laban the Aramean Intended

Text h: After concluding this hint and putting down the wine cup, we pick up our story where we left off with a long midrashic exegesis on Deuteronomy 26:5–8, the Viddui Bikkurim, the confession said when bringing first fruits to the Temple, which began at Shavuot and continued through Sukkot. The three pilgrimage festivals are all linked. Every word is examined and new meanings are derived from tiny hints in the text. The analysis stops pointedly before the ninth verse: "He brought us to this place and gave us this land, a land flowing with milk and honey." We interpret four verses and leave the fifth unspoken, just as we drink four cups and leave the fifth untouched.

Louis Finkelstein has used an equally close reading of this part of the Haggadah to bolster his argument that it derives from pre-Maccabean times. First, the Viddui would have been familiar to everyone during Temple times, an obvious choice for interpretation. Then, our text mentions the Shekhinah in a passage that implies that the Israelites actually saw the divine presence. The word for the terror (*mora*) of God witnessed by the Israelites during the Exodus is related to the vision (*mareh*) of the Shekhinah. This was contrary to the later rabbinical position, but in line with the view of the pre-Maccabean Jews.

Finally, Deuteronomy 26:5 reads, "An Aramean (Syrian) on the brink of perishing was my father (Jacob)," meaning, when Jacob first settled in Egypt. The clear meaning of this verse is, "My father (Jacob) was a wandering Aramean." The Haggadah understands these words to mean, "An Aramean (the Syrian, Laban, Jacob's father-in-law) would have destroyed my father (Jacob)," meaning, so that is why Jacob fled to Egypt, to evade Laban. In Jewish thought, key individuals in the Bible stand for whole peoples. Syria, the Seleucid Empire, the opponent of the Maccabees of the Chanukkah story, represented here by Laban, comes off as a greater enemy of the Jews than even the Pharaoh of the Exodus.

According to Finkelstein, this was to placate the Ptolemaic rulers of Egypt who controlled Palestine at the time this part of the Haggadah was composed. When we arrive at this passage in the Haggadah today, the introduction of Laban at this point seems forced. The commentary opens by abusing, for no apparent reason, our long-time foe Syria and leaps from that to our descent into Egypt. The land of the Pharaohs in this scenario is the lesser of two evils, so that is why we went. Finkelstein's argument makes a smooth transition out of what is otherwise an abrupt jump cut. Again, this is intriguing, but speculative. We might also link up the line "In every generation, there arise . . ." with Laban as a pertinent example. Further, we might hear *ha-Romi* (the Roman) instead of *Arami* (the Aramean), and change the time frame completely.

Smooth or not, this odd, abrupt opening leads to an intensive analysis of a capsule version of the Exodus. The Haggadah avoids ever telling the whole story in a linear or connected way. We seem to jump all over and around it without ever just saying, "Moses, of basket in bulrushes fame, spoke with a burning bush and then led the Israelites out of Egypt after inflicting ten plagues on the Egyptians. He split the Red Sea, drowned the Egyptians, led the Children of Israel (Israel, alias Jacob, the great-great-grandfather of Moses) to Mount Sinai to receive the Torah, then to the Promised Land and died without entering himself."

In fact, Moses has no role in the Haggadah. The rabbis wanted to emphasize that God was the redeemer, not a human being, even one as great as Moses. By minimizing his role, they were separating themselves from the Karaite position. This Jewish fundamentalist sect, which began in the eighth century and still has adherents to this day, rejected the talmudic interpretation of Judaism in favor of a direct apprehension of the Bible. Their Haggadah excluded all the Mishnaic, talmudic, and midrashic material, emphasizing the literal understanding of the Exodus story and the role of Moses in our deliverance. They reject the levels of metaphor that enrich our Haggadah, and they also make their matzo from barley.

The Haggadah need not tell us about Moses, though. Everyone knows already. We are all permeated with these stories long before we get to the seder table. The more we know, the more resonant the symbols, rituals, words, melodies, and foods become. And what if we do not know? The less we know, the more wonderful to see it all for the first time. For the child, watching the preparations, there are hundreds of questions to elicit the story long before the night of the seder. Every year we each take on the different roles of the four children. At first we do not even know what to ask, then come simple questions, and finally complicated ones. Perhaps in some years we veer off into wayward, rebellious, or wicked directions. Still we come to the seder and ask questions.

As we have seen, a tremendous amount of material is available to us without any liturgy, even more with just a minimal text. The Haggadah has a much more poetic and philosophical aim than to merely tell the story. Any number of forgotten books have told the story. Many have told it better, but none has replaced the Haggadah. What the *Zohar* has to say about the Torah can as well be said of the Haggadah:

> *If a man looks upon the Torah as merely a book presenting narratives and everyday matters, alas for him! Such a Torah, one treating with everyday concerns, and indeed a more excellent one, we too, even we, could compile. . . . But the Torah, in all of its words, holds supernal truths and sublime secrets.*

—*Zohar* III:152 a

Ritual action 11: Remove three, ten, and three drops of wine.

Blood, Fire, and Columns of Smoke

Text i: The capsule summary of the Passover story brings us to the ten plagues, the most ominous part of the seder. The first three drops are removed as we say: *Dahm* [Blood] *va-Aysh* [and Fire] *ve-Simrote Ahshahn* [and Columns of Smoke] (Joel 3:3).

Now we actually say the ten plagues inflicted on the Egyptians:

*D*ahm	Blood
*Tz*fardayah	Frogs
*K*inim	Lice
*A*hrove	Flies
*D*ehvehr	Blight
*Sh*echine	Boils
*B*ahrahd	Hail
*A*rbeh	Locusts
*Ch*oshak	Darkness
Makkot *Be*-Chorot	Striking of the Firstborn

Our last three drops are spilled over Rabbi Judah's acronymic mnemonic of the first letters of each plague grouped into three words. Supposedly, these were engraved on the staff Moses used to effect the plagues so he could inflict them in the proper order. You wouldn't want to have boils before lice, after all. The plagues are mentioned in a number of places in the Bible and never in the same order. Rabbi Judah's mnemonic gives us the order of the plagues as given in Exodus—*D'tzak Adash B'Achab*—which can be construed to mean: The scorpion stung the uncle. I have never heard any sensible explanation of this nonsensical sentence, but a certain amount of enigma is appropriate to this evening. More to the point, the dangerous, intelligible ten plagues have been collapsed into a harmless, meaningless, even protected three.

Rabbi Yose of Galilee Says

Text j: Three midrashic interpretations of the ten plagues from Rabbis Yose of Galilee, Eliezer, and Akiba are given, showing that actually there were as many as 300 plagues by the time Pharaoh's army was drowned at the Red Sea. This returning to Akiba suggests a continuity in the performance of the seder that includes all of us as well as all past sedarim. It is as if we were at one end of an incredibly long table, our family closest to us and all the rest of our people stretched out to the far end. Way down near that end Uncle Akiba throws in his playful *jeu d'esprit*. This learned rabbinical joke has become as dry and beloved after two millennia as matzo. Since Rabbi Yose begins the derash by assigning the ten plagues in Egypt to the finger of God, this makes an elegant linking of text with the last ritual action, where we used our fingers to remove drops of wine for each plague. Note that this section includes the one incidental mention of Moses in the whole Haggadah.

How Many Are the Favors

Text k: Having gotten past the plagues and the splitting of the Red Sea, we come to what is probably the most famous song of the Haggadah, "Dayyenu," which explains in fifteen steps all the miracles God performed for the Israelites:

> If he had brought us forth from Egypt, but had not punished them, it would have been enough (or sufficient).

Thirteen more kindnesses are enumerated, ending with:

> If he had brought us into the Land of Israel, but had not built us the Temple, it would have been enough.

This rollicking recital concludes with a paragraph reiterating all the reasons we have to be thankful to God:

God (1) brought us forth from Egypt, and (2) punished the Egyptians, and (3) punished their gods, and (4) slew their firstborn, and (5) gave us their wealth, and (6) split the sea for us, and (7) led us through it on dry land, and (8) drowned our foes in it, and (9) sustained us in the wilderness for forty years, and (10) fed us with the manna, and (11) gave us the Sabbath, and (12) brought us to Mount Sinai, and (13) gave us the Torah, and (14) brought us to the Land of Israel, and (15) built the Temple for us to atone for all our sins.

These fifteen *ma'alot* (ascending steps), or divine favors, correspond to the fifteen steps of the seder, the fifteen semicircular steps in the Temple, and the fifteen Shir ha-Ma'alot (Pilgrim Songs, Songs of Ascent) from the book of Psalms. The Levites would have recited these Psalms as they went up the Temple steps. When you go to the Holy Land, you make aliyah, you go up; while leaving is going down, like Jacob and his family fleeing the famine in Canaan by going down to Egypt. One of these Shir ha-Ma'alot is sung just after the seder meal is concluded. Fifteen is also the numerical value of one of God's names, the letters Yod He, or Yah. An important motif here is that our liberation is only complete after the revelation at Sinai. This sets up the expectation of Shavuot fifty days after the first seder.

At this point in the text (or just past it, when saying "In every generation"), some Sephardim have the custom of lashing one another with leeks and scallions. This is based on the Israelites' complaint to Moses: "We remember the fish that we used to eat free in Egypt, the cucumbers, the melons, the leeks, the onions, and the garlic" (Numbers 11:5). The whippings are to remind us of what went with the free lunch. At the same time, onions function as an anti-demonic. Remember, for example, that vampires hate garlic.

Rabban Gamaliel Said

Text 1: Our telling and questioning pick up again with a passage from the Mishnah in which Rabban Gamaliel explains the minimum recital necessary for the Passover. Now the questions are not the random outbursts of curiosity, nor the self-revealing queries of the uninitiated. They have become the focused inquiry of a great teacher:

> Rabban Gamaliel said, "Whoever has not explained these three things on Passover has not fulfilled his obligation, namely:
>
> Pesach   Matzo   Maror
>
> The paschal sacrifice that our ancestors ate at the time when the Temple still stood. What was the reason for it? Because the Holy One passed over the houses of our ancestors in Egypt, as it says, "You shall say, 'It is the Passover offering to the Lord who passed over the houses of the Children of Israel in Egypt when he smote the Egyptians and spared our houses.' And they bowed their heads and the people prostrated themselves." (Exodus 12:27)

Obviously, the reason God passed over the Israelite homes was that they were in the non-smoting section.

Since we no longer make the paschal sacrifice, we do not lift or point to the shankbone. Oddly, the single most powerful, the central symbol of the ancient Passover, the Pesach, the paschal offering itself, is now missing, represented by only a tiny bit of the whole. From this splinter we must regenerate that whole. Rabban Gamaliel was already living at a time when the telling of the story had to replace the original action of sacrificing the lamb. This loss and substitution led to the creation of the seder, the Haggadah, and the elaborate web of meaning and metaphor that they are able to produce. For those who had made the paschal sacrifice in Temple times, there was no interpretation necessary or really possible. The lamb they ate was because of the lamb that had been sacrificed and eaten on the night we had become a people. Ironically, the meaning of Jewish practice was enriched by the destruction of the

Temple. Judaism became far more than an ancient Near Eastern national cult.

Ritual action 12: Point to the matzo.

Text l: This passage continues with the explanation of the matzo, Matzo *zoh:*

> This matzo which we eat, what is the reason for it? Because the dough of our ancestors had not yet leavened when the King over all kings, the Holy One, was revealed to them and redeemed them. As it is said, "And they baked unleavened cakes of the dough which they brought forth out of Egypt, for it was not leavened; because they were thrust out of Egypt, and could not tarry, nor had they prepared any provisions for themselves." (Exodus 12:39)

Ritual action 13: Point to the maror.
Text l: The passage continues, Maror *zeh:*

> These bitter herbs which we eat, what is the reason for them? Because the Egyptians made the lives of our ancestors bitter in Egypt. As it is said, "And they made their lives bitter with hard service, in mortar and in brick, and in all manner of service in the field; in all their service, wherein they made them serve with rigor." (Exodus 1:14)

After these three key components of the evening have been explained, the whole is summed up in these memorable words, *Be-Chol Dor va-Dor:*

> In every generation it is our duty to regard ourselves as if we personally had come forth out of Egypt. As it is said, "And you shall tell your child on that day, saying, 'It is because of that which the Lord did for me when I came forth out of Egypt'" (Exodus 13:8). It was not only our

> ancestors that the Holy One redeemed, but ourselves as
> well were redeemed along with them. As it is said, "And
> God brought us out from thence, that we might be
> brought in, to give us the land which had been promised
> to our ancestors." (Deuteronomy 6:23)

Again, the Haggadah links our original redemption with our future redemption and our hope to be returned to the Land of Israel.

Ritual action 14: Raise and lower the wine cup.

Therefore It Is Our Duty

Text m: This, Lefichach, is the first of three similar praise paragraphs. The others are the Yehalleluchah before the Great Hallel and the Yishtabach after the Nishmat. Our deliverer is again toasted via a piling up of praises, an expansion of a talmudic passage that connects the praise due to God with our liberation from bondage. We do not drink at this point. There are five forms of slavery and five forms of freedom mentioned. These are sometimes equated with five periods of Jewish history:

> from slavery to freedom, the release from Egyptian
> bondage
>
> from grief to joy, the return of the exiles from Babylonia
>
> from mourning to festivity, the foiling of Haman at
> Purim
>
> from darkness to great light, the defeat of the Seleucids
> by the Maccabees at Chanukkah
>
> from servitude to redemption, an end to our current
> exile

The significance of five—as in the fifth unstated verse about redemption; the fifth unconsumed cup; and the letter *he,* whose value is five and which stands for matzo—is reiterated here in the fifth example of freedom, our future redemption. These five pairs are connected to the following list of ten modes of praise. Just as our current exile is not over, so we cannot yet sing the new song, the final form of praise. We constantly take our story up to the very edge of history.

Lefichach tells us we owe God these ten forms of praise, which are analogous to the ten plagues and sefirot: thank, extol, praise, glorify, exalt, honor, bless, elevate, acclaim, and song. This litany climaxes with a shout of Hallelujah, which leads naturally into the next passage, Psalm 113, the Hallelujah.

Praise the Lord

Text n: Lefichach flows into the first part of Hallel, Psalms 113, the Hallelujah, and 114, Betzait Yisrael. These first two psalms refer to what God has done for us in the past and how we were delivered from slavery by divine intervention. The rest of Hallel after the meal points toward a future redemption in another Nisan to come. Passover is the only time that Hallel is said at night, sitting down, and without an introductory blessing. In this context the Hallel becomes part of the larger mitzvah of performing the seder. Hallelujah combines the word for praise, Hallel, with one of God's names, Yah. Psalm 114 is especially notable for its beauty of expression and parallel construction. There is no rhyme in the Bible. Instead, poems repeat their ideas in each line:

> When Israel went out of Egypt
> Jacob's household from a people of strange speech

You can hear the same cadences and see the same structures used in writers as diverse as the Elizabethans, Walt Whitman, and Gertrude Stein. If you are more of a fan of animation than literature, listen to the last set of paired images in this psalm:

> Who turned Bedrock into a pool of water
> The Flintstones into a fountain.

Ritual action 15: Raise the wine cup and drink the wine, while leaning to the left. As we saw in the last chapter, there are some extra benedictions here preceding the usual blessing over the wine. This concludes the Maggid section.

Step VI. Rachtzah
Ritual action 16: Wash hands again, with a benediction.

Step VII. Motzi
Ritual action 17: Hold the matzot, and say a benediction, Motzi.

Step VIII. Matzo
Ritual action 18: Hold the upper and middle matzot, and say the second benediction, Matzo.

Ritual action 19: Eat from the upper and middle matzot, while leaning to the left.

Step IX. Maror
Ritual action 20: Say the benediction, then eat the bitter herb dipped in charoset.

Step X. Korekh
Ritual action 21: Eat the Hillel sandwich made from the bottom matzo.

In Memory of the Temple
Text o: We have said the benedictions and eaten the prescribed foods separately. Now, out of respect for Hillel, we eat the prescribed foods together as he did. There is no special benediction for this action, since we have already said benedictions over matzo and maror. Instead we remember Hillel:

In memory of the Temple, we do as Hillel did in Temple times: he put bitter herbs between matzot and ate them as one, to fulfill what is said, "They shall eat it with unleavened bread and bitter herbs." (Numbers 9:11)

Step XI. Shulchan Arukh

Ritual action 22: Eat the hard-boiled egg, dipped or mixed in the saltwater, while leaning to the left. This action usually goes unmentioned in most Haggadot, although those Sephardim who observe this custom say:

> *Zechar le-Korban Chagigah.*
>
> In remembrance of the Festival Offering.

At this point an elaborate meal, Shulchan Arukh, of traditional foods can be eaten, although the hard-boiled egg stands for the whole meal.

Step XII. Tzafun

Ritual action 23: Eat the afikoman, while leaning to the left. Nothing more may be eaten for the rest of the night.

Step XIII. Barekh

Ritual action 24: Pour the third cup of wine, lift the cup, and drink, while leaning to the left. We sing the Grace after Meals over this third cup of wine.

A Pilgrim Song

Text p: When the meal is finished and before the formal grace, Barekh, it has become traditional to sing Shir ha-Ma'alot, Psalm 126, a pilgrim song, or a song of ascents, since to be a pilgrim means ascending to Jerusalem. It begins with this beautiful image:

> When the Lord returns us to Zion, we will be like those
> in a dream.

Another interesting couplet reminds us of the parallel between interring the decomposing, dead seeds in the winter—in other words, burying the dead, and harvesting the reborn grain in spring:

> They that sow in tears shall reap in joy. Though he walks
> along weeping, bearing the bag of seed, he shall come
> back with joyous song, bearing his sheaves.

Everything hints at a wished-for future redemption, another end to exile. This Psalm is followed by the Grace discussed in the last chapter. It concludes with the benediction over the third cup of wine. If you go back to the text of the Grace in the preceding chapter, you will find that we request that Elijah the prophet be sent to us. That leads to our next text and action.

Ritual action 25: Pour the wine for Elijah and open the door for him.

Pour Out Your Wrath

Text q: We pour this cup after we have had our third cup. Although we pour it for Elijah, we do not share it with him. Instead, with the door open in expectation, we say, *"Barukh haba!"* ("Blessed be he who comes in the name of the Lord!"), which is not in the Haggadah, and then these words:

> Pour out Your wrath upon the nations that do not know
> You, upon realms that do not invoke Your name. For
> they have devoured Jacob and laid waste his home
> (Psalm 79:6–7). Pour out Your wrath upon them and
> may Your fierce anger overtake them (Psalm 69:25).
> Pursue them in anger and destroy them from under the
> heavens of the Lord. (Lamentations 3:66)

Obviously, we do not share in this cup of wrath, linked to the cup of wrath that Pharaoh had to drink. As we pour the cup for Elijah, by sympathetic magic, we hope that God will pour out heavenly wrath upon the nations, literally goyim, just as was done when our ancestors were redeemed in Egypt. This has long been a controversial passage. The Reform movement took it out of its first Haggadah and restored it in the second. Even earlier the rabbis explained that since Christians and Moslems worship the same God as us, they are not referred to in this passage, which is aimed at pagans. That seems like an intellectual shell-game. Since goyim means gentiles, non-Jews, to all Jews, then we are asking God to pour divine wrath upon them. This is in line with the illustrations in many Haggadot that picture, not the Pharaoh of Egypt, but the contemporary Czar or Kaiser or whatever despot was oppressing us at that moment.

The Golem legend, in which a superhuman robotic being is created by a wonder-working rabbi to protect the Jews from the usual Passover pogroms is another expression of the Jews' prayers for divine intervention. Given the almost two millennia of anti-Semitism that reached its crescendo only a half century ago in the Holocaust, it seems premature to remove this passage, a reminder of the not so distant past.

Ritual action 26: Close the door.

Step XIV. Hallel

Ritual action 27: Pour the fourth cup of wine . . .

Not for Our Sake

Text r: The Hallel is recited over the fourth cup of wine, a continuation of the joyous praises of God that began in the Grace. These are a group of linked Psalms that were chanted by the Levites during the sacrifice of the paschal lamb. When we recite them today, we look backward to the glory of Temple days and also forward to a future redemption. Before the meal we recited Psalms 113 and 114. These refer to our original deliverance from Egypt. After the meal we begin with 115 and continue through 116, 117, and 118. These six are the Egyptian Hallel. They point toward and urge God to bring a future redemption. Before continuing with Psalm 136, the Great Hallel, we say the paragraph known as Yehalleluchah, which dates from talmudic times.

Psalm 115, the first of the psalms to be read following the words "Pour out Your wrath," begins:

> Not for our sake, Lord, not for our sake, but for Your Name's sake, grant glory.

This makes a natural continuation from our plea for the destruction of our enemies. Ours is not a selfish request, but one we desire for the sake of Heaven. For the divine honor, God should show up their gods as idols of silver and gold.

The general tendency of the Hallel poems is to praise God—Hallelujah. Two motifs from Psalm 118 are worth examining in some detail. The fifth verse proclaims:

> *Min ha-metzar karati Yah;*
>
> Out of the straits I called upon the Lord;

In some medieval Haggadot, this passage is illustrated by showing King David, the reputed author of the Psalms, wedged between steep rocks, plucking away at his harp. The steep rocks are the straits, the narrow, confined place, *ha-metzar,* from the same root as Mitzrayim, Egypt. For anyone listening to the Hebrew, Egypt cannot be just the geographical location in North Africa. It is also the limitations life imposes on us, from which we have our second birth as fully realized individuals shaped by the experiences and failures of life.

Ehvehn ma'ahsu ha-bonim, ha'yesaw le-rosh pinah.

The stone which the builders rejected has become the chief cornerstone.

This, the twenty-second verse, has been important to both alchemists and Freemasons. For alchemists, this is the stone of the philosophers, the achievement of the Magnum Opus, the Great Work, that stone which reconciles male and female, sulphur and mercury, that gives life eternal and transmutes everything it touches into gold. For Freemasons, the rejected stone is the slain master builder, Hiram Abif, whose death and resurrection is the secret of the Master's, or third, degree. For both, this is a veiled metaphor for Jesus and represents the same appropriation and reinterpretation of Jewish symbols we have seen earlier.

Pinchas Lapide, a scholar of Jewish-Christian relations, once said that in the Middle Ages the only people who lived or imitated the life of Christ were the Jews. For us, this stone is ourselves as a people. It is also Jacob's pillow, the gateway to heaven, the rock on which he slept at Bethel when he dreamed of the ladder on which the angels ascended and descended. We can see Jacob asleep on this stone on the first page of the alchemical *Mutus Liber.* It is the stone on which Solomon built his Temple on the hill of Zion in Jerusalem. Moslems assume that this spot is where the Dome of the Rock is today. We can see the builders as Christianity and Islam rejecting their own cornerstones, the Jewish people.

The rejected stone is the thirty-six hidden saints, the *lamed-vav,* for whose sake the world is preserved, another synecdochal emblem of the Jewish people. The numerical value of the Hebrew letters *lamed* and *vav* equals thirty-six. These people walk among us as the lowest of the low: a shoemaker like the biblical Enoch, uniting the upper and lower worlds as he nailed uppers to soles; a fool; a storyteller; a musician. The Chasidim have many tales about them. They have all failed in the normal world and so are hidden:

> *Success is to be the achievement of a goal known, open,*
> *given. Failure, achievement of a goal not known yet, hidden*
> *and to be discovered.*

—Léo Bronstein

What is the goal of Jewish history? What is the role of the Jewish people in history? Why are we continuously uncovered and covered, visible and invisible, revered and despised, like our matzot? This reminds us also of our afikoman, our hidden matzo which must be dis-covered. It stands for the paschal lamb, which in turn is a symbol of the Jewish people:

> *. . . that for generations Yiddish was despised should serve as*
> *a sign that great treasures of folklore, wisdom, and unique-*
> *ness are hidden in it. Yiddish shared and is still sharing the*
> *lot of the Jew who resigned from the promises of this world,*
> *its vanities, and its wickedness. He will remain hidden until*
> *there will be justice for all.*

—Isaac Bashevis Singer

The Breath of Every Living Thing

Text s: Following Psalm 136 we close this section with the Nishmat, one of the most beautiful of all Hebrew prayers. It is a regular part of the morning service on Shabbat and festivals. Nishmat means both "breath" and "soul." Its earliest strata go back to the Mishnaic period, while successive layers date from talmudic and gaonic times. Here are a few particularly expressive verses:

> The breath of every living thing shall bless Your name, O
> Lord our God, and the spirit of all flesh shall glorify and
> exalt Your remembrance, our King, forever. . . . Though
> our mouths were as full with song as the sea and our
> tongue with rejoicing like the roaring of its waves, and
> our lips with praise like the vastness of the heavens, and

our eyes with the light of the sun and moon, and
our hands spread like the wings of the eagles of the
sky, and our feet as swift as the deer, we should still be
unable to thank You enough, O Lord our God and God
of our ancestors, and to bless Your name, for one of the
thousands of thousands and myriads of myriads of the
favors You did for our ancestors and us. . . . Therefore,
the limbs You have spread out in us, and the spirit and
breath You have breathed into our nostrils, and the
tongue which You have placed in our mouths shall
give thanks, and bless, and extol, and glorify, and exalt,
and reverence, and sanctify, and crown Your name, our
King. . . .

Clearly, God does not need our praises. So why do we ramble
on with these extended adorations? One of the seder night strate-
gies is to get on God's good side, to thank the Lord for everything
we have. Even if we have *gornisht* (nothing), we say it is sufficient.
We mention how wonderful and powerful our God has always
been, especially compared to all those second-raters. Do nothing
on our account but only for the sake of your own name, says Psalm
115. These are hints that we hope will elicit tangible demonstra-
tions of God's power and munificence in our favor. We want the
nice things we say about God to come true.

At the same time, we do want to remind ourselves of the wonder and delight that is being alive. Whatever misery we experience
is as nothing compared to the pleasures of the natural world, family, children, friends, the arts, study, food, sleep. Life is a miracle of
joy and pain that we constantly take for granted. Through the poetry of Nishmat, we can push aside the inconsequential and focus
on what is real.

Finally, these poem-prayers allow us to enter the realm of the
numinous. In rattling off these strings of superlatives, these heaps

of divine adjectives, we transcend language and arrive at the state of ecstasy, or at least of contemplativeness. Our limited human knowledge is certainly incapable of describing or praising God, yet we make the attempt. We pile up one honorific after another until the words become emptied of meaning and we pass from inadequate description into the actual experience of the holy. Again, the specific sounds of Hebrew, the repetitions of the names and epithets of the sefirot—Hod, Netzach, Gedolah, Gevurah, Malkhut, Rachamim, Chesed, Tzaddikim, Tiferet—all help to create a circularity of meaning that spirals us inward toward the still, small voice beyond meaning that we refer to as God.

Nishmat closes with the Yishtabach, another litany of divine praises like the Lefichach and the Yehalleluchah that precedes the Great Hallel. This one has fifteen (a repeated seder motif) forms of praise that are owed to God: song, praise, glorification, hymn, strength, dominion, victory, grandeur, power, renown, beauty, holiness, sovereignty, blessings, and thanks. The phrase Ki Lechah Noeh, "For to him is due," used here, is picked up in two of the post-seder songs.

Ritual action 27: . . . lift the cup and drink, while leaning to the left.

Step XV. Nirtzah

The Passover Seder Is Finished

Text t: Following this, we recite the brief passage called Nirtzah, a plea for acceptance of our seder. These four verses are excerpted from the close of a long *piyyut* by the eleventh-century French Rabbi Joseph ben Bonfils. The complete poem, explaining all the laws of the seder and erev Pesach, was intended for use at Shabbat ha-Gadol, the Sabbath before Passover. There is an implication that we have kept our part of the bargain, the covenant. Now it is time for God to make good on the divine side, to literally deliver.

> *The Passover seder is finished down to the last detail, with*
>   *all its customs and laws.*
> *As we have been privileged to plan it, so may our perfor-*
>   *mance be accepted.*
> *You who are pure, dwelling on high, raise up your congrega-*
>   *tion without number.*
> *Speedily lead the shoots of your stock, redeemed, to Zion in*
>   *joyous song.*

The final words of the actual seder are now said:

> *La-Shanah Ha-Ba'ah Bi-Yerushalayim!*

> Next year in Jerusalem!

Those in Israel add the word *Ha-Benuyah*, "Rebuilt." This final plea returns us to the opening of the Maggid section: "Next year in the land of Israel." That puts the *chatimah* (seal) on the whole ceremony, our final and most important wish for the night, may all we have done produce the desired result.

Following this, on the second night, we count the omer, as explained in the last chapter. Even though the seder has ended, we hate letting go. Over the centuries, the Ashkenazim have developed an extended coda of six *zemirot* (songs), an expression of exultation in carrying out our self-appointed task, which contains some of the most memorable portions of the Haggadah. Over the years they have been adopted by the Sephardim, some even being translated into Ladino. Continuing the theme of order that pervades the evening, the first four are alphabetic acrostics, the fifth a counting song from one to thirteen, and the last a sequence of ten linked actions that move from lowest to highest.

It Came to Pass at Midnight

Text u: The first one, "Vayehi Bachatzi ha-Laylah," "It Came to Pass at Midnight," is sung on the first seder night. Through a series of elliptical references, it mentions all the times in the Bible that God saved us in the middle of the night and pleads that it should happen again soon in the refrain, Kahrev Yom, "Bring near the day." *Kahrev,* "bring near," comes from the same root as korban, "sacrifice," as in korban Pesach, the paschal offering. In the days of the Temple, the sacrifices brought us close to God and brought God close to us. Now we hope that our prayers will effect the same result. This is the first of the post-seder songs to use material from the Yishtabach in its refrain. Written in the form of an alphabetical acrostic, it is attributed to Rabbi Yannai, a piyyutin who flourished in the Holy Land sometime during the sixth to eighth centuries C.E. Since God has redeemed us so often in the middle of the night, why not now?

And You Shall Say This Is the Feast of Passover

Text v: "Va-Amartam Zavach Pesach," "And you shall say this is the feast of Passover," is sung at the second seder and, with equal erudition, mentions all the times God saved us on Passover. It was written by the greatest writer of piyyutim, Eleazar Kallir, a pupil of Yannai, who also lived in the Holy Land. Again, since God has redeemed us so often on the night of Passover, why not now? These first two zemirot both derive their refrains from phrases in Exodus 12. This one imposes two kinds of order on its material. Besides being an alphabetical acrostic, it marshals its examples in chronological order as well. The last line of the penultimate stanza cobbles together two phrases from Isaiah 21:5, one of which echoes through the whole seder: "The lamps were lit, the table set. . . ." This is the ultimate source for our Shulchan Arukh.

For to Him Praise Is Proper

Text w: "Ki Lo Naeh," "For to Him praise is proper," is the third alphabetical acrostic. It is also known as "Addir bi-Melukhah," "Mighty in Kingship." The anonymous author, who may be Kallir or some later French or German Jewish poet, took inspiration from a line in the Yishtabach that concludes the Nishmat, but borrows many biblical phrases as well. The earliest mention of this song is from the thirteenth century. This is another numinous piling up of accolades, abetted by the frequent repetitions of the short syllables *ki* (for), *lo* (to Him) and *lechah* (to You). Each line has two forms of praise followed by one group of angels doing the praising.

Mighty Is He

Text x: A similar set of adjectives is used in the fourth and final alphabetical acrostic "Addir Hu," "Mighty is He," popular since the fourteenth century. It originated in Germany, but has become popular throughout the Jewish world. For some, the alphabetical construction of these poems is merely a mnemonic, a way to remember all the lines, but it also suggests that God contains everything from A to Z, or *alef* to *tav.* The anonymous author both prays to and encourages God to rebuild the Temple soon.

Who Knows One

Text y: "Echad Mi Yode'a," "Who Knows One," takes us from the order of the alphabet to that of numbers. It was added to the Haggadah in the fifteenth century. Both this song and the next are based on gentile models, specifically from France and Germany. The Christian originals only count to twelve, while our Jewish version naturally goes on to thirteen. Note the use of the word *yode'a* for knowledge, another reference to the kabbalistic concept of *Da'at.*

This children's counting song gives us something from Jewish tradition to associate with each of the numbers one through thirteen, one for the one God and thirteen for the classical number of *middot* (divine qualities). Hebrew letters all have a numerical value, and the letters of *echad* (one) add up to thirteen. The linear counting from one to thirteen is transformed into a circular movement from the One, to the One that is contained in the thirteen. We begin and end with God.

For the children, it is fun. For the learned, there are further lessons. The Haggadah teaches everyone simultaneously, on their own level, without driving a wedge between the generations. It disagrees with Paul's rigid remark, "But when I became a man, I put away childish things" (1 Corinthians 13:11). Here is the last stanza, which contains the content of the first twelve:

> Who knows thirteen? I know thirteen. Thirteen divine qualities, twelve tribes of Israel, eleven stars in Joseph's dream, ten commandments, nine months of pregnancy, eight days before circumcision, seven days in a week, six orders of the Mishnah, five books of Moses, four mothers (Sarah, Rebecca, Leah, and Rachel), three fathers (Abraham, Isaac, and Jacob), two tablets of the covenant, one God who is in heaven and on earth.

One Kid One Kid

Text z: One of the most famous songs of the seder comes at the very end because it was the last addition to the Haggadah in the fifteenth century. Perhaps its position added to its prominence, but "Chad Gadya," a medieval Aramaic song structured like "The House That Jack Built," is a natural favorite with children and adults. It tells the story of the little kid that father purchased for two *zuzim,* two coins, and ends with God putting an end to death. This ending describes a future Messianic era, in keeping with the theme of the postprandial part of the seder. Its theme makes a fitting conclusion to the Haggadah. The continual movement of Gevurah, Severity or Judgment, through the song, can only stop when God eliminates death. That final killing is the killing of the attribute of Gevurah:

The long mysterious Exodus of death.

—Henry Wadsworth Longfellow, "The Jewish Cemetery at Newport"

This movement from the lowest to the highest reminds us of other similar medieval patterns: the chain of being that moves from the bottom of society to the top and then through the cosmos and angels until it ends with God. Another is the dance of death, showing how death spares no one from the pauper through the emperor and pope. In Petrarch's poem "The Triumphs," there is a similar movement from love through chastity, death, fame, and time to eternity. This was borrowed, along with the other patterns mentioned, to construct the series of Triumphs or trumps of the card game of Tarot, where we move from the fool at the bottom through emperor and pope to love, death, and eternity.

Although it may be a simple children's song, "Chad Gadya" can also be allegorized to represent the history of the Jewish people. In this scenario the Jewish people are the kid. In Temple times either a kid or lamb could be offered as the paschal sacrifice, so this connects the Jewish people to the paschal offering. Father is God, who purchased us with two zuzim, the two tablets of the Covenant, the Ten Commandments, already referred to in the previous song. The cat who ate the kid is the Assyrians; the dog, Babylonia; the stick, Persia; the fire, Alexander the Great and the Seleucid and Ptolemaic powers; the water, the Roman Empire; the ox, the Saracens; the slaughterer, the Crusaders; and the Angel of Death, the Ottoman Turks. Each of the devourers of Israel was in turn devoured. Unfortunately, though our enemies have been punished, the Jewish people were always caught in the crossfire. When the Crusaders went to fight in the Holy Land, they killed all the Jews they could get their hands on along the way. Whole communities were decimated in the Rhineland. The blood libel was born in England at that time. The movement from the one kid to the Holy One occurs in ten steps.

Another element in these songs, especially those that become more complex and tongue-twisting as they go on, is the hilarity of trying to sing them after four bumpers of wine. Here is the final stanza of "Chad Gadya":

> *Ve-ata ha-kadosh Baruch Hu, ve-shachat le-malach ha-mahvet, de-shachat le-shochet, de-shachat le-toraw, de-shatah le-mayim, de-chavah le-nurah, de-soraf le-chutrah, de-hecaw le-chalbaw, de-nawshak le-shunrah, de-awchal le-gadya, de-zabin abaw beetray zuzay, chad gadya, chad gadya.*

> And then the Holy One slew the exterminating angel, that slew the slaughterer, that slaughtered the ox, that drank the water, that quenched the fire, that burned the stick, that beat the dog, that bit the cat, that ate the kid, that father bought for two zuzim. One kid, One kid.

One striking symmetrical feature in the order of the haggadah is that the Maggid section begins in (ancient) Aramaic with Ha Lachma Anya and proceeds to a set of (four) questions. As we leave the haggadah, we step out in reverse, a chiastic, X-shaped, or mirror image of our entry, by first posing a set of (thirteen) questions and then returning to (medieval) Aramaic.

The Song of Songs Which Is Solomon's

If you want to go on to the next plateau, you can read Shir ha-Shirim, the Song of Songs, until the sun comes up and it's time to say Shema. The Song of Songs' beautiful poetry of springtime and erotic love was later read symbolically by the kabbalists as the story of God's longing for the Shekhinah:

> *The wonderful time, the most joyous time of the year has come. . . . The sun is high in the sky . . . the air is free and*

fresh, soft and clear. On the hill are the first sprouts of spring grass—tender, quivering, green. . . . With a screech and a flutter of wings, a straight line of swallows flies overhead, and I am reminded of the Song of Songs. "For lo, the winter is past, the rain is over and gone, the flowers appear on the earth, the time of singing is come."

—Shalom Aleichem

"And the voice of the turtle is heard in our land." So we have come full circle, from the primitive agricultural festivals celebrating the showering of blessings on us in the form of wheat, barley, grapes, and lambs; through the liberation from bondage in Egypt and its commemoration in the Temple sacrifice; to the two millennia of exile and hoped-for redemption and, finally, back again to the continual celebration of the return of spring.

Where's my Serpent of Old Nile? —Shakespeare

After looking at all that text, you might still be wondering, "Where's the story?" People often ask for a Haggadah that tells the story in a linear, connected way. No traditional Haggadah, and only a few untraditional ones, do this. The superficially abrupt and disjointed nature of the traditional "telling" has a modernistic feeling. The various details must be held in suspension, all existing at once, beyond the mere historical moment of that first seder in Egypt. Indeed, that is what has kept the Haggadah relevant for all moments of our history. Its structure has its own coherence, which far from being prosaic, is more like William Carlos Williams's *Patterson* or James Joyce's *Finnegan's Wake* than Cecil B. DeMille's *The Ten Commandments*.

Passover cannot be explained away with a simple, linear account of the Exodus from Egypt. That would maintain the too prevalent idea that what we are doing at the seder is merely a commemoration or reenactment of specific events that took place once some three millennia ago. The Haggadah constantly insists that we are to regard ourselves as having personally gone forth from Egypt. Our own redemption is implied as well. It is at once both history and myth, and myth, eternally returning on itself, need not be sequential. The Haggadah was not constructed to be coherent, linear, and connected. It is our guide through the seder, but not always an obvious and lucid one:

> *For as well the Pillar of Cloud, as that of Fire, did the*
> *Office of directing.*
> —John Donne

If you still desire a coherent narrative, though, I have constructed the following arrangement of the Maggid section almost solely from words of the traditional Haggadah. For the observant, the story is there in the traditional telling. I have tinkered with the language just enough to make it intelligible and gender neutral. I will not claim that my achievement is as grandiose as that of the Byzantine Empress Eudoxia, who patched together a life of Jesus from Homeric verses, but it should convey the story of the Exodus clearly. If read and discussed line by line, it might generate further table talk.

Maggid

Our ancestors dwelt of old time beyond the River, even Terah, the father of Abraham, and the father of Nahor. In the beginning our ancestors were idolaters and served other gods. And God said unto Abram: "Know of a surety that your seed shall be a stranger in a land that is not theirs, and shall serve them; and they shall afflict them four hundred years; and also that nation, whom they shall serve, will I judge; and afterward shall they come out with great substance."

And God took our father Abraham and our mother

Sarah from beyond the River, and led them throughout all the land of Canaan, and multiplied Abraham's seed, and gave Sarah, Isaac. And God gave unto Isaac and Rebecca, Jacob and Esau; and gave unto Esau, Mount Seir, to possess it; and Jacob and his children went down into Egypt, and they said unto Pharaoh: "To sojourn in the land are we come; for there is no pasture for your servants' flocks; for famine is sore in the land of Canaan. Now therefore, we pray you, let your servants dwell in the land of Goshen."

Jacob went down into Egypt with threescore and ten persons, few in number; and became there a nation, great, mighty, and populous. And it came to pass in the course of those many days that the king of Egypt died. And the Egyptians considered us evil and said, "Come, let us deal wisely with them, lest they multiply, and it come to pass, that, when there befalleth us any war, they also join themselves unto our enemies, and fight against us, and get them up out of the land."

Therefore they did set over us taskmasters to afflict us with our burdens. And we built for Pharaoh treasure-cities, Pithom and Ramses. And the Egyptians laid upon us heavy bondage and made the children of Israel to serve with rigor. And they made their lives bitter with hard service, in mortar and in brick, and in all manner of service in the field. And Pharaoh said, "Every Hebrew son that is born you shall cast into the River Nile." And we cried unto the Lord, the God of our ancestors, and the Lord heard our voice, and saw our affliction, and our toil, and our oppression.

God heard our groaning, and God remembered the covenant with Abraham and with Isaac and with Jacob. These make up the ten plagues that the Holy One brought upon the Egyptians in Egypt: blood, frogs, lice, beasts, murrain, boils, hail, locusts, darkness, the slaying of the firstborn. The Lord went through the land of Egypt on the night of the first seder and smote all the firstborn in the land of Egypt, both man and beast, but the Holy One passed over the houses of our ancestors in Egypt.

And we baked unleavened cakes of the dough that we brought forth out of Egypt, for it was not leavened; because we were thrust out of Egypt, and could not tarry, neither had we prepared for ourselves any provisions. The dough of our ancestors had not yet leavened when the King over all kings redeemed us. This is the bread of affliction, which our ancestors ate in the land of Egypt.

The Lord did take us out of Egypt, and executed judgments on them, and judgments on their gods, and slew their firstborn, and gave us their substance, and tore the sea apart for us, and brought us through it dry, and sunk our oppressors in the midst of it, and satisfied our needs in the desert for forty years, and fed us manna, and gave us the Sabbath, and brought us to Mount Sinai, and gave us the Torah, and brought us into the land of Israel, and built us the Temple to atone for all our sins.

We were slaves unto Pharaoh in Egypt, and the Lord our God brought us forth from a people of a strange tongue with a mighty hand and an outstretched arm, and with great terribleness, and with signs, and with wonders. And if the Holy One had not brought our ancestors forth from Egypt, then we and our children and our children's children would still be slaves unto Pharaoh in Egypt.

A Pattern Language

Apart from telling the story clearly, might there be some other pattern in the Haggadah?

We begin with acts of sanctification (candle lighting and the first cup of wine) and purification (hand washing). We have a bite of green vegetable dipped in purifying saltwater, an appetizer, and break bread, but we do not eat anything else for a while.

> *Text a:* Our first text is an invitation with a slight hint of our origins in slavery and a hope of future redemption. All of the themes of the evening are laid out immediately in capsule form.

> *Text b:* The text asks the four questions that move us forward to the answer given in text c.

> *Text c:* We were once slaves. We have continued through millennia to tell the story, at the correct moment and at length, and that is meritorious.

> *Text d:* Indeed, once five of the greatest Jewish scholars got together and told the story all night.

> *Text e:* The Torah, in four separate passages, specifically commands us to tell the story to our children. It implies by this that there are four types of children to be told. Again, each child poses one of four questions.

> *Text f:* Now we back up and start again, but not with our slavery. We go all the way back to God's promise to Abraham, which includes the foreknowledge of our bondage in Egypt and our ultimate redemption.

> *Text g:* We pause to thank God for that promise.

> *Text h:* Returning to the specifics of the story, we move along to Jacob reaching Egypt. That allows us to go

through the particulars of our bondage, which culminate in text i.

Text i: The ten plagues.

Text j: Using these ten plagues as a yardstick, we perceive the parting of the Red Sea as an even greater achievement.

Text k: We burst into song, thanking God for all the divine favors. This passage also sketches the totality of our relationship with God from the end of slavery, through the wilderness to the entry into the Promised Land and the building of the Temple.

Text l: We come down from that plateau a bit to explain the symbols of pesach, matzo, and maror.

Text m: We pause to thank God again, always with the element of a hoped-for future redemption.

Text n: That appreciation continues with two psalms of thanks for past favors. Finally, we toast God and drink the second cup. We purify ourselves by hand washing again and eat the symbolic foods, including that in text o.

Text o: We eat the Hillel sandwich. The banquet, in the present, follows.

Text p: With the repast over, we sing a psalm that hints at redemption and say Grace after the meal. That is concluded with the third cup of wine. Our mood has slid gradually from the historical events of the past, emphasized in the preprandial part of the ceremony, to the hoped-for future redemption that dominates the postprandial portion of the seder.

Text q: One of the signal elements of future redemption is the arrival of the prophet Elijah heralding the Messianic era. We pour a glass of wine for him, open the door to him, and ask God to pass judgment on our oppressors. This is a key transitional moment from past to future that brings everything together into the present. We open the door in the here and now, along with the rest of our wandering Aramean kin around the world, with the expectation of Elijah entering. When the door is closed, we turn from the past and present to a future redemption.

Text r: We begin the Hallel, praises to God, by disclaiming any selfishness in our desire to see our enemies destroyed. We only wish it for God's sake. The praises continue with text s.

Text s: The Nishmat is another form of praise, universal in nature, from a different time and perspective. That brings us to the fourth cup, in text t.

Text t: As we drink the fourth cup, we close with the plea that our seder performance be accepted. The last words we say are our bottom line: "Next year in Jerusalem."

Texts u–z: But we do not want to stop now, so we have five or six songs that continue the mood of extravagant thanks and wished-for redemption.

A linear story? No, but a clear program none the less. Each piece unfolds from its predecessor in an incredible display of stylistic variety, more apparent in Hebrew and Aramaic than in English. In some ways, there is no real movement in the book. Only a few themes are presented, but each presentation is unique in its method of conveying and cross-pollenizing those themes. Somehow, this patchwork of material from so many times and places becomes welded together into one experience. As we participate annually in the making of a seder ceremony, we too are welded to that same experience. Our comments, thoughts, and variations all have a chance to make their way into the Haggadah of the future.

Perhaps this is a sufficient seder. But for those who still have questions, we need to find out who knows one.

A Catalogue of Haggadot

Compared to the festival of Passover, the Haggadah is a recent creation. When the Temple existed, the paschal sacrifice was brought to the Temple Mount and slaughtered while the Levites sang Hallel. After the destruction of the Temple in 70 C.E., the tannaim who created the Mishnah also created the seder pretty much as we know it today. The ten rabbis named in the Haggadah are all tannaim. Chapter 10 of the talmudic tractate Pesachim has many of the Haggadah passages and seder ceremonies with which we are familiar. Others can be found in the various corollary works to the Talmud. The story of the five rabbis is unique to the Haggadah, although a similar story about Rabban Gamaliel can be found in Tosefta (supplement to the Mishnah). The Hallel was taken from the Temple service. Most of the benedictions, the Kiddush, and the Birkat ha-Mazon, had already come into being, some given final form by the Men of the Great Assembly, the Grace finished at the time of the Bar Kokhba revolt. The Nishmat is also mentioned in the Talmud, although it has been lengthened over the centuries. The Nirtzah and the Kadesh Urchatz mnemonic were added in the eleventh century. The six zemirot were added from the sixth through fifteenth centuries.

The Haggadah as a book came into being when the ninth-century Rav Amram Gaon compiled his prayer book, which included the seder service. It is remarkably like our Haggadah. The Haggadah is also contained in Maimonides' *Mishneh Torah*. The first independent Haggadah manuscripts were probably created in the twelfth century. By the time of the beautiful *Darmstadt Haggadah* in the fourteenth century, four of the six zemirot had been added. The last two seder songs finally appeared in print in a Prague Haggadah of 1590. Although close to 4,000 Haggadot have been published since the first one in 1482 in Spain, there has really been little variation in the standard text over the centuries.

Still, that has not stopped people from producing hundreds of elaborations, variants, ornamentations, parodies, and commentaries. The listings of haggadot and other titles included in this book makes no pretense to completeness, an impossible task even if attempted, but they do make mention of the most important and available items by title, author or editor, illustrator, publisher, year of publication, number of pages, and least expensive available binding. Information concerning prices, and whether a book is currently in or out of print, have been omitted because they are so variable. Similar Haggadot are grouped together by category for ease of comparison. Every Haggadah is described as to language, abridgment, transliteration, musical notation, illustration, commentary, and quality of type size and face. Unless otherwise stated, all Haggadot are in Hebrew and English, unabridged, and without transliteration, notation, illustration, and commentary, and are acceptably printed.

Orthodox: Ashkenazic

The largest Orthodox congregational organization is the Union of Orthodox Jewish Congregations of America. Its rabbinical branch is the Rabbinical Council of America. To my knowledge neither of these groups has promulgated their own Haggadah, but any traditional text of the Haggadah is Orthodox. There may be slight variations, though, in the positioning of the Nirtzah and the six final zemirot.

Abarbanel Haggadah, translated and abridged by Yisrael Herczeg, Mesorah, 1990, 160 pages, paper. The fifteenth-century commentary of Don Isaac Abrabanel (there are many variant spellings of this name), unfortunately abridged and adapted. Still valuable.

American Heritage Haggadah, compiled by David Geffen, translated by Moshe Kohn, introduction by Stuart Eizenstat, Gefen, 1992, 100 pages, cloth. Scrapbook of Passover in America. Hebrew text is facsimile of an 1857 American Haggadah. Wonderful.

Anah Dodi Haggadah, Rabbi David Feinstein, Mesorah, 1993, 149 pages, paper. Feinstein's insights into the text of the Haggadah. Includes interpretive translation of Song of Songs indicating which verses are said by God and which by Israel. A ruler on back cover allows you to measure your *ka-zaytim.*

Archaeological Passover Haggadah, translated by Cecil Roth, edited by Beno Rothenberg, introduction by Michael Avi-Yona, Adama, 1992, 119 pages, cloth. An earlier shorter version (1986, 76 pages) included many photos of Sinai. The 1992 version focuses on Egypt and adds the Song of Songs, with photos of Israeli wildflowers.

Basic Haggadah, translated by Rabbi Aryeh Kaplan, Moznaim, 1982, 141 pages, paper. Good translation, clearly laid out, lots of transliteration. Everything is explained, even for the first-time seder-giver, and lines and paragraphs are numbered. English translations of songs can be sung to the familiar melodies.

Birnbaum Haggadah, Philip Birnbaum, Hebrew Publishing, 1976, 187 pages, paper. Excellent translation, typeface, and background information, including a midrashic version of Exodus and copiously detailed running commentary. It also has good black and white illustrations of old Haggadot and ritual objects, music for seven songs, and an annotated Song of Songs. This unpretentious volume is one of the finest Hebrew-English Haggadot ever produced. One of my favorites.

Commentator's Haggadah, Haggadah text and translation from Hirsch Haggadah, commentary edited by Rabbi Yitzchak Sender, Philipp Feldheim, 1991, 319 pages, cloth. Sender brings together widely scattered comments and insights about the Haggadah text, the seder, and Passover from many Torah scholars and halakhic authorities.

Commentator's Seder, Haggadah text and translation from Hirsch Haggadah, commentary edited by Rabbi Yitzchak Sender, Philipp Feldheim, 1992, 309 pages, cloth. Sender continues his presentation of insights into the Haggadah by our great sages.

Deluxe Haggadah, translated by Abraham Regelson, notes and supplement by Rabbi Sidney Hoenig, music by Cantor Joshua Weisser, art by Siegmund Forst, Shulsinger, 1950, 172 pages, cloth. Slightly old-fashioned translation with sentimental illustrations by Forst and arrangements of a dozen seder songs. What makes this a great Haggadah, though, is the material collected at the English end of the book: primary material in English and vocalized Hebrew and Aramaic from all the classical sources. One of my favorites.

Diaspora Haggadah, translation by Jeremy Hyman, art by Shlomo Katz and Mira Sheffer, Yaniv, 1988, 64 pages, cloth. Although this is the only completely transliterated haggadah, the art is garish and the translation is uninspired. Available in both large leader's format or smaller participant's format.

Family Haggadah, translation by Rabbi Nosson Scherman, commentary by Rabbi Avie Gold, Mesorah, 1981, 95 pages, paper. This volume has a good translation, nice layout and typeface, and brief marginal commentary.

Family Seder, Rabbi Alfred Kolatch, Jonathan David, 1967, 123 pages, paper. This volume has a complete Hebrew text, interpretive and explanatory English text, some illustrations, a fair amount of transliteration, supplementary material on Soviet Jews and the Holocaust, and many quotes about freedom drawn from world literature.

Feast of History, Chaim Raphael, W. H. Smith, 1972, 256 pages, cloth. This is two books in one. When you begin at the Hebrew opening, you find a Haggadah. When you begin at the English opening, you learn about the history and customs of the holiday. Throughout the book there are numerous illustrations, many in color. Raphael does more than provide information, though. He presents ideas as knots of possibility with which we must grapple. It is both a sumptuous volume and one full of humor, learning and insight. One of my favorites.

Haggada, translated by Harold Fisch, Koren, 1991, 127 pages, cloth. This volume is enhanced with eleven plates from the fifteenth-century *Ashkenazic Erna Michael Haggadah.*

Haggadah, Rabbi Joseph Elias, Mesorah, 1977, 226 pages, paper. This haggadah adds an extensive commentary to Mesorah's *Family Haggadah.*

Haggadah, Cecil Roth, art by Donia Nachshen, Soncino, 1975, 112 pages, paper. The excellent introduction and marginal notes fully explain ritual, holiday, text, and history. One of my favorites.

Haggadah for Pesah, Rabbi Reuven Bulka, Machon Pri Ha'aretz, 1985, 144 pages, cloth. This volume is Orthodox yet gender neutral. It interprets the traditional text from a psychological perspective.

Haggadah for the American Family, Rabbi Martin Berkowitz, Haggadah Institute, 1975, 51 pages, paper. From the Hebrew opening, there is a complete Hebrew Haggadah with English instructions. From the English opening, there is an English interpretive Haggadah with some Hebrew, a fair amount of transliteration, minimal illustration, and music for three zemirot. I find this format confusing, but it may be perfect for those who want to use Hebrew only or minimal amounts of Hebrew.

Haggadah Treasury, edited by Rabbi Nosson Scherman, Mesorah, 1980, 200 pages, paper. This is the Mesorah Haggadah text plus materials from the classic commentators chosen by the students of Zeirei Agudath Israel.

Hirsch Haggadah, commentary edited by Rabbi Mordechai Breuer from the writings of Samson Raphael Hirsch, Philipp Feldheim, 1993, 291 pages, paper. Hirsch (1808–1888) was a German rabbi who created Neo-Orthodoxy, the antimystical, allegorized, moralizing form of Judaism that dominates much of Orthodoxy even today. This Haggadah brings together Hirsch's scattered references to the seder text. It is hard not to be affected by such thoughts as: "Here at the feast of the redeemed, no priest consecrates the meal, passes the cup or breaks bread. This People has no need for priests. Where the heart reaches out to God, all are priests and ministers of holiness. Every hovel is a sanctuary, every table an altar, every head of the family a priest of God, and all their sons and daughters are acolytes in His ministry."

Israel Passover Haggadah, Rabbi Menachem Kasher, Shengold, 1983, 346 pages, cloth. Kasher adds 100 chapters of running commentary to his haggadah to give explanations for the text and rituals of the seder. Also included are rare illustrations from ancient Egypt, medieval Haggadot, the Holocaust, and reborn Israel. One section deals with Moses and another with the propriety of the fifth cup. A great achievement.

Kol Dodi Haggadah, Rabbi David Feinstein, Mesorah, 1990, 160 pages, paper. This is the Mesorah Haggadah preceded by a ninety-page detailed explication of the laws of the seder as understood by the strict Feinstein. If you choose to deviate from his understanding of the law, Feinstein admits that family custom overrides his rulings. Comes with a ruler on the back cover.

Land of Israel Haggadah, commentary by Yona Zilberman, art by Haim Ron, Adama, 1992, 144 pages, cloth. An ambitious Haggadah, but photographically disappointing. The supplementary material and commentary are the strongest parts of the book.

Lehmann Haggadah, Rabbi Marcus Lehmann, Philipp Feldheim, 1969, 358 pages, paper. Lehmann (1831–1890), a German Orthodox rabbi, presented the treasures of Talmud and Midrash to a public that no longer knew Hebrew and Aramaic. Included are thirty-one illustrations from rare Haggadot.

Maharal Haggadah, Judah Loew ben Bezalel, edited and translated by Shlomo Mallin, prelude by Rabbi Aryeh Carmell, Horev, 1993, 384 pages, cloth. This volume collects Rabbi Judah Loew's discussion of the seder text from his *Book of Divine Power,* the Grace after Meals from another work, and his sermon for Shabbat ha-Gadol of 1588. Unfortunately, we must view the Maharal through the subjective filter of the compiler. Still, we get unique thoughts about a fifth cup of wine and an interesting discussion by the compiler on the pattern of the seder plate. One nice touch is the use of illustrative material from the *Prague Haggadah* of 1526.

Malbim Haggadah, translated, adapted, and annotated by Jonathan Taub and Yisroel Shaw, Philipp Feldheim, 1993, 320 pages, cloth. The Malbim was the acronym for the Rumanian Rabbi Meir Loeb ben Jehiel Michael (1809–1879). This commentary to the Haggadah is in his style and based on his thought, but is probably the work of Rabbi Naftali Maskil LeAison, another nineteenth-century scholar.

Me'am Lo'ez Haggadah, Rabbi Jacob Culi, translated by Rabbi Aryeh Kaplan, Moznaim, 1978, 209 pages, paper or spiral binding. This is the same Haggadah listed with the Sephardic Haggadot, but adapted by Kaplan for Ashkenazim. It omits the section on Passover laws, but includes all the zemirot.

Metsudah Linear Passover Haggadah, Rabbi Avrohom Davis, KTAV, 1993, 101 pages, cloth. This volume presents a literal, line-by-line translation of the Haggadah. Besides the close translation, the ritual is explained and there is a running commentary in the margin. One of my favorites.

Passover Haggadah, edited by Nahum Glatzer, Schocken, 1989, 154 pages, paper. The text is beautifully printed in Hebrew with an excellent English translation, informative notes, and beautifully reproduced illustrations from early printed Haggadot. Glatzer provides an excellent introduction and supplementary material. One of my favorites.

Passover Haggadah, translated by Rabbi Nathan Goldberg, KTAV, 1966, 96 pages, paper. Clean, clear Hebrew typeface with accurate English translation, numbered lines and simple, bold, black linoleum block illustrations. Also comes in annotated (1987) version with the same numbering of lines and brief notes in the bottom margin. Large-type version in identical format, recording, and sheet music are available separately. This is one of the most perennially popular of Haggadot.

Passover Haggadah, edited by Nachman Ran, Terra Sancta Arts, 1986, 60 pages, cloth, accordion folded, gift box. This uniquely formatted gift item combines the text of the *Copenhagen Haggadah* (listed with the facsimiles) with illustrations from other Haggadot and of rare ritual objects.

Passover Haggadah, translation by Rabbi Yaakov Reinman, introduction by Rabbi Avraham Marmorstein, art by Chana Zakashanskaya, C.I.S., 1994, 175 pages, paper. Good translation based on Rashi's understanding of the text, nicely printed and laid out—a pictorial code in the margin tells what step you are at in the seder. The introduction has a thorough summary of laws and fresh insights.

Passover Haggadah, Rabbi Shlomo Riskin, KTAV, 1983, 169 pages, paper. Riskin is an Orthodox rabbi whose Haggadah commentary takes the form of short, relevant essays in touch with the contemporary world.

Passover Haggadah, Rabbi Adin Steinsaltz, Carta, 1989, 155 pages, cloth. Steinsaltz's excellent Haggadah commentary indicates a profound knowledge of traditional thought. He has a scholarly historical perspective and is a master stylist. Decorative illustration.

Passover Haggadah, commentary by Elie Wiesel, art by Mark Podwal, Simon and Schuster, 1993, 144 pages, paper. Elie Wiesel bears witness to one of the most painful episodes in either Jewish or twentieth-century history, the Holocaust. One cannot begrudge him his melancholy. He is aware of it, and has even found Chasidic forbears who were also born under Saturn, but his books always leave me feeling that he is withholding or stingy in what he will give his readers. This Haggadah, with beautiful Hebrew typography, good translation, and fine calligraphic illustration, left me with the same disappointment.

Passover Haggadah: Legends and Customs, Rabbi Menachem Hacohen, art by Haim Ron, Adama, 1987, 184 pages, cloth. This treasure trove of Passover curiosa begins with a full explanatory introduction to laws and customs, and follows that with hundreds of stories, parables, and legends running alongside the text. Ron's illustrations are poor, but he has some clever decorated borders and letters.

Passover Haggadah: The Complete Seder, Rabbi Arthur M. Silver, Menorah, 1980, 185 pages, cloth. This is actually two books, one an excellent Haggadah and the other, beginning at the English opening, a study of the laws and historical rulings from the great halakhic authorities who have determined our performance of the seder rituals today. Along the way, the whole seder is explained, recipes are provided for the meal, and we begin to understand the conversation between the sages that has gone on for millennia. One of my favorites.

Pesach Haggadah, Rabbi Shalom Wallach, Mesorah, 1989, 221 pages, paper. This volume features the Mesorah Haggadah text in the upper half of the page with a sequence of pertinent stories on the lower half from the great exponents of the Musar movement, the ethical school founded by Rabbi Israel Lipkin of Salant (1810–1883). These stories stress the combination of learning, performance of mitzvot, and perfection of behavior that characterizes Musar.

Polychrome Historical Haggadah, Rabbi Jacob Freedman, Freedman Liturgy Research Foundation, 1974, 134 pages, cloth. This is one of the most bizarre, informative, and wonderful Haggadot ever produced. The Hebrew text is printed in seven colors according to the date of composition. Freedman's marginal notes give further information on sources and dating. There are color plates from illuminated manuscripts and dozens of other illustrations from printed Haggadot and of ritual objects. One of my favorites.

Secrets of the Haggadah, Rabbi Mattiyahu Glazerson, Raz-Ot, 1987, 188 pages, cloth. Glazerson gleans the words of the Haggadah for mystical *raz ot,* "secrets of the letters," using *gematria,* deriving meaning from the numerical value of words. Many of the secrets were more allegorical and moralistic than symbolical and mystical. I did enjoy his linking of the word Haggadah with *aguda* (union), since it is the recitation of the Haggadah at the seder that unites individuals into families and families with the Jewish people as a whole.

Sinai Haggadah, translation and commentary by J. Sinason, guide to seder laws and customs by Rabbi A. Weiss, Philipp Feldheim, 1982, 112 pages, cloth. On the one hand, this is a good Haggadah with full annotation. On the other hand, those texts that are not unique to the Haggadah are left untranslated, such as Kiddush, benedictions, Grace after Meals, Hallel, and Nishmat.

A Singing Haggadah, edited and illustrated by Ellen Egger, translated by Rabbi Arthur Chiel, L'Rakia Press, 1986, 275 pages, paper. The late Ellen Egger wanted to present the traditional Hebrew and English text of the Haggadah alongside musical notation and transliteration for the vast bulk of it. The songs were supplied by Rabbi Chiel, his wife Kinneret, and their children, and transcribed by Egger from their performances. "Eliyahu," "Ani Ma'amin," and "Avadim Hayinu," are included. There is some commentary and background material, as well as Egger's charming, simple illustrations.

Soncino Koren Haggada, translated by Harold Fisch, art by R. Ben-Ari and Irina Lyampe, Soncino, 1965, 128 pages, paper. Beautifully printed in Hebrew and English, minimal illustration and commentary.

Vayaged Moshe Haggadah, compiled from the writings of Rabbi Moshe Feinstein by Rabbi Yosaif Asher Weiss, Mesorah, 1991, 137 pages, paper. Feinstein was known as the greatest halakhic authority of our time, but this volume presents his more expansive thoughts on the text of the Haggadah and the seder ritual. A ruler is included on the back cover.

Vilna Gaon Haggadah, compiled by Yisrael Herczeg from the commentary of the Vilna Gaon and his son Rabbi Abraham, Mesorah, 1993, 136 pages, paper. A Mesorah Haggadah with classic commentary from Elijah Zalman, the Gaon of Vilna, and his son Abraham. Like Herczeg's other compilation, the *Abarbanel,* this presents wonderful material, but it does abridge and interpret. Still, this is a fascinating work and shows one of the great Jewish thinkers creating a quite idiosyncratic seder (see my diagram of the Vilna Gaon's seder plate in chapter 2) from his interpretation of tradition.

Yeinah Shel Torah Haggadah, Rabbi Binyamim Adler, translated by Yaakov Lavon, Philipp Feldheim, 1993, 273 pages, cloth. Available in Hebrew since 1978, this Haggadah is studded with classic material that brings fresh insight to our understanding of the text. One I particularly enjoyed was the punning of matzot and mitzvot, which are spelled the same, but vocalized differently. We are told to guard the matzot, make them quickly, so that they do not leaven, become chametz. Likewise, when we have the chance to perform the mitzvot, we should rush to do them with joy and not a sour, or chametz, attitude.

Yeshiva University Haggada, compiled by Steven Cohen and Kenneth Brander, Student Organization of Yeshiva University, 1985, 182 pages, paper. The Hebrew text is the same as that of the Soncino Koren Haggadah, the translation and typography are excellent, and the commentary is both scholarly and interesting. Appended to the Haggadah are nine brief essays on the Haggadah, halakhah, and philosophy by scholars of contemporary enlightened Orthodoxy.

Orthodox: Sephardic

Sephardic Passover Haggadah, Marc Angel, KTAV, 1988, 112 pages, paper. Rabbi Angel compiled this Haggadah with bits of commentary from the great Sephardic sages, Sephardic customs, plus a few texts in Ladino. Not only for Jews whose roots go back to the Spanish expulsion of 1492, but for all who are fascinated and curious about Sephardic Jewry.

Sephardi Haggadah, Rabbi Jonathan Cohen, Feldheim, 1988, 159 pages, cloth. Besides the Sephardi text of the Haggadah, Cohen provides complete explanations, laws, and details on ritual, *kashrut,* and seder preparation, and a glossary. There are four color illustrations.

Passover Haggadah Me'am Lo'ez, commentary by Rabbi Jacob Culi, translation by Rabbi Aryeh Kaplan, Moznaim, 1989, 278 pages, cloth. This is the Haggadah from Rabbi Culi's classic Ladino commentary to the Torah, *Me'am Lo'ez.* Rabbi Culi's discussion of the laws of Passover follows the Haggadah. Ashkenazic variants are given throughout the Haggadah to show differences in custom.

Chasidic

There is no central Chasidic organization. The publishing arm of Lubavich or Chabad Chasidism is Merkos L'inyonei Chinuch.

Breslov Haggadah, Rabbi Yehoshuah Starret, Chaim Kramer, and Moshe Mykoff, Breslov, 1989, 252 pages, cloth. This is the Haggadah used by the followers of Rabbi Nachman of Bratslav. It has much Breslov lore, a commentary to the Haggadah, and midrash on the Exodus, omer period, and Shavuot. Excellent.

Chassidic Haggadah, Rabbi Eliyahu Touger, Moznaim, 1988, 175 pages, cloth. A Haggadah whose running commentary is a group of pertinent Chasidic tales, it also has laws, symbols, and explanations. Excellent.

Haggadah for Pesach, edited by Rabbi Menachem Schneerson, translated by Jacob Schochet, Kehot, 1985, 74 pages, paper. The Lubavichers publish a number of Haggadot in Hebrew, with and without the commentaries of seven generations of Rebbes. This one presents the cream of that material. Much kabbalistic lore and unique Chabad customs. Like all Lubavich Haggadot, this one leaves out the Nirtzah and the six zemirot. One of my favorites.

Haggadah for Pesach, Rabbi Jacob Schochet, art by Nachum Waldman and Baruch Gorkin, Merkos L'inyonei Chinuch, 1987, 64 pages, paper, comes in large format with color art or in an inferior, black and white, smaller version. Two different artists have illustrated a complete Lubavich Haggadah for children. One has painted some beautiful pictures, while the other is a hack who spoils what could have been a beautiful Haggadah.

Haggadah of the Chasidic Masters, Rabbi Shalom Wallach, Mesorah, 1990, 208 pages, paper. Another Haggadah whose running commentary is a collection of pertinent Chasidic tales. Very little overlap between this and *Chassidic Haggadah.* Excellent.

Photographic Facsimiles

All of these Haggadot are reproductions of one-of-a-kind illustrated Haggadot, or of rare early printed Haggadot. The text, in every case, is secondary to the beauty of the book. Some of them, in spite of their original cost, still show the wine stains that indicate their use at the seder table. Incidentally, less than forty medieval illuminated Haggadot are extant, mainly because of Christian destruction of Hebrew books.

Abecassis Haggadah, Razim Art, 1993, 84 pages, cloth, gift box. Raphael Abecassis's work combines elements of Russian folk art with Blue Rider colors and both wild and precise abstraction. Like other contemporary Jewish artists, he has an element of kitsch, kept in check here, but he makes a fine book illustrator.

Agam Passover Haggadah, translation by Moshe Kohn, Gefen, 1993, 119 pages, paper. Yaakov Agam is a well-known optic and kinetic painter from Israel who places colors and shapes together for both striking and subtle effect. For this Haggadah, he has done both the Albers-like illustrations as well as the mechano-lettering. If you are not proficient in Hebrew, it takes some getting used to. The translation is a little rough in spots.

Amsterdam Haggadah 1695, Adama, 1983, 58 pages, cloth. A beautifully printed facsimile of one of the most influential Haggadot of all time. The illustrations were done by Abraham ben Jacob, a proselyte, whose copperplate engravings are remarkably like the alchemical cycles of plates being done at that time. This should come as no surprise, since he swiped his illustrations from Matthaeus Merian, who himself was responsible for so many of these alchemical engravings. The illustrations in this Haggadah were copied in many of the eighteenth-century hand-illustrated Haggadot.

Ashkenazi Haggadah, translation and commentary by David Goldstein, Abrams, 1985, 138 pages, cloth, slipcase. Beautifully reproduced mid-fifteenth-century manuscript, classic illuminations and Hebrew calligraphy by Joel ben Simeon. The original manuscript includes a marginal commentary attributed to Eleazar ben Judah of Worms. This edition includes a translation and transcription of the whole manuscript. The illuminations include the hare hunt; stunning zoomorphic initial letters; and micrography, the shaping of text into animal or other forms, a medieval Jewish type of concrete poetry.

Bordeaux Haggadah, Nahar, 1987, 146 pages, cloth. Hebrew-French manuscript executed by Isaac and Jacob Zoref in 1813. The illustrations and initial letters copy the *Amsterdam Haggadah* of 1712. Sephardic rite with some Ladino in a Napoleonic Imperial style.

Breslau Haggadah, introduction by Chaya Benjamin, Turnowsky, 1984, 54 pages plus 8-page introductory pamphlet, cloth, slipcase. Another manuscript version based on printed models, this one done by Nathan ben Abraham Speyer of Breslau in 1768.

Chagall Haggadah, Leon Amiel, 1987, 111 pages, cloth, slipcase. Also available in smaller format with paper binding. A traditional Hebrew-English Haggadah, including both the Ashkenazic and Sephardic versions of Grace, with a cycle of twenty-five watercolor paintings on the theme of the Exodus by Marc Chagall, one of the great masters of twentieth-century art.

Copenhagen Haggadah, introduction by Chaya Benjamin, Rizzoli, 1987, 68 pages plus 8-page introductory pamphlet, cloth, slipcase. This is a recreation right down to the binding of the original done by Uri Pheibush in Altona-Hamburg in 1739. It includes the commentary of Don Isaac Abrabanel, a brief kabbalistic commentary, and Yiddish and Ladino translations of parts, as well as many charming naive paintings, most based on the *Amsterdam Haggadah* of 1695.

Four Haggadot, Turnowsky. This unusual package consists of a box holding four miniature facsimile Haggadot, a 32-page English translation of the Haggadah, and a 16-page bilingual pamphlet describing the four treasures. The copies are of a reduced 94-page Haggadah, another production of the *Ashkenazi Haggadah* artist, full of beautiful miniatures, cloth; an enlarged 55-page Haggadah excerpted from a Mantuan siddur done in 1480 with delicate filigree illuminations, cloth; a reduced 51-page Haggadah by Simmel of Polin, Moravia, 1719, with simulated tooled leather binding and French marbled end papers, adapted from the Amsterdam Haggadot, cloth; and a reduced 37-page nineteenth-century Yemenite *Haggadah* by Yosef ben Yosef Hammami with minimal embellishment, paper.

Kaufmann Haggadah, Hungarian Academy of Sciences, 1957, 113 pages plus 30-page introductory booklet by Alexander Scheiber, cloth. This beautifully illuminated fourteenth-century Sephardic Haggadah has some resemblances to the Rylands Haggadah. Unfortunately, it has suffered quite a bit of water damage over the years so that the outer pages containing the narrative paintings have had a lot of their color washed away. Still, much that is beautiful in the calligraphy, decorations, and paintings remains.

Kaufmann Haggadah, Kultura International, 1990, 128 pages plus 23-page introductory booklet by Gabrielle Sed-Rajna, leatherbound, silvered edges, boxed. In 1987 the Kaufmann Haggadah was restored. This facsimile presents the results of that restoration, and includes the blank pages left out of the 1957 edition. It comes in a strange coffin-like box, for some reason, but the paper, the photography, the printing, and the binding—creamy, fragrant leather—are all superior to the earlier production.

Leipnik Haggadah, Turnowsky, 1985, 44 pages, cloth, slipcase, includes a 16-page pamphlet with the 1898 English translation of the Haggadah by Aaron Asher Green and a separate sheet with notes by Shlomo Zucker. Another handmade version of the 1712 *Amsterdam Haggadah,* this one done in 1733 in Darmstadt by Joseph ben David Aharon of Leipnik, Moravia.

Moravia Haggadah, Palphot, 42 pages, cloth, slipcase. This is another eighteenth-century manuscript, dated 1737, copying the Amsterdam Haggadot. The scribe-artist is unknown, but the manuscript is called, after one of its later owners, the *Floersheim Haggadah.*

Moss Haggadah, Bet Alpha, 1990, 114 pages, cloth, plus 20-page English translation pamphlet (also sold separately) and one paper-cut. In 1980 David Moss began a three-year project of creating a unique Haggadah for a specific patron, which is now available in this gorgeous facsimile edition. This is one of the most beautiful books in the long history of the Jewish book. More than just sumptuous illustration and masterful calligraphy, every bit of decorative elaboration is linked to a resonant knot of Jewish thought, emotion, and experience. The whole Jewish manuscript tradition is referred to and then extended.

This is a profound artistic meditation on the contents of the Haggadah. For example, Psalm 114 is musical notation with the heads of the marching Israelites as the notes of the song. When we are asked to consider ourselves as having been redeemed, we see two pages of our ancestors interspersed with mirrors that include us in the picture. One of the paper-cuts shows a bird cage whose doors are the gates of Auschwitz. Through the cutout bars we see the bird-headed Jews, proto-Foghorn Leghorns, from an early Haggadah that avoided the human image. The text is, "We were slaves to Pharaoh . . ." This instant family heirloom is a work of genius that repays close study.

Ottingen Haggadah, introduction by Chaya Benjamin, Nahar, 1985, 64 pages plus 8-page introductory pamphlet, cloth, slipcase. Another late manuscript, this one done by Jacob ben Michael May Segal of Innsbruck in Ottingen, 1729, and patterned after Amsterdam models.

Prague Haggadah 1526, Shulsinger, 1964, 84 pages, cloth, originally packaged with Charles Wengrov's *Haggadah and Woodcut.* Gershom Cohen's *Prague Haggadah* of 1526 was the first illustrated Haggadah to be printed from movable type. It influenced all of the illustrated Haggadot that followed. It stands today as one of the masterpieces of the art of printing. The Hebrew typeface is clear and fluid. Even more worthy of note are the woodcut initial letters, illustrations, and elaborate borders, reminiscent of Dürer's borders, Tarot cards, and bookplates. When copperplate engravings were later introduced, they were seen as an improvement; but for all their detail and subtlety, they never achieved the virile boldness of these woodcuts.

Prague Haggadah 1526, Ravin, 1987, 78 pages, cloth, plus 8-page introductory pamphlet by Joseph Tabory, comes in gift box. Unlike the beautiful printing, paper and binding of the Shulsinger volume, this has a cheap, tacky binding, a textured faux parchment paper, and a glitzy use of gold for all of the woodcut initial words and letters, that virtually destroys the value of this book as a beautiful object. The pamphlet by Tabory is excellent.

Rosenstein Haggadah, Aberbach Fine Art, 1986, 143 pages, cloth. Yossi Rosenstein, an Orthodox rabbi and talented painter, adheres to the strict interpretation of "no graven images." He will not show faces or any body parts, even of animals. The camels are wooden ships of the desert with carved camel figureheads. The result is this weirdly surrealistic Haggadah, in which all the protagonists are like mannequins. The intention is more symbolic than magical, but the result is a compression of time in which Pharaoh finally gives Moses an enormous key to the concentration camps, or Israeli soldiers hold up Moses' arms in the battle with Amalek. Printed in gold and white on black and filled with both the Haggadah text and many biblical quotes that amplify the paintings, this book has a certain enjoyable kitsch quality common in "Jewish" art, but is still compelling.

Rylands Haggadah, introduction and translation by Raphael Loewe, Abrams, 1988, 190 pages, cloth, slipcase. Full of elaborate, decorated initial letters and words, micrography, fanciful grotesques, and a complete illuminated story of Passover from the burning bush through the crossing of the Red Sea, this is one of the greatest of all Haggadah manuscripts. It was created in the mid-fourteenth century in Catalonia. Besides the Haggadah and the cycle of Passover illustrations, this manuscript includes eighty-three Hebrew poems for liturgical use during the Passover season.

Sarajevo Haggadah, commentary by Cecil Roth, Jugoslavija, 1967, cloth, 196 pages, slipcase. This fourteenth-century Sephardic Haggadah is probably the single most famous medieval Hebrew manuscript. Besides the beautiful calligraphy, decorated initial words and letters, gold leaf, and charming text illustrations, this book is famous for a complete cycle of Torah illustrations preceding the text. Beginning with the spirit of God hovering over the face of the deep and ending with the death of Moses and the ensconcement of Torah scrolls in an Ark, the unknown artist "pictured" the whole Pentateuch. By bracketing the Passover story between these two images, he linked creation, redemption, and revelation.

Sarajevo Haggadah, Prosveta-Svjetlost, 1983, 280 pages plus 45-page introductory pamphlet by Eugen Werber, cloth, slipcase. This improves on the earlier facsimile both photographically by bringing out more detail and by the inclusion of the additional hymns, which were left out of the earlier reproduction.

Shalom of Safed, Terra Sancta, 1992, 88 pages, cloth, gift box. Shalom Moskovitz, an Israeli Grandpa Moses, was born in 1887 and began painting his primitive canvases at age seventy. In them, he combined his own Chasidic background, knowledge of kabbalah, and vision of the Holy Land to create these fresh perceptions of the Bible, Haggadah, and Israeli landscape. This Haggadah brings together illustrations from two separate Haggadah cycles. Oddly reminiscent of the Little King, they are truly naive and magical.

Szyk Haggadah, edited by Cecil Roth, Massadah and Alumoth, 92 pages. This book originated as an English limited edition on vellum in 1939. Roth did his usual excellent job in translating and commenting on the text, Arthur Szyk created an inspired, now-classic view of the seder, the Bible story, and midrash. The Beaconsfield Press, publisher of the limited edition, did a masterful job of printing, both Hebrew and English, and layout. The pages are accordion-folded so they are only printed on one side, which reduces show-through. Children will love the fairy tale illustrations, while adults will be amazed at the wealth of detailed information packed into every image. The ornamental calligraphy opens up the magic of the sinuous curves and evocative strokes of the Hebrew letters. It has been photographically reprinted in the same format on paper many times since then. This twentieth-century creation evokes the feeling of the finest medieval illuminated manuscripts.

Washington Haggadah, Library of Congress, 1991, 77 pages, leatherbound, plus 212-page commentary volume edited by Myron Weinstein, cloth, boxed. Another of the exquisite productions of Joel ben Simeon, creator of the *Ashkenazi Haggadah,* this is simpler, but still a masterpiece of calligraphy and ornamentation. The pictures not only illustrate, but guide the reader through the text showing when to pour wine or when to toast. When it is time to point to the matzo, a monkey shaking a tambourine in the margin provides a dramatic drum roll. The seder uses many methods of communicating information: symbol, ritual, text, music, food. These involve apprehending information through all five senses, which strengthens the memory and the impact of information through association. One other element was the use of illustration in Haggadot:

> *It was an old heirloom, with ancient wine stains on it, which had come down from the days of her grandfather, and in which were many boldly and brightly colored pictures, which she had often as a little girl looked at so eagerly on Passover evenings.*
> —Heinrich Heine, *The Rabbi of Bacherach*

Before we understood the words, there were the pictures, whether painted parchment or woodcuts and engravings on printed paper. The *Washington Haggadah* must have charmed many a child in its day. It has lost none of its power over the centuries. The companion volume is both erudite and fascinating.

The Wolloch Haggadah in Memory of the Holocaust, calligraphy and micrography by Yonah Weinrib, art by David Wander, Goldman's Art Gallery, 1988, 114 pages, cloth. A powerful memorial to the 6 million, adapting the images of the Passover to our most recent enslavement. The pyramids we built for Pharaoh are here a pile of the cheap suitcases we took to the camps. The blood, fire, and pillars of smoke are the crematoria. The usual wine stains are blood; the matzot, all burnt; the charoset, actual bricks; the greens, dipped in blood. You may not want to bring this to the seder table, but it is an eloquent and moving perception of the eternal meaningfulness of the holiday.

Foreign Languages

Over the centuries the Haggadah has been translated into almost every conceivable language. There is even a Haggadah of the Chinese Jews from the seventeenth or eighteenth centuries, some in Marathi for Indian Jews beginning in the last century, and more recently, one in Japanese. Certain songs, translated into Yiddish or Ladino (see listings under Sephardic), have become as standard as the original Hebrew and Aramaic. Besides these languages, I have seen Haggadot in French, Spanish, Portuguese, Italian, and Russian. The last language has generated many new editions because of the recent flood of Russian émigrés previously barred from Jewish education and now eager to learn about their heritage. Years ago I longed for Russian Haggadot but could not find any. Now there are more than half a dozen.

Conservative

The official Conservative congregational organization is United Synagogue of America. Its rabbinical branch is the Rabbinical Assembly.

Passover Haggadah: The Feast of Freedom, edited by Rachel Rabinowicz, art by Dan Reisinger, Rabbinical Assembly, 1982, 144 pages, paper. This first-ever Conservative Haggadah is a fairly traditional, though mostly gender neutral (God is still male), text with bold, colorful graphics and some incredible supplementary materials. Changes from the traditional Haggadah include: replacing the rabbinic expansion on the ten plagues with a collage of Exodus verses on the miracle at the Red Sea; a choice of a long or short Grace after Meals; omission of the last paragraph of the parable of the four children, the Great Hallel and the first two closing zemirot; and placing the Nirtzah after the remaining zemirot. An excellent tape and coloring book are also available.

This extract from the prison journal of Soviet Jewish dissident Shimon Grilius comes from the *Feast of Freedom:*

> We held the seder in a hurry, as in the time of the Exodus from Mitzrayim, since the camp authorities prohibited the holding of a seder. Instead of maror, we ate slices of onion, and for zero'a, we used burnt soup cubes. We read from one Haggadah, the only copy we had, and when we reached korekh, we had nothing to put between the matzot. Then Iosif Mendelevich said, "We do not need

a symbol of our suffering. We have real suffering and we shall put
that between the matzot."

The Art of Jewish Living: The Passover Seder, Dr. Ron Wolfson with Joel
Grishaver, Federation of Jewish Men's Clubs, 1988, 330 pages, paper. This
is a teaching text, not actually a Haggadah, though it contains most of the
Haggadah—in this case the *Feast of Freedom Haggadah.* Because of that
and because the Federation is an arm of the Conservative movement, I include it here. Wolfson, a gifted teacher, moves through the text systemati-
cally, showing what materials are needed and how and why we perform the
rituals. His explanations are clear, thoughtful, and reassuring. Everything
is transliterated. A variety of specific sedarim are represented with inter-
views and photos. A second section goes into the preparations for the
seder. A tape and Russian edition are available. A Workbook (64 pages)
and a Teacher's Manual (45 pages) expand the activities for learning given
in the book. One of the few thorough books on the holiday from a non-
Orthodox viewpoint.

The Passover Haggadah, compiled by Rabbi Morris Silverman, revised by
Jonathan Levine, art by Ezekiel Schloss, Prayer Book Press, 88 pages,
1987, paper. Morris Silverman's traditional Haggadah with commentary
and supplementary material, though never endorsed by the Rabbinical
Assembly, has become a standard for many Conservative Jews. With simple, bright, two-color illustrations, this now classic version gives equal
weight to the voice of the past and the call of the present. Over a dozen
songs plus the benedictions are transliterated.

Reform

The official Reform congregational organization is the Union of American
Hebrew Congregations. Its rabbinical branch is the Central Conference of
American Rabbis. The Old Union Haggadah (1923), now out of print,
with English opening and minimal Hebrew, omitted the ten plagues,
"Pour out Your wrath," and "Next year in Jerusalem" sections. The New
Union Haggadah is bilingual with Hebrew opening, and returns to the
traditional text and rituals.

New Union Haggadah, edited by Rabbi Herbert Bronstein, art by Leonard
Baskin, Central Conference of American Rabbis, 1982, 123 pages, paper.

This is the current Reform Haggadah, as renowned for its return to the traditional text as for the memorable color illustrations. Some parts of the text have been adapted and rearranged, some of the zemirot and parts of Hallel have been omitted, and many supplementary readings have been appended. Much of the text is arranged for group or responsive reading. Music and transliteration for over thirty songs can be found at the back of the book. No evasion of tradition here, but an active struggle and response instead. A Russian edition is available.

Gates of Freedom, Rabbi Chaim Stern, introduction by Rabbi Eugene Borowitz, art by Todd Siler, Behrman House, 1982, 129 pages, paper. This beautifully illustrated Haggadah, unfortunately no longer available in color, is peppered with quotations about freedom from world literature that work as analogs to the classic text. Most of the traditional text is retained with fresh, gender neutral translations, much transliteration and music for fourteen songs. An alternative Reform Haggadah.

Reconstructionist

Reconstructionism began when Orthodox Rabbi Mordecai Kaplan defected to Conservatism, then broke with that and founded the Society for the Advancement of Judaism in 1922. Its current congregational organization is the Federation of Reconstructionist Congregations and Havurot.

New Haggadah, edited by Mordecai Kaplan, Eugene Kohn, and Ira Eisenstein, art by Leonard Weisgard, Behrman House, 1978, 176 pages, paper. This recently revised Haggadah was first done in 1941. It abbreviates Hallel and omits much of the exegesis, some of the zemirot, and the "Pour out Your wrath" passage. Most of the Hebrew text is traditional, but the fresh, heartfelt translation freely paraphrases and adapts. Many unique readings about Moses and the Exodus story. Includes notation and transliteration for twenty songs.

Alternative

The following Haggadot, about a quarter of our listings, represent a variety of contemporary texts. Some remain quite traditional, merely abridging the usual text. Others ring the changes on the familiar words in a new key, showing the adaptability of Passover concepts to our modern problems.

Family

These Haggadot are specifically constructed to keep the attention of children without losing that of the adults.

Family Haggadah, Shoshana Silberman, art by Katherine Kahn, Kar-Ben, 1987, 64 pages, paper. A traditional, familiar, but shortened Haggadah with many fresh ideas for activities that keep children from fidgeting, yet do not seem childish to adults. It is neither too long and dry, nor too short and simple. Two-color graphics enliven the page. It emphasizes songs and provides lots of transliteration. An accompanying tape and two adjunct children's books, *Passover Fun for Little Hands* and *My Very Own Haggadah,* are available.

We Tell It to Our Children, Mary Ann Wark, art by Craig Oskow, Mensch Makers, 1988, 116 pages, spiral bound. This Haggadah involves children in the seder by using puppets in a dramatic performance to tell the Exodus story. Includes traditional blessings and rituals, unusual charoset recipes, new English songs set to familiar melodies, notation and transliteration for five traditional songs, and Hebrew and transliteration for blessings and the four questions. Leader's edition available with nine illustrations on card stock for making stick or finger puppets, plus pocket for storing.

Feminist and Egalitarian

The seder text for women is currently the most active arena for alternative Haggadah creation. The original story of freedom from oppression almost begs for feminist adaptation. All of these Haggadot demonstrate prolonged meditation on the traditional text and come under the rubric, "Whoever expands upon the story of the Exodus deserves praise."

And We Were All There, Rabbi Sue Levi Elwell with Members of the Center, American Jewish Congress Feminist Center, 1993, 56 pages, paper. This ambitious project is traditional but with a feminist focus that includes women in our history, our sacred texts, our worship, and our perception of the divine. Blessings are in male and female forms, all Hebrew transliterated.

Egalitarian Hagada, Aviva Cantor, Beruriah, 1992, 16 pages, paper. Cantor created her *Ur-Haggadah* in 1971 and first published this version in Lilith magazine in 1982. It is egalitarian, not specifically feminist, but it gives equal space to both male and female roles in the Exodus story. No Hebrew, but much transliteration.

New Haggadah: A Jewish Lesbian Seder, Judith Stein, Bobbeh Meisehs Press, 1985, 20 pages, spiral binding. This is a quite traditional feminist Haggadah that makes a rightful claim to our history and customs, but with an emphasis on our foremothers, like Sarah, Jocheved, Miriam, Judith, and more recently, Hannah Szenes. Mostly English with some transliteration.

San Diego Women's Haggadah, edited by Jane Zones with Members of the Institute, Woman's Institute for Continuing Jewish Education, 1986, 84 pages, paper. A great deal of creative liturgy has come from the Woman's Institute. Their Haggadah emphasizes the role of women in Jewish history and life and especially in the story of the Exodus. Thirteen songs, lots of transliteration, graphics.

The Telling, E. M. Broner with Naomi Nimrod, HarperSanFrancisco, 1993, 216 pages, cloth. This is both the story of Broner's creation, with Naomi Nimrod, of what was one of the first women's Haggadot, published in *Ms.* magazine in 1977, as well as about an incredible pride of feminists, the Seder Sisters—Gloria Steinem, Bella Abzug, Grace Paley, Letty Cottin Pogrebin, Phyllis Chesler, and Michele Landsberg, among others—who have met every year since then to celebrate Passover. Many original sedarim are described and Broner's revised English Haggadah closes the book.

Women's Haggadah, E. M. Broner with Naomi Nimrod, HarperSan-Francisco, 1994, 69 pages, paper. Once you have read Broner's *The Telling,* you might want to use a set of her *Women's Haggadah* at your seder. This compact volume gives the complete English text plus the Hebrew (with transliteration) for many of the passages. Broner has written a new introduction explaining the origin of her feminist liturgy.

Jewish Renewal Movement

The Jewish Renewal Movement represents a post-Sixties response and commitment to Judaism: New Jewish Agenda, Aquarian Minyan, Zalman Schachter, Shlomo Carlebach, the *Jewish Catalogs, Tikkun.* It seems appropriate at this point to mention the Haggadah insert, edited by Michael Lerner, that appears in *Tikkun* magazine every Passover season. It addresses today's issues in light of the ancient holiday, and there are new texts every year.

Passover Haggadah, Meryam, Hercules, 1990, 40 pages, paper. Traditional but much abbreviated Haggadah using explicit metaphors of conception and birth to describe the movement from spiritual ignorance to consciousness that can take place during the seder ritual. Key parts in Hebrew and transliteration, mostly English with new translations, computer graphics.

Santa Cruz Haggadah, Karen Roekard, art by Nina Paley, Hineni Press, 1991, 73 pages, paper. Karen Roekard, long associated with the Bay Area's Aquarian Minyan, has created a Haggadah for evolving consciousness. Its central theme is the attempt to put aside chametz—habitual patterns of thought and action that enslave us—so we can leave Mitzrayim, the narrow place of self-limitation. The psychological text is balanced by light-hearted cartoon illustrations. Key parts in Hebrew and transliteration. A 168-page, spiral-bound leader's copy with commentaries, complete Hebrew text, and exercises is also available.

Shalom Seders, introduction by Arthur Waskow, preface by Grace Paley, Adama, 1984, 104 pages, paper. Three different Haggadot from three different New Jewish Agenda affiliates: *Rainbow Seder,* by Arthur Waskow—liberation, ecology, peace; *Seder of the Children of Abraham,* by Philadelphia Chapter of New Jewish Agenda—reconciliation between Israeli and Palestinian, full of information from two peoples who love the Holy Land; *Haggadah of Liberation,* by the Seattle Affiliate, Kadima—feminist and more. You can either choose one or mix and match. Although radically different from the traditional Haggadah, they display an awareness of, and struggle with, tradition. Some transliteration, illustrated.

The Telling: A Loving Hagadah for Passover, Dov Ben-Khayyim, Rachamim Press, 1989, 48 pages, paper. Dov, who died last year of AIDS, was a sweet, gentle person, part of the Aquarian Minyan, a creative circle of San Francisco Bay Area Jews who came out of the Sixties hippie period and applied that to the concept of being Jewish. Eastern mysticism, kabbalah, multi-culturalism, feminism, and ecology are all a part of his egalitarian Haggadah. He wanted it to be inclusive, so there is a strong emphasis on songs, transliteration, both male and female forms of the blessings, interesting illustrations of Pesach in many cultures, and everything you remember fondly of the Haggadah, but in a much briefer format. The female forms of the berakhot are addressed to the Shekhinah. This is just one of the ways that Dov emphasized the spiritual core of the holiday.

Miscellaneous

Bay Area Jewish Forum Hagadah, Ralph Kramer and Philip Schild, art by Bezalel Schatz, Benmir, 1986, 69 pages plus sheet with transliterations, paper. The origins of this poetic reconstruction of the Haggadah go back to a 1947 adaptation of the Reconstructionist Haggadah. It was recast over the years until it reached its present state. Notation for seven songs, minimal Hebrew.

Becoming Free, Howard and Judith Rubenstein, Granite Hills, 1993, 166 pages, paper. The Rubensteins take a fundamentalist, one might say Karaite, approach in their highly idiosyncratic Haggadah. They want to return to the Torah injunctions about the paschal sacrifice, at least roast lamb, and the blood on our doorposts. They reject many rabbinic ordinances, since they feel that we should be vigilant, not relaxed and reclining, at the seder. They believe that the celebration of Passover has led to a complacency in dangerous times, like the Holocaust, that lulled us into a sense of freedom we did not have. For their Hillel sandwich, they eat roasted lamb with matzo and maror. The Haggadah is abridged and supplemented, all Hebrew is transliterated. A songbook is also available.

Concise Family Seder, Rabbi Alfred Kolatch, Jonathan David, 1987, 48 pages, paper. This Haggadah is an abridgement of Kolatch's *Family Seder.* In some portions it reduces the Hebrew and updates and expands the English. Much of the remaining Hebrew is transliterated. It eliminates four of the zemirot and most of the midrash, shortens Grace after Meals, and reduces Hallel to Psalm 114.

A Family Seder in 20 Easy Steps, Maida Hoffman, Anvil, 1992, 26 pages, some Hebrew, all transliterated. By reducing the postprandial part of the seder to two cups of wine and opening the door for Elijah, this is indeed a very brief seder. Although most of the rest of the Haggadah is boiled down to nine blessings, this slimmest of Haggadot manages to include at least a token amount of all fifteen steps. Simple, effective illustrations. Perfect as the most minimal of bases on which to begin construction of your own Haggadah. Also available in a 52-page, spiral-bound edition that adds menus, recipes, games, glossary, customs.

Haggadah for the School, Hyman Chanover, art by Uri Shulevitz, United Synagogue, 1963, 77 pages, paper. A slightly abridged Haggadah for use in religious schools and at model sedarim. The translation paraphrases the text in words that children can understand. The more abstruse rabbinic passages are replaced by straightforward narrative. Simply illustrated, slight commentary.

Israel Haggadah, Meyer Levin, Abrams, 1991, 128 pages, paper. Famous as the author of *Compulsion,* Levin was less well-known as a pioneer in the early kibbutz movement. Out of that experience came this fresh adaptation of the traditional Haggadah, first published in 1968, which eliminates midrash in favor of narrative and dramatic recitation. Here is much of the old ritual and familiar song but in the context of the modern-day return of the Jewish people to the Holy Land. The poetic English text, with key parts in Hebrew, all transliterated, is supplemented with thirteen songs and over fifty beautiful color photos of Israel and one original painting by Reuven Rubin.

Maggid Haggadah, edited by Kiva Shtull, Ann Rae, 1993, 125 pages, paper. This Haggadah substitutes long extracts from the Bible for the Maggid section, abridges Grace after Meals and Hallel, omits the first four zemirot, and adds back the four questions, "Dayyenu," and Rabban Gamaliel.

Model Seder, Rabbi Harry Nelson and Harry Malin, Jonathan David, 1981, 48 pages, paper. First done in 1954 for use at model sedarim in religious schools, this abbreviated text has explanations and some wonderful photos. It eliminates or simplifies much of the midrash, Grace, Hallel, and zemirot.

New Model Seder, Rabbi Sidney Greenberg and Allan Sugarman, Prayer Book, 1991, 33 pages, paper. First done in 1971, this brief, simple Haggadah retains the memorable while recasting the text. Includes photos, explanations, and supplementary material from spirituals, the Holocaust, Dr. Martin Luther King, and Anne Frank.

On Wings of Freedom: The Hillel Haggadah for the Nights of Passover, Rabbi Richard Levy, KTAV, 1989, 153 pages, paper. Los Angeles Hillel Rabbi Richard Levy saw a need for a traditional, gender neutral Haggadah that would delve more deeply into the text and ritual actions while also connecting these with contemporary events. The result is this fresh translation with lots of transliteration, additional comments, and a dramatic sense of the seder's reenactment of the first seder. Both playful and deep thought are at work here. The midrash of the three rabbis on the ten plagues and the first two zemirot are omitted. A leader's edition with 40-page pamphlet is also available. Though its poetic qualities are occasionally strained, this is one of my favorites.

Passover Celebration, edited by Rabbi Leon Klenicki, Anti-Defamation League of B'nai B'rith and Liturgy Training Publications of the Archdiocese of Chicago, 1980, 58 pages, paper. This simple, brief, ecumenical, yet completely Jewish Haggadah of interfaith understanding is perfect for a seder with gentile guests or for Jews who are just beginning to observe Passover. The clear text will explain the Passover rituals to Jews and non-Jews alike. In place of "Pour out Your wrath," there is a touching passage from Anne Frank. Lots of notation and transliteration, little Hebrew, most songs in English, tape available.

Passover Haggadah, Roe Halper, Bayberry Press, 1990, 37 pages, paper. Graphic artist Roe Halper wrote, illustrated, and published this Haggadah. Minimal Hebrew, blessings transliterated, quotes from world literature, text rewritten, with linear narrative, ritual simplified.

Passover Seder: Pathways through the Haggadah, Rabbi Arthur Gilbert, art by Ezekiel Schloss and Uri Shulevitz, KTAV, 1970, 64 pages, paper. While eliminating much of the text, this Haggadah focuses instead on the traditional Passover order, the seder. Each action is here, from the sanctification of the meal with wine to the ritual closing. This simple, inviting volume, illustrated in two colors, and with Rabbi Gilbert's thoughtful telling of the story and explanation of the symbols, provides a fresh look at the traditional Haggadah. Key parts are transliterated, and Moshe Nathanson's arrangements for eight songs are included. An accompanying tape is also available.

Non-Jewish: African-American

The Overcome: A Black Passover, Peter Bramble, C. H. Fairfax, 1989, 203 pages, paper. Bramble, a black Episcopalian priest from the West Indies, now rector of a church in Baltimore, believes that blacks need a cyclical ritual proclaiming their victories so that they do not become bogged down in seeing their history as a linear sequence of unremitting frustrations and tragedies. Without making point-by-point comparisons to our seder, Haggadah, and Passover, he uses these as analogs for the creation of contemporary black ritual. He realizes that somehow, in spite of millennia of persecution, the Jewish people retained a positive sense of themselves. Though physically enslaved, our hearts, minds, and souls remained free. His Overcome ritual would attempt to do the same thing for African-Americans who, unlike us, were stripped of their language, names, food, culture, and calendar when they made the Middle Passage.

Instead of the Exodus from Egypt, Bramble uses the assassination of Martin Luther King (has anyone else noticed that his initials, MLK, mean King in Hebrew?) on April 4, close to spring, Passover, Good Friday, and Easter, as the moment of transition from bondage to freedom. Dr. King's life and work achieve an epiphany at the moment of his death, just as, at the moment of our first seder, our matzot changed from bread of affliction to bread of freedom. The book has great ideas, but it would have been more productive to actually write an Overcome Haggadah and seder ritual than to just write about it. Hopefully, Bramble will do this soon.

Non-Jewish: Christian and Ecumenical

For Christians, Passover comes close to Easter and reminds them that the Last Supper of the Gospels was supposedly a Passover seder. Although the original texts are ambiguous on this point, positive parallels between the two holidays are better than negative. The following books provide a modified seder for the increasing number of Christians who want to participate in a Last Supper seder, or to interpret the holiday from a Christian point of view. I omit one item, a Haggadah from Jews for Jesus. I don't mind sharing my holiday, but I don't want someone beating me about the head with it.

Jesus and Passover, Anthony Saldarini, Paulist, 1984, 116 pages, paper. A study of what Passover was like in the time of Jesus by a Christian scholar of Judaism.

Celebrating an Authentic Passover Seder, Joseph Stallings, Resource, 1994, 140 pages, paper. Stallings provides background, aids to performance, and a Haggadah for Christians to use at home or large church gatherings. He understands the Passover through the lens of Jesus, but he obviously loves our holiday.

Passover Seder for Christian Families, Sam Mackintosh, Resource, 1986, 31 pages, paper. A Christianized version of the seder.

Rediscovering Passover, Joseph Stallings, Resource, 1988, 352 pages, paper. Stallings's first book on Passover, giving his views on what Passover was like at the time of Jesus.

Secular

These Haggadot eschew the use of the word God, yet they are none the less Jewish for that. Connection to Yiddishkeit, wanting to engage in Jewish custom, though others may call it law, and even hoping that one's children will be lucky enough to find Jewish mates—none of that requires dogma or belief. These Haggadot celebrate spring, family, and freedom in a Jewish way.

Haggadah for a Secular Celebration of Passover, Elsie Levitan, Max Rosenfeld, and Bess Katz, art by Ruthie Rosenfeld, Sholem Aleichem Club of Philadelphia, 1977, 64 pages, paper. Some Hebrew and Yiddish, some transliteration, seven songs. This charming Haggadah emphasizes Yiddish culture through wonderfully relevant selections from Aleichem, I. L. Peretz, Chaim Zhitlowsky, and Yiddish songs of rejoicing and resistance. With simple graphics and calligraphy, reminiscent of Ben Shahn, our uniqueness as a people is both observed and celebrated. One of my favorites.

Hagode for Passover, edited by Joseph Mlotek, Naomi Kadar and Chava Reich, Workmen's Circle, 1991, 80 pages, paper. The Arbeiter Ring, or Workmen's Circle, was founded in 1900 as a fraternal order, a kind of socialist B'nai B'rith. Their Haggadah never mentions God, but it salutes our glorious history with the traditional songs and poems of the Haggadah as well as new songs from Hirsh Glick, Bunim Heller, and H. Leivick. If you want to learn to sing the four questions in Yiddish, you will find them here. Hebrew, English, and Yiddish, completely transliterated, minimal illustration. Although no ritual is mentioned, it can be inferred from the sequence of songs.

Humanist Haggadah, Rabbi Sherwin Wine, Society for Humanistic Judaism, 1994, 24 pages, paper. This brief, simple Haggadah uses the food symbols of the seder to emphasize the importance of freedom and hope in Judaism and the story of the Exodus. Twelve songs with transliteration.

Vegetarian

Appropriately, our alphabetical list of alternative Haggadot ends with the "Chad Gadya," the paschal sacrifice.

Haggadah for the Liberated Lamb, Roberta Kalechofsky, Micah, 1988, 159 pages, paper. In this first vegetarian Haggadah, not just the Israelites, but the lamb as well is liberated. This text is a poetic improvisation on the original text as viewed from the perspective of kindness to all animal life. The question asked is, "Do we master both human and Mother nature or free them?" Ten songs with music and transliteration. Extensive notes, recipes, graphics. Also available in an earlier, slightly different, more concise, English-only edition (1985, 96 pages).

Haggadah for the Vegetarian Family, Roberta Kalechofsky, Micah, 1993, 72 pages, paper. An adaptation of the earlier Haggadah for families with children. Includes ten songs, transliterations, recipes, graphics.

If you are interested in receiving a more extensive, annotated, 110-page review of over 500 Passover books and items, please send a check in the amount of $12.00 to: Ira Steingroot, P.O. Box 8464, Berkeley, CA 94707.

Chapter Six

Echad Mi Yode'a:
Who Knows One?

The Power of Numbers

The Egyptians believed in the power of words and spells. The Babylonians had the same faith in numbers. The Jews took both concepts and merged them into their own system. In Hebrew each letter has a numerical value. This led to the science of *gematria,* from the word geometry, in which two words of equal value may be connected in some way. For instance, since the word for "one" is *echad,* whose numerical value is thirteen, you have the makings of a good case for the equivalence of the one God and the thirteen divine qualities.

In actual practice, however, gematria can become quite a bit more complicated. The sacredness of the text has the effect of both emptying it of specific meanings and opening it to the possibility of unlimited meanings. Every word, phrase, and sentence is like a black hole whose enormous gravitational pull draws meanings to it. When you throw in the fact that there are no vowels in Hebrew, and that the simple tri-consonantal roots can cover an enormous area of meaning, the field is wide open for a kind of extravagantly spirited word play that might make James Joyce duck and cover.

Besides signifying quantity, numbers can also contain magical power. Odd, masculine numbers are considered to be strong; and even, feminine numbers are considered to be weak. Logically, the strongest number should be one; but just as there can be no myth in a strictly monotheistic world, so there is no magic in the number one by itself. You cannot do anything with it. That makes three the strongest number, because it allows for complex interactions. To thicken the plot, three becomes a substitute for one, and four becomes a substitute for two. In the ancient Greek performances, the step from choral singing to the birth of the drama took place when Thespis stepped out in front of the chorus. He understood what Heraclitus meant when he called strife the mother of all things. There is no story without opposition.

The seder symbols and much of the Haggadah are permeated with the dialectic of three and four. We swing back and forth between these numbers all evening, sitting upright, then leaning, as we rebalance our psychic scales. Every spring we need spiritual re-alignment. In this context there is no value judgment to the terms strong and weak, or for that matter, masculine and feminine. Both are needed for wholeness: the bone and the egg, the bitter and sweet, the unleavened bread and the wine.

Odd numbers are powerful and protective, with three, seven, and nine, in that order, being the most popular. Even numbers, pairs, are usually feared. But on Passover, a night of watching, of God watching out for us as well as of our watching out for God, we need not fear pairs. That is why we have four cups of wine, a practice normally avoided. Multiples of numbers are intensifications of their strength.

I Know One

The Haggadah is shot through with the symbolism of numbers. Since there are only ten numbers from which all the rest are generated, correspondences are not that difficult to make. Still, the consistency of the symbols and the coherence of the total range of numerical symbols is quite impressive. Throughout the seder and the Haggadah, numbers have been used for both magical and mnemonic purposes. In this chapter we will brush our prepared table, mute book, *berakhot,* and Haggadah text against the grain in search of numerical material. From one to thirteen, we will first list the answers given in the song "Who Knows One." We will then discuss some other numbers that are significant in the context of the seder.

1: One is the one God who is in heaven and on earth. The Hebrew word for "one" is echad. Our profession of faith is, "Hear, O Israel, the Lord our God, the Lord is One" (Deuteronomy 6:4).

2: Two are the two tablets of the covenant, Shenei Luchot ha-Brit, that Moses brought down from Mount Sinai. The first commandment reminds us of the Exodus: "I am the Lord your God who brought you out from the land of Egypt, from the house of bondage. You shall have no other gods before Me" (Exodus 20:2–3). In the Ladino adaptation of "Who Knows One," two are Moses and his big brother, Aaron. We dip twice at the seder: the *karpas* into saltwater and *maror* into *charoset.* We wash our hands twice during the seder: once before eating the greens, and again before eating the matzo that commences the meal. In the Diaspora we have two sedarim.

3: Three are the patriarchs, Abraham, Isaac, and Jacob. They are represented at the seder by the three ceremonial matzot, which are also associated with: the three surviving tribal groupings of Kohen, Levi, and Yisrael; the three unleavened cakes that Sarah made for the three angelic messengers who came to tell her of the impending birth of Isaac; the three measures of meal that a freed captive brought to the Temple as a thanksgiving offering. There are three pilgrimage festivals, Pesach, Shavuot, and Sukkot, and three parts to the Tanakh (the Bible), an acronym for *T*orah (Five Books of Moses), *N*evi'im (Prophets), and *Kh*etuvim (Writings). Then there are Rabban Gamaliel's three words that need to be said at the seder: pesach, matzo, and maror. The odd, strong, three unites with the three male patriarchs and the three male matzot (discussed in chapter 3).

4: Four are the matriarchs, Sarah, the wife of Abraham, Rebecca, the wife of Isaac, and Rachel and Leah, the wives of Jacob. The mothers of the Twelve Tribes are four: Rachel and her handmaid Bilhah, and Leah and her handmaid Zilpah. Since there are really, then, six matriarchs, we see the symbolic necessity of the number four in this context. It continues the symbolism of the weak, feminine, even, four connected to the four cups of wine in opposition to the three matzot and its corollary attributes. There are four children in the parable, four promises of redemption (Exodus 6:6–7), four explicated verses (Deuteronomy 26:5–8), and four questions. Likewise, there are four corners to the tallit and four species used at Sukkot. Four, like seven, represents all or the whole, as in the four corners of the earth or the four seasons of the year. Four questions or four children stand for all questions and all children.

5: Five are the books of the Torah: Bereshit (In the Beginning), Genesis; Shemot (Names), Exodus; Va-Yikra (And Called), Leviticus; Be-Midbar (In the Wilderness), Numbers; and Devarim (Words), Deuteronomy. The cup of Elijah is the fifth cup left unconsumed for the fifth form of redemption, bringing us into the land (Exodus 6:8), just as the fifth verse (Deuteronomy 26:9) that refers to our being brought to the land is left unread. The numerical value of the letter *he* is five, and this letter is associated with the word matzo, a symbol for redemption. Five, like eight, represents the resolution or completion of the whole. There are five rabbis at Bene-Berak. There are five benedictions in a Saturday night seder Kiddush, and they are remembered by the mnemonic *yaknehaz.*

6: Six are the *sidre* (orders or parts) of the Mishnah: (1) Zera'im (Seeds); (2) Mo'ed (Appointed Season); (3) Nashim (Women); (4) Nezikin (Damages); (5) Kodashim (Holy Things); and (6) Tohorot

(Cleanliness). There are six symbolic foods on the seder plate: *zero'a, betzah, maror, charoset, karpas, chazeret.*

7: Seven are the days of the week. There are seven weeks between Passover and Shavuot, the Festival of Weeks. Seven are the number of days of Passover ordained by the Torah. The world was created in six days, and on the seventh God rested. God asserts that what has been created is good on seven occasions in the Genesis story. From God resting on the seventh day, we derive the Sabbath, the day of rest. The three dimensions, up and down, right to left and back and forth, find their center and a state of rest, Shabbat, in seven. Ancient Babylonian astronomy knew of seven planets, wandering stars. The seventh was Saturn, a baleful, ominous, heavy, black, leaden, melancholic planet. His day was Saturday, the seventh day, Shapatu, when no one ventured out for fear of his malevolence. Jewish practice adopted and inverted Shapatu into Shabbat, a day of rest given to us by God as a blessing. In this, among many other examples, we can see that whatever is powerful can either be hallowed or demonized. Seven, the sum of three and four, resolves these contraries.

8: Eight are the number of days after birth before the covenant of circumcision is performed. Eight are the number of days of Passover in the Diaspora as ordained by the rabbis. Eight represents a completed cycle in both these examples, just as it does in the octave in music, or the ogdoad, the eighth heaven above the seven heavens.

9: Nine are the months until birth.

10: Ten are the utterances of the Ten Commandments. Ten are also the utterances of the creation. God speaks ten times to create the universe. There are ten *sefirot,* the emanations of God. (They are listed and explained in chapter 2.) Ten pieces of bread are hidden before the search for *chametz.* Ten people are needed for a minyan, the quorum necessary in order to take out the Torah, perform the marriage ceremony, or recite the Kaddish for the dead. God inflicted ten plagues on the Egyptians, and they are remembered by the ten-letter mnemonic *D'tzak Adash B'Achab.* There are ten steps from the one kid to the Holy One in "Chad Gadya." Ten rabbis are named in the Haggadah: Eliezer, Joshua, Eleazar ben Azariah, Akiba, Tarfon, Ben Zoma, Judah, Yose of Galilee, Rabban Gamaliel, and Hillel. There are ten forms of praise mentioned in the Lefichach.

11: Eleven are the stars in Joseph's dream. They symbolize himself and his ten brothers (before the birth of Benjamin).

12: Twelve are the tribes, the sons of Jacob. By implication, the twelve brothers correspond to the twelve constellations of the zodiac and the twelve months of the year. The brothers, in order of birth, were Reuben, Simeon, Levi, and Judah by Leah; Dan and Naphtali by Rachel's handmaiden, Bilhah; Gad and Asher by Leah's handmaiden, Zilpah; Issachar and Zebulun by Leah again; and Joseph and Benjamin by Rachel. That is the order as given in Genesis 29–30; but when Jacob blesses them in Genesis 49, it is in the order given below, starting with Reuben and ending with Benjamin. The following table shows the correspondences between the Jewish months, the zodiacal signs, and the sons of Jacob:

Nisan	Aries	Benjamin
Iyyar	Taurus	Reuben
Sivan	Gemini	Simeon
Tammuz	Cancer	Levi
Av	Leo	Judah
Elul	Virgo	Zebulun
Tishri	Libra	Issachar
Heshvan	Scorpio	Dan
Kislev	Sagittarius	Gad
Tevet	Capricorn	Asher
Shevat	Aquarius	Naphtali
Adar	Pisces	Joseph

For what it's worth, note that Judah, whose ensign is the Lion of Judah, is associated with the astrological sign of Leo the Lion; that Rosh Hashanah and Yom Kippur occur in Tishri, connected to Libra, the scales, when our souls are weighed in the balance and light and dark are balanced in the day; that Joseph's sign is Pisces, two fish, and his tribe is divided in two; that Passover occurs in Nisan, assigned to Aries, the male sheep or ram and the time of the sacrifice of the paschal lamb, the male baby sheep.

The fact that the oldest son, Reuben, is assigned to Taurus suggests an awareness of the precession of the equinoxes, the backward movement of the zodiac every 2,000 years. That is why classical astrology has spring begin in the sign of Aries, even though it has begun in Pisces for the last 2,000 years and is now sliding into Aquarius for the next 2,000. Before Aries, spring began in Taurus. Worship of the sacred cow in India, of the bull Apis in Egypt, and bull worship in Minoan Crete point to this earlier period, as do later remnants of this worship evidenced in the slaughter of the sacred bull in Mithraism and the various surviving Mediterranean bull cults, best exemplified in Spanish bullfighting.

Twelve is the product of three times four. Both three and four are at the root of the seven planets and the twelve Zodiacal constellations.

Twelve is the age of bat mitzvah, when a girl becomes a woman.

13: Thirteen are the *middot,* the divine qualities of mercy, which are to be construed from the words of Exodus 34:6–8:

> YHVH, YHVH, a God compassionate and gracious,
> slow to anger, abounding in kindness and truthfulness,
> extending kindness to the thousandth generation, forgiving iniquity, transgression, and sin; yet not remitting all punishment, but visits the iniquity of parents upon children and children's children, upon the third and fourth generations.

The numerical value of the word for one, echad, is thirteen. This connects the one God with the thirteen divine qualities. Joseph had two sons, Ephraim and Manasseh, and they were each counted as a tribe, so there were actually thirteen tribes. The thirteenth month is the second Adar added during leap years. Notice that Joseph is assigned to Adar, the month that can be doubled, and Joseph had two sons, each counted as a tribe. This ambiguity between twelve and thirteen tribes represents the difference between the solar and lunar years, although the Torah explains this discrepancy by dividing up the Land of Israel among the twelve tribes excluding Levi, who as the priests and their assistants in the Temple, had no land. A further thirteen can be found when we look at the actual number of children (as opposed to sons) that Jacob had. His daughter Dinah by his wife Leah gives Jacob a total of thirteen children, and again emphasizes the feminine nature of the Jewish lunar calendar as opposed to the twelve months of the solar calendar.

Thirteen is the age of bar mitzvah, when a boy becomes a man, and it is the number of principles of faith as drawn up by Moses Maimonides. Thirteen is not an unlucky number to Jews as it is to non-Jews. It probably became unlucky since Judas, the archetypal betraying Jew to Christians, was the thirteenth person at Jesus' last supper. In the Tarot deck, for instance, the thirteenth card of the trumps is the death card. None of this has any meaning in Jewish tradition, though the transformation of lucky thirteen into unlucky implies a rejection of the feminine Jewish lunar year in favor of the masculine Christian solar year.

15: Passover takes place on the fifteenth of Nisan. There are fifteen steps in the order of the seder, and there were fifteen semicircular steps leading from the forecourt to the inner court in the Temple. As the Levites ascended these steps, they sang the fifteen Shir ha-Ma'alot, the pilgrim songs, or songs of ascent, from the biblical book of Psalms. "Dayyenu" mentions fifteen favors or *ma'alot,* ascending steps, which conclude with the building of the Temple. The Yishtabach at the end of Nishmat mentions fifteen forms of praise owed to God. There are fifteen words in the priestly benediction that we say at the beginning of the seder to bless the children. There were fifteen generations, or steps, between Abraham, the father of the Jewish people, and Solomon, who built the Temple. The numerical value of Yah, one of God's names, is fifteen.

16: We remove sixteen drops of wine from our second cup in remembrance of the ten plagues.

18: The numerical value of the word for "life," *chai,* is eighteen. This is universally regarded as a number for good luck among Jews. Monetary gifts are given in multiples of eighteen. Candles are lit eighteen minutes before sundown. From the time water is added to flour in the making of matzo until it comes out of the oven, no more than eighteen minutes may elapse. The central prayer of the liturgy, the Amidah (standing), is usually referred to as the Shemoneh Esreh, meaning eighteen, even though there have been nineteen benedictions in it for at least two millennia.

22: These are the names of the twenty-two letters of the *alef bet* (Hebrew alphabet), with their numerical values: *alef* (1), *bet* (2), *gimmel* (3), *dalet* (4), *he* (5), *vav* (6), *zayin* (7), *chet* (8), *tet* (9), *yod* (10), *kaf* (20), *lamed* (30), *mem* (40), *nun* (50), *samekh* (60), *ayin* (70), *pe* (80), *tzadi* (90), *kof* (100), *resh* (200), *shin* (300), *tav* (400), final *kaf* (500), final *mem* (600), final *nun* (700), final *pe* (800), final *tzadi* (900). The final forms of the letters can also have the same value as the initial forms for the purposes of gematria.

Four of the closing songs of the seder are alphabetical acrostics in which the key words of the songs are arranged in alphabetical order. This is quite common in the *siddur* and earlier in the psalms. Besides being a mnemonic, helping us to remember the lines in order, it implies that God contains everything from *alef* to *tav,* just as Azusa, California, has everything from A to Z in the USA. Later, the New Testament book of Revelations was composed in twenty-two chapters for the same reason. It was from this model, not directly from the Hebrew alphabet, that the Tarot deck borrowed the number twenty-two, for the twenty-one Trump cards plus the Fool, as a symbol of completeness. There is no other connection between the Tarot and the Hebrew alphabet.

26: The numerical value of the letters of the Tetragrammaton, the original four-letter word, YHVH, is twenty-six. There are twenty-six verses of praise to God in the Great Hallel, Psalm 136, which concludes the chanting of Psalms after the seder meal. There were twenty-six generations between Adam and the revelation at Sinai. The Friday night Kiddush begins with the last sentence of the first chapter of Genesis and the opening verses of the second chapter, in order to recite in sequence the words:

> . . . *Yom Ha-shishi. Va-yechulu Ha-shamayim . . .*

> . . . the sixth day. And thus were completed the
> heavens . . .

The complete passage about God resting is important to the moment, the beginning of Shabbat, but these words are important for themselves because their initial letters spell the Tetragrammaton. This is a *notarikon,* the finding of new words in the initial or final letters of the words of a phrase.

33: The period between Passover and Shavuot, the counting of the omer, is considered ominous, a time of semi-mourning. This is based on the legend that many of Rabbi Akiba's students died of plague during this period. Some believe this plague was the Romans, who killed so many Jewish students and rebels at this time. In our own time, the Warsaw ghetto uprising took place during the omer period. Today we avoid marriages during these forty-nine days except on the thirty-third day, the minor holiday of Lag Ba-Omer. *Lamed* plus *gimmel* equals thirty-three, or *lag.* The plague supposedly let up on this day. Clearly, the double three is a strong magical number. Since the holiday falls on the eighteenth of Iyyar, eighteen meaning "life," that reinforces the positive aspects of the day.

36: There are thirty-six hidden saints, *lamed-vav,* on whose account the world is preserved. Double *chai* is thirty-six.

40: The Israelites wandered in the wilderness for forty years. Moses fled Egypt at age forty, returned at eighty, and died at 120. He ascended Mount Sinai for forty days and forty nights on two occasions. Forty represents an ominous period, probably based on the forty-day disappearance of the stars known as the Pleiades. It rained for forty days and forty nights to cause the Flood of Noah's time.

49: We count the omer for forty-nine days, just as the Israelites waited forty-nine days, from Passover to Shavuot, to receive the Torah at Sinai. There are forty-nine gates to understanding and repentance.

50: According to Rabbi Yose of Galilee, God inflicted fifty plagues on the Egyptians at the Red Sea, since the plagues in Egypt were as a finger, but at the Red Sea they felt the strong hand of God, hence fifty. The fiftieth gate of Binah (understanding) and *teshuvah* (return or repentance) is Shavuot itself, the revelation of the Torah.

60: The total of the ten plagues in Egypt and the fifty at the Red Sea is sixty.

70: When Jacob went down to Egypt, his family consisted of seventy people. The Sanhedrin consisted of seventy judges.

72: Exodus 14:19–21 is made up of three sentences, each containing seventy-two letters. When arranged correctly, these form the seventy-two-letter name of God. Quadruple *chai* equals seventy-two.

200: According to Rabbi Eliezer, since each plague in Egypt can be considered as four, they received forty in Egypt and 200 at the Red Sea.

240: The total of the forty plagues in Egypt and the 200 at the Red Sea is 240.

250: According to Rabbi Akiba, since each plague in Egypt can be considered as five, they received fifty in Egypt and 250 at the Red Sea.

300: The total of the fifty plagues in Egypt and the 250 at the Red Sea is 300.

600,000: The number of Israelite men of military age who left Egypt and received the revelation at Sinai. This figure, then, does not include the additional numbers of women and children who also left Egypt. *Karpas,* the green vegetable, can be read backward as the letter *samekh* and the word *parakh,* meaning "crushing oppression," as in "And the Egyptians made the Children of Israel serve them with crushing oppression" (Exodus 1:13). The letter *samekh* has a value of sixty. So the karpas comes to symbolize the sixty myriads, or 600,000, Israelites in harsh bondage at the time of the Exodus. The constant implication of the 600,000 is that all the people of Israel were freed from bondage and all received the revelation at Sinai. This is not the story of Moses, but of a people made up of 600,000 individuals. We are included in the 600,000 in a way that we are not included if the story is about one great hero.

Chapter Seven

Shir Ha-Ma'alot:
A Pilgrim Song

The Songs of the Seder

So far, we have brought everything to our prepared table, performed the rituals of the mute book, added the simple words of *Barukh Attah,* Blessed are You, to those rituals, and answered the questions *Mah Nishtannah ha-Layla Hazeh?* Why is this night different? and *Echad Mi Yode'a?* Who knows one? For some, *Dayyenu,* this might be a sufficient seder, but for many of us, a key element is still missing: the songs. The meaning of the words of the Haggadah remains in our minds because the tunes that carry them have already entered our hearts:

> *Mournfully merry, seriously playful, and fabulously mysterious is the character of this nocturnal festival, and the usual traditional singsong chant in which the Haggadah is read by the father, and now and again echoed in chorus by the hearers, at one time thrills the inmost soul as with a shudder, then calms it as if it were a mother's lullaby, and anon startles it so suddenly into waking that even those who have long fallen away from the faith of their fathers and run after foreign joys and honors are moved to their very hearts when by chance the old well-known tones ring in their ears.*

—Heinrich Heine, *The Rabbi of Bacharach*

Heine knew whereof he spoke. He had forsaken the faith of his fathers by allowing himself to be baptized to gain his "entrance ticket to European civilization," his acceptance as a German, not Jewish, writer, and had then pursued foreign joys and honors by leaving Germany for France to escape the repressive Prussian government. In his heart he remained Jewish, and once admitted, "I have not returned to Judaism because I never left it."

There is an interesting conflict in this passage between the mother's lullaby and the faith of our fathers. Similarly, in the passage called Lefichach (text m), a toast over wine, we are enjoined to sing a new song, *shirah chadashah*. Shirah is the feminine form of song. Three paragraphs later, when we say the benediction over the second cup of wine, we refer to another new song we will sing in Messianic times, but this time the new song is masculine, *shir chadash*. In our pre-Messianic world, the feminine is the source of song. We have already seen that wine is feminine. Now wine and song together are linked to the feminine:

> . . . *wreathéd friezes intertwine*
> *the viol, the violet, and the vine.*
> —Edgar Allan Poe

Only in the post-Messianic world can the fully realized masculine originate song. As we saw in chapter 3, it takes both the female and male working in conjunction to complete the transmutative operations of the seder ceremony.

Without a Song

Lacking song, the Haggadah, our telling, would indeed be as dry, cold, and fixed as the bones of Ezekiel's vision, or our *shemurah* matzo. As the eating of unleavened bread demands the drinking of wine, so the words of the Haggadah demand melody. A seder without song does not lean to the left. The resulting upright attitude generates the feeling that we are to endure an interminable recitation of unintelligible Hebrew. With song, we understand and enjoy the text without understanding each word. Although we may not follow every nuance of the rabbis' complex midrashic reasoning, we cannot forget the lyrical beauty of the Kiddush, the simplicity of "Mah Nishtannah," the full-tilt, jubilant, tongue-twisting boogie of "Dayyenu," or the bittersweet hopefulness of "Eliahu ha-Novi."

Now that we have our texts, we can learn to sing some of them and learn some new ones that, oddly enough, are not in the Haggadah. To help you to add melodies to the texts, the end of this chapter lists sources of sheet music and tapes that teach the Passover music of Ashkenazic, Sephardic, Chasidic, and Israeli traditions, as well as more recently composed songs and melodies.

> . . . *songs which float between divine mystery and the*
> *jesting mood begot by wine* . . .
>
> —Franz Rosenzweig

There is no way that a book can actually teach you to sing songs (unless you can read sheet music, and even that is a mere approximation). The same is true of transliterations. Unless you listen to the words of the Haggadah on recordings, you will never learn to speak them correctly. The best way to learn the songs is to get a good teaching recording (tapes are easiest) that presents the songs simply and with their traditional melodies. The tape that most fulfills these requirements is from the Rabbinical Assembly. It features a minimal amount of spoken instruction and a maximum amount of songs from Shira Belfer. Her voice is clear, sweet, slightly folky, and she accompanies herself on the guitar.

Another option is to learn the melodies, but to sing them in English. The listing of recordings will highlight those that translate the songs into English. Scattered among the recordings, you will find English versions of seven seder tunes.

Once you have chosen whatever recording of Passover songs takes your fancy, you will want to have the text in front of you while you learn it. On the trickier songs, it can help to plot out the actual repetitions of words and returns of phrases in transliteration until you actually master the melodies. Of course, if you read music, all of this is laid out for you on paper already. You do not have to learn every song the first time. What you cannot sing this year, you will learn for another seder. This year "Dayyenu," next year "Ve-Nomar Le-Fanav"; this year it will be enough, next year let us sing a new song.

Before the Parade Passes By

Besides the main text of the Haggadah, we should also mention the *berakhot.* Most recordings ignore the bulk of the benedictions, seeing them as too brief and familiar. The exceptions are the blessing over wine, the Kiddush and the She-Hechiyanu, usually treated as a piece, and the first paragraph of Grace after Meals. Once you have learned the melody said over the wine—*borey peri ha-gefen*—you can use it to chant the rest of the simple blessings. Chapter 4 contains the transliterations of these benedictions in the correct sequence.

The Kiddush melody is one of the most beautiful in the Jewish liturgy, at once exalted and lyrical. It is derived from the ancient melody of the Akdamut prayer said at Shavuot. Its purpose is to sanctify the time and place, over wine, clearing a hallowed space for all that follows. The "She-Hechiyanu," which completes the Kiddush, combines a dreamy movement from the everyday into the festival mode with an exultant sense of arrival.

In chapter 4 we presented the English translation of the *kavvanot* for the first cup of wine. Many families have the custom of chanting the first words of this before the Kiddush. Here, in transliteration, are the Hebrew words that are sung:

> *Hineni mookawn oomzuman le-kayem mitzvot kos rishon . . .*

> Herewith I am prepared and arrayed to fulfill the
> command of the first cup . . .

Even before this statement of intention, we chant the mnemonic table of contents to our seder procedure, Kaddesh Urchatz. These fifteen steps (which can be found in chapter 3) outline what will follow during the evening. The old melody is the simplest of chants, breaking the sixteen words into four equal, almost identical, lines. There is a slight chordal variation in the third line that becomes a bridge to the resolution in the concluding line. Among the Sephardim it is traditional to sing the chant before each step, up to the step they are about to do.

One song that has been consistently added to the seder recital, at least since the Fifties, is the old Negro Spiritual "Go Down, Moses," often called "Let My People Go" because of the repetition of this key phrase from Exodus 5:1. The African-American identification with the plight of our ancestors in Egypt is paralleled in the Jewish identification with the plight of African-Americans in the New World. This song can be added anywhere, but just before text i will fit with the history well. The rest of the melodies will be treated according to their position in the text as outlined, alphabetically, in chapter 5.

Text a: "Ha Lachma Anya," a passage with an ancient melody. We announce that this is the bread of affliction. In this tune we hear the paradoxical blending of joy and yearning, celebration and sadness, that epitomizes the music of the seder:

> *There's not a string attuned to mirth but has its chord in*
> *melancholy.*
> —Thomas Hood

Text b: "Mah Nishtannah," another ancient text and melody. In this one we can hear the traditional singsong of the scholar half-chanting, half-reading, the words of the Talmud. Just as the medieval monks sat in their carrels, caroling the texts they copied and studied, so the ancient rabbis chanted as they learned the Mishnah and Gemarah, turning study into prayer. This is usually sung by the youngest child at the seder. A variant is to learn the Yiddish words of the *fier kashes* and to sing them to the old melody interweaving the Hebrew with the *mama-loshen* (mother tongue, Yiddish).

Besides the familiar ancient melody, a newer, more lively tune has become popular. It bears the imprint of the joyous music of the Israeli *chalutzim,* the Zionist pioneers who settled the Holy Land before the creation of the state of Israel. In these new songs, shirah chadashah, the minor, modal, melancholic qualities of Hebrew song are replaced with the spirited melodies of peasants returning to the land.

Text c: At this point we recite or chant the text, "Once we were slaves . . . ," followed by a lively modern song by S. Postolsky that couples the first two words of this text, *Avadim Hayinu,* with the last two words of text a, *Bnai Chorin,* "children of freedom." To feel some of the affect of this song, let us look at a translation of these words in the same format as the Hebrew. The result is akin to avant-garde poetry, something between John Giorno and Jackson MacLow.

> *Avadim Hayinu Hayinu*
> *Atah Bnai Chorin Bnai Chorin*
> *Avadim Hayinu Atah Atah Bnai Chorin*
> *Avadim Hayinu Atah Atah Bnai Chorin Bnai Chorin*
>
> Slaves we were we were
> Now children of freedom children of freedom
> Slaves we were now now children of freedom
> Slaves we were now now children of freedom children
>   of freedom

Text d: The final quadruplicate benediction of this section, *Baruch ha-Makom,* is sung to a sprightly march, somewhat like the themes from *Hogan's Heroes* and *Raiders of the Lost Ark,* a delighting in our God and the gift of Torah. This was composed by R. Koeningberg in the Seventies and has already become well known.

Text g: The Haggadah is simply recited for awhile until we reach the happy, reassuring toast "Ve-hi Shayamdah," "And it is this promise."

Text h: The Shenemar section from the midrash on Deuteronomy 26:7, "And we cried to the Lord God of our ancestors," is rarely done but emotionally moving. It allows the singer tremendous freedom of elaboration around the repeated refrain, "Shenemar," "As It Is Written."

Text i: The enumeration of the ten plagues in sets of three, ten, and three is done in a somber, keening chant. The Sephardim have a more lighthearted tune for their expanded rendering of this.

Text j: The Chasidim sing the rabbis' discussion of the ten plagues to a melody adapted from the cantillation of the Torah on the High Holidays, but I know of no recording of it.

Text k: One of the most over-the-top songs of the seder, "Dayyenu," represents a specific peak of enjoyment following the horrific enumeration of all the plagues. The familiar melody is among the best-known of the seder, but you will have to decide on whether to say *"Illu Illu Hotzianu"* or *"Illu Hotzi Hotzianu."* The concluding paragraph, "Al Achat Kama Ve-Kama," has a traditional spirited melody, but is rarely heard on record.

Text l: The last paragraph in this section, "Be-chol Dor Va-Dor," following the pointing at the matzo and *maror,* has a plaintive melody.

Text m: The last five words of this paragraph make a simple praise to God. The Chasidic melody is at once glorifying, yet subdued:

> *Ve-nomar le-fanav shirah chadashah. Hallelujah.*
>
> Let's sing before him a new song. Praise the Lord.

Text n: With the Hallelujah we begin the Egyptian Hallel that starts before the meal and finishes after it. This first part consists of Psalms 113 and 114. The first combines awe and mournfulness in its slow, stately repetition of the key word Hallelujah.

Psalm 114, "Betzait Yisrael," is a joyous paean to our deliverer at the Red Sea. The second part, "Mah Lechah Ha-Yam," has its own more pensive melody.

Text p: The Grace after Meals, Barekh, is part of the benedictions, but it is customary to sing "Shir Ha-Ma'alot," Psalm 126, before commencing the Grace. This upbeat hymn about returning to Zion leads naturally into the equally lighthearted Grace. The first paragraph is the best-known section, but all of it can be sung. The transliteration of the opening portion can be found in chapter 4.

Text q: Opening the door while saying "Pour out Your wrath" was done long before the time of the Kos Eliyahu and the singing of "Eliyahu Hanovi." Since the Holocaust, it has become common practice to sing "Ani Ma'amin" at this point as well. Neither song is actually in the Haggadah. Both songs, from different times and points of view, express a people's yearning for redemption. "Eliyahu Hanovi" has all the pathos and longing of those who have been homeless for millennia. It dates from the Middle Ages and is sung at the end of every Shabbat as one of the traditional *zemirot.* "Ani Ma'amin" is heartbreaking, even more so when we realize that this statement of belief, the twelfth of Maimonides' thirteen principles of faith, was sung by the martyrs of the Holocaust as they marched to their deaths.

> *Eliyahu ha-novi Eliyahu ha-Tishbi*
> *Eliyahu Eliyahu Eliyahu ha-Giladi*
> *Bimheyrah be-yomenu yavo Elenu*
> *Im moshiach ben Dovid Im moshiach ben Dovid*
>
> Elijah the prophet Elijah the Tishbite
> Elijah the Gileadite

Come to us quickly in our days
Bringing the Messiah son of David

The prophet Elijah hailed from Tishbi, a village in Gilead. A friend's brother would always ask at their sedarim, "Where was Elijah from?" and no one could ever remember Tishbi, even though they had just sung the song.

> *Ani ma'amin be-emunah shlayma be-viat ha-moshiach ve-af ahl pi sheyitmahmayach im kol zeh achakeh lo be-chol yom sheyavo.*

> I believe with a perfect faith in the coming of the Messiah and although he may tarry I daily await his coming.
>
> —Moses Maimonides

Maimonides's thirteen principles were highly controversial in their day, but eventually, possibly because of the popularity of the number thirteen, they became generally accepted. There is a pun in the word for belief and the patronymic of the author: *ma'amin,* from the word *emunah* (faith), and Maimon, the father of Maimonides.

Text r: The same melody can be used for the singing of Hallel at the seder as is used in the synagogue. That includes the two Psalms sung before the meal. There are also many alternative melodies as well. The most frequently sung parts of the post-prandial Hallel are "Yevarek Et Bet Yisrael," Psalm 115: 12–18; "Ha'amanti," Psalm 116:10–11; "Mah Ahshiv la-Adonai," Psalm 116:12–19; "Hallelu," Psalm 117, whose two verses are the short-est chapter in the Bible; "Hodu L'adonai," Psalm 118:1–4; "Min Ha-Metzar," Psalm 118:5; "Azi ve-Zimra," Psalm 118:14; "Kol Rinah," Psalm 118:15; "Pitchu Li Sha'arei Tzedek," Psalm 118:19; "Odekha," Psalm 118:21–24; "Anah Adonai," Psalm 118:25–26; "Eli Attah," Psalm 118:28–29; and "Hodu L'adonai," Psalm 136, the Great Hallel. All of these praises of God continue the shift in mood from the preprandial joy in our past liberation to the awe and solemnity of the after-dinner portion of the seder.

Text s: "Nishmat" can be sung with the same tune sung in the synagogue.

Text t: "Chasal Siddur Pesach" is sung with the feeling of a job well-done. "La-Shanah Ha-Ba'ah Bi-Yerushalayim" caps this formal conclusion to the seder with this single line being repeated joyously over and over. It can also be done wistfully without any repetition. At the second seder, you can sing the benediction for the counting of the omer.

Text u: "Karev Yom," or "Vayehi Bachatzi Ha-Layla," has a haunting refrain that pleads for an end to this long Exile. Not as well known as the last four songs of the post-seder section, its drama and pathos deserve to be rediscovered.

Text v: There must be a melody for "Uve-chain va-Amartem Zehvach Pesach," but I have never found a recording of it. This can best be explained by its relegation to the second seder only.

Text w: "Ki Lo Naeh" hints at the playfulness that will close the seder. There are a few different melodies for it, but the one by Moishe Oysher is the best, full of delight in the short, repeated syllables of the refrain.

Text x: The simple "Addir Hu" returns to the stately awe of the Hallel. Indeed, the traditional melody for this song predates it and often turns up earlier in the seder in the priestly blessing, the Kiddush and Hallel.

Text y: By the time we reach "Echad Mi Yode'a," we are ready for the pure fun of this counting song. The choruses go faster and faster as we count higher and higher, each time ending our zestful enumeration with the glorious love of God. Although these last six zemirot were created by the Ashkenazim, they have been enthusiastically adopted by the Sephardim. Indeed, "Echad Mi Yode'a" and "Chad Gadya" have been translated into beautiful Ladino versions that you might want to learn. They will give your seder a unique flavor. "Echad My Yode'a" even traveled to India, where the Jews there sing it all year long.

Text z: At last comes "Chad Gadya," a tongue-twister of repeated phrases that become more difficult as we move up the chain of being from the one kid to the Holy One. In addition to the most familiar tune, there are many alternative melodies, but all involve singing at breakneck speed.

Following this full evening of song, you can sing the Song of Songs. Use the same melody as is used in the synagogue, or just sing some of the popular excerpts.

A Catalogue of Recordings and Sheet Music

Even though we think we know the correct tunes for the most familiar Passover songs, there are actually many alternatives from which to choose our seder melodies. There are no wrong ones. You might start by trying to recall familiar tunes from your family past, or pick those easy enough for everyone to sing. They can be simple or complex, joyous or mournful, pensive or silly, melancholy or exuberant, defiant or resigned. Indeed, it would be hard to sing all of these texts without expressing the full range of human emotions.

The possibilities come from every corner of the globe. Perhaps you will want to compose your own melodies for some of the Passover texts. Your seder singing may combine elements of family nostalgia, Chasidic fervor, Sephardic romance and lightheartedness, Israeli exhilaration, or cantorial traditionalism. By listening and choosing from the broad range of Jewish music, you can create the seder songfest that is just right for your gathering. Even the list of recordings that follows can in no way be considered definitive. Every family and every community have their own variations on even the most familiar tunes. No one can know all the melodies that have been created to praise God at the seder, so be sure to bring along your ancestral melodies to your performance of the ancient texts.

The following recordings are devoted to the music of Passover, primarily the seder tunes, but often songs of spring or the synagogue liturgy of the season as well. They can be divided into two groups: those that are artistic and entertaining, to be enjoyed for their intrinsic beauty, and those that are educational and instructive. Sadly, most of the available recordings fall short of the level of artistry at which they aim. I should admit a prejudice against most choirs, especially those of children; glitzy, overproduced, pop arrangements, especially with drums and horn sections; synthesized sound; narration that cannot hope to be interesting after a few listenings; operatic grandstanding; and the transformation of the simply holy into some kind of kitsch, pompous "Art."

That leaves us little to enjoy. The greatest Passover recording is the double LP of Sidor Belarsky. The recent reissue of this material on tape unfortunately left out some of the best tracks from the original album, notably a heartbreaking, yet defiant version of "Ani Ma'amin." Also in the category of great is the work of Moshe Koussevitzky. Most of the other recordings pale in comparison. Still, most of us cannot hope to sing like Koussevitzky and Belarsky. Their free ornamentations are beyond us. Simpler versions will be more helpful in actually mastering the seder melodies. The following list is in rough chronological order, though it was necessary to approximate in many cases.

Recordings

Leil Shimurim, Prayers for Passover and the Omer Counting Days, Jacob Koussevitzky (1903–1959) and Moshe Koussevitzky (1899–1966), Zavel Kwartin (1874–1953), Israel Bakon, Misha Alexandrovich, David Moshe Steinberg, Leib Glanz (1898–1964), Benjamin Ungar (1907–?), Israel Music 1072. This is a historic collection of rare cantorial masterpieces with overall good sound quality. The only seder songs included here are a beautiful reading of "Betzait Yisrael" by Glanz; an elaborate omer blessing and the "Hineni Mookawn," the mystical intention, that precedes it, by Alexandrovich; the omer blessing by Ungar, with unfortunately poor fidelity; and a lovely traditional singing of "Nirtzah" by Moshe Koussevitzky, taken from his *Passover Seder* recording. We cannot sing like these giants, but we can hear the angelic choirs when we listen to them.

The Moishe Oysher Seder, Moishe Oysher, Abraham Nadel Chorus, narration by Barry Gray, Banner Records BASC 1021, 1950s(?). The narration is intrusive and annoying, but there are excellent and unique performances of

"Ha Lachma Anya," "Dayyenu," "Yevarek," the "Great Hallel," "Ki Lo Naeh," and a magnificent, virtually scat-sung, version of "Chad Gadya." The ten plagues are chanted, as is the "Korekh" paragraph. One of the most infrequently sung parts of the Haggadah, "Shenemar," is done here in an intricate, arabesque improvisation. The opening section of "Grace" is talked over, while parts of the later, less-well-known sections are given full elaboration. The four questions are sung in English. Oysher was a great cantor, who sang with authority in a personal, ornamental style. He retained many of the Oriental elements favored in Eastern Europe, but he had a tendency to grandstand and a penchant for indulging in an annoying bleating on a couple of tunes. Still, at his best, he is among the greatest Jewish singers.

Seder Nights, Sidor Belarsky, choir conducted by Vladimir Heifetz, Musique Internationale CM535B, 1962. For pure depth of emotion, this is my favorite recording of the music of Passover. The only disappointment here is that half of the original double-length album was left out of this tape, notably a moving version of "Ani Ma'amin" and the four questions in Yiddish. Most of the other omissions, fortunately, are of non-seder songs. What has been reissued, though, is breathtakingly moving, a mixture of traditional and unique melodies. Among the best tracks are "Ha Lachma," "Be-Chol Dor Va-Dor," sung heartbreakingly in free tempo, heightening the melancholic effect, and "Karev Yom," but this is like picking rubies out of a bag of diamonds. Belarsky was a successful opera singer in his own time, but he deserves to be remembered as one of the great performers of Jewish music.

Malavsky Family Passover Seder Service, Chazzan Samuel Malavsky and His Daughters, Banner Records BASC 1013, 1950s(?). At times, Malavsky sings movingly, with a pathos American cantors have yet to achieve. One of his daughters gives a powerful performance on the rarely heard last three verses of Psalm 113. The other pieces worth mentioning are a Yiddish version of the four questions, the opening to the midrash beginning with our enemy Laban, a bit of Psalm 118, and an elaborate version of the traditional counting of the omer that begins "Ribono Shel Olam." These little pearls are scattered in a sea of kitsch.

Seder Service, Jan Peerce, Israel Music EASTK 2019, 1960s(?). The only pieces worth mentioning are the singing of the actual "Avadim Hayinu" paragraph and one of the later paragraphs from Grace.

Passover Seder, Moshe Koussevitzky, Ben Friedman and his choir, Berel Aneis, Israel Music 1036, 1963(?), includes song sheet. Moshe Koussevitzky was arguably the greatest cantor of his generation. On this recording he gives fresh, powerful performances of most of the familiar seder songs. This double-length album was made just a few years before his death, yet his strength seems unlimited, never strained. There are no highlights here, every track is remarkable. Of special note are the Yiddish versions of the four questions and "Chad Gadya" by Aneis, the "Rachem No" from the Passover liturgy, the "Yalle Ve-Yovoi" from the third sequence of benedictions from the Grace, a moving "Ribono Shel Olam" from the omer counting, the traditional chanting of the "Avadim Hayinu" passage, a kind of Jewish yodeling on the "She-Hecheyanu," and the exquisite "Ki Lo Naeh." The choir never gets in the way but truly provides support for the free movement of Koussevitzky's improvisations. In his heartbreaking broken notes and extended ululations, we can hear the Ancient Near East, the Chasidic *niggun* (wordless melody), and the free ornament of the klezmer clarinet. This is one of the great landmarks in the recording of Jewish music.

Passover Seder Festival, Richard Tucker, choir conducted by Sholom Secunda, narrated by Ben Irving, CBS 72293, 1960s(?). Tucker never seems to sink his teeth into this material, except for the solo feature "Ribono Shel Olam" from the omer counting. There are also versions of the prayers for dew and the "Pitchu" from Hallel.

Music for The Passover Seder: Pathways through the Haggadah, Cantor Nathan Lamm, Alisa and Nina Golden, KTAV, 1970s(?), comes with song sheet with some lyrics. This tape is a companion resource for the KTAV *Pathways* Haggadah. It has the usual songs, including benedictions for candles, wine, *karpas,* hand washing, *motzi,* matzo, and *maror.* "Echad Mi Yode'a" and "Chad Gadya" are sung in English. There is an abbreviated "Kiddush," "Go Down, Moses," and the rarely performed *zimmun* (invitation) to the Grace. The song sheet and tape are keyed to the specific pages (off by two pages) in the Haggadah, where transliteration can often be found. Anyone who uses this Haggadah will want this tape.

Sounds of the Seder, Samuel Rosenbaum and the Media Judaica Chorus and Ensemble directed by Samuel Adler, Prayer Book Press, 1970s(?). This tape is a companion to the Prayer Book Press's Silverman Haggadah. The familiar tunes are done with no surprises except for an alternative performance of

"Betzait Yisrael." The real interest of this tape is in the four parts of Grace after Meals that are done here beyond the first paragraph: "Ve-Al Ha-Kol," "U-Venai Yerushalayim," "Ha-El Avinu," and "Migdol Yeshuot."

Passover Songs, Nira Rabinovitz, Shlomo Nitzan, Hed Arzi BAN 14116, 1973. The best tune here is the least familiar, "Al Achat Kama Ve-Kama," which follows "Dayyenu" in the Haggadah. They give this a spirited run through.

The Songs of the Haggadah, Cantor Binyamin Glickman and the Boys' Choir of Hillel Hebrew Academy of Los Angeles, Tara 59012, 1974(?). The only interesting track here is the beautiful "Kiddush," sung solo by Cantor Glickman. Otherwise, what is good is the wealth of songs and melodies, many in alternative versions, and the fact that the recording is keyed by page and line number to KTAV's *Goldberg Haggadah.* Besides all the familiar seder songs, there are versions of "Lefichach," "Mah Lechah Ha-Yam," from Psalm 114, and "Baruchim Atem," from Psalm 115.

Seder Melodies, Velvel Pasternak and the children of Congregation Sons of Israel, Woodmere, New York, Board of Jewish Education of New York, 1976, available with song booklet. When Velvel Pasternak sings, there is no distancing of the singer from the audience. He affects no pompous or formal style. Instead, we hear his real voice singing a variety of Passover melodies, often with a choir of children, but just as often alone. Of special interest here is the blessing for lighting the candles, "Hineni Mookawn," "Baruch Ha-Makom," "Ve-hi Shayamdah" done with the Chasidic melody of Saul Jedidiah Eleazar of Tel Aviv, the Modzhitz "Rebbe," and an unusual, happy melody for "Karev Yom." "Chad Gadya" is done in Hebrew and English. This is that rare accomplishment, Jewish music sung naturally and without affectation.

The Brothers Zim Present Sol Zim, Joy of the Passover Seder, Sol Zim, Zimray 110, 1979. The one song worth noticing here is the rarely done "Shenemar," a poignant tour de force.

Pesach Songs for Children and All the Family, Yehoram Gaon, Shula Chen, the Parvarim and others, CBS 40-53686, 1970s(?). The strength of this tape is in these seder song performances: "Avadim Hayinu," "Ve-hi Shayamdah," "Dayyenu," "Betzait Yisrael," "Karev Yom," "Echad Mi Yode'a," and "Chad Gadya." The arrangements are a combination of klezmer, Israeli, and pop, but they work because of the tremendous spirit that informs the performances. The words, no, the very letters, are enunciated with great feeling and meaning. Shula Chen's version of "Dayyenu" is just about my favorite.

Passover Songs in the Oriental Tradition, Reuven Erez, Aviva Nir, Alexandra, Aliza Azikri, Shimon Hatuka, Oshik Levi, Uzi Meiri, Uri Shevach, Dudu Zar, CBS 54121-4, 1979. The only reason to get this inferior recording is for the Sephardic melodies. There are versions, sometimes more than one, of "Kadesh Urchatz," "Ha Lachma," "Odekha," "Chad Gadya," "Echad Mi Yode'a" in Ladino, the four questions, "Ki Lo naeh," "Min Ha Metzar," "Pitchu Li," "Anah Adonai," and a few songs not from the Haggadah.

Passover, Yehoram Gaon, Tal Dunski, Cilla Dagan, Cantor A. Nachmias, Shula Chen, CBS 67243-4, 1970s(?). Six of these songs are the same tracks as on *Pesach Songs.* The two other tunes worth mentioning are Gaon's "Ki Hine Ha-Stav Avar," from the Song of Songs, and a beautifully traditional "Kiddush" by Nachmias. There is nothing pretty or professional about this performance, but it reeks of authenticity.

Songs for Passover in the Sephardic Tradition, Yehoram Gaon, House of Menorah CBS 80668, 1970s(?). This is a beautiful album of Ladino songs and seder songs in Sephardic melodies. Gaon performs "Kaddesh Urchatz," an expanded and lighthearted "Ten Plagues," "Dayyenu," "Addir Hu," "Betzait Yisrael," "Odekha" from Hallel, and "Ki Lo Naeh" in Hebrew, but with lilting melodies from the Sephardim. Three songs are done in Ladino including catchy versions of "Echad Mi Yode'a" and "Chad Gadya." There is also a Hebrew-Ladino version of the first few lines of the Song of Songs and the Hebrew of the lines beginning "tanned by the sun."

Songs for the Seder Meal, Cantor David Politzer, Liturgy Training Publications, 1980. This tape is a companion to the ecumenical Haggadah *The Passover Celebration.* Traditional melodies are used and key Hebrew phrases and terms are explained, with "Dayyenu," "Adir Hu," and "Chad Gadya" done in English. There is also a performance of "Go Down, Moses."

Passover Songs and Commentary for "The Feast of Freedom," Shira Belfer, narration by Rabbi Max Routtenberg, Rabbinical Assembly, 1982. This will be the standard against which all other teaching tapes will be judged. Belfer has a sweet, pure voice and sings the songs in a simple, straightforward manner. She performs "Kaddesh Urchatz," "Kiddush," "Ha

Lachma," the four questions in both versions, "Avadim Hayinu," "Ve-hi Shayamdah," "Ten Plagues," "Dayyenu," "Hallelujah," "Betzait Yisrael," "Shir Ha-Ma'alot," the first paragraph of Grace, plus "U-Venai Yerusha-layim" and "Ha-Rachaman," "Ani Ma'amin," "Eliyahu," selections from Hallel ("Yevarek," "Hodu," "Min Ha-Metzar," "Odekha," and "Anah Adonai"), "Chasal Siddur Pesach," "Ki Lo Naeh," "Addir Hu," "Echad Mi Yode'a," and "Chad Gadya." I will not mention any of these songs in the other listings unless the rendition is particularly unusual or beautiful. If you get this and one of the tapes with the simple benedictions, you can learn to sing most of the text of the Haggadah.

A Singing Seder, Cindy Paley with Ann Brown and children's chorus, Cindy Paley, 1980s(?), comes with songbook. The highlights of this tape are versions of "Hineni Mookawn," "Go Down, Moses," an English ren-dering of "Chad Gadya," the rarely sung "Be-Chol Dor Va-Dor," and even rarer, "Ki Hine Ha-Stav Avar" ("For lo, the winter is past") from the Song of Songs. If you want to add a part of Shir ha-Shirim to the end of your seder, you could not pick a more beautiful passage. One interesting track is the "Kiddush," where an uncredited, perhaps Israeli, man sings in his nat-ural voice. In spite of an occasional wavering in pitch, this has some meat to it. The tape as a whole contains most of the familiar tunes and is appro-priate for children.

Songs for Pesach, Linda Hirschhorn, Oyster Records, comes with translit-erated song sheet, 1980s(?). I believe Linda is letting this go out of print, which is a shame because there is nothing else like it. She goes through many of the seder songs word by word, first pronouncing them and then singing ten familiar seder songs, including the rarely sung "Mah Lechaw Ha-Yom," from Psalm 114. She also includes more blessings than usual: wine, "She-Hecheyanu," karpas, hand washing, motzi, matzo and maror, all in a strong, sweet, clear voice.

Paul Zim Invites You to Come to My Seder, Paul Zim and the Hillcrest Jew-ish Center Youth Chorale, Simcha 41386, 1986. Whatever they are teach-ing in the academy that makes *chazzanim* want to sing in a pompous, formal, bombastic way will not be found here or on his other Passover recordings. What you will find is a charming, informative shmoos from Zim between songs and a fairly complete seder. Blessings for wine, karpas, hand washing, matzo, motzi, and maror are here, as are most of the famil-iar seder songs. Less familiar tunes include the "Baruch Ha-Makom,"

"Oseh Shalom" from the Grace, the Mandel melody for the four questions, the Rockoff melodies to the first paragraph of Grace and "Ki Lo Naeh," a Chasidic march for Psalm 117 and 118:1–4, and Shlomo Carlebach's "Adir Hu." Zim also sings Moishe Oysher's beautiful Sephardic-influenced "Ha Lachma," and there is a lagniappe of Oysher's "Ki Lo Naeh" and "Chad Gadya."

Haggadah Songs, Chaim Parchi, C.P. Music, 1987. Parchi performs fifteen songs in multiple versions. Variants represent the communities of Salonika, Babylonia, Jerusalem, Sarajevo, Bucharest, Casablanca, Pilipopoli (Plovdiv, Bulgaria), the traditional Ashkenazic melodies, and eleven tunes by Parchi himself. Most of the songs are familiar, but there are rare performances of "Be-Chol Dor Va-Dor" and "Karev Yom."

Songs for a Family Seder, Cantor Robert Freedman and students of the Princeton Jewish Center Religious School, narrated by Shoshana Silberman, Kar-Ben Copies, 1987. Kar-Ben Copies' *A Family Haggadah* by Shoshana Silberman has achieved incredible popularity since its publication, because it takes into account the natural responses of children without ignoring the needs of adults. This accompanying tape is intended to help every family using that Haggadah to add music to their seder. Besides the most familiar seder songs, the ample tape includes the blessings for karpas, motzi, matzo, maror, and omer. There are a number of English children's songs from Kar-Ben's popular *My Very Own Haggadah,* as well as "Go Down, Moses" and a Yiddish-English rendition of Holocaust victim Hirsh Glick's "Partisan Song," the anthem of the Vilna partisans. The less frequently performed seder songs included here are "Baruch ha-Makom," "Be-Chol Dor Va-Dor," "Ve-Nomar Le-Fanav," "Mah Lechah Ha-Yom," one of the closing sentences from the Grace, "Eli Attah," from Psalm 118, and "Dodi Li," from the Song of Songs 2:16.

Let's Sing Pesach Songs, Adi and Esthy Sulkin, Acum 16, 1987, comes with booklet with transliterated songs. Adi Sulkin is an Israeli educator with a beautiful, spirited voice. The songs on the first side of this tape are about spring and Passover, but are not seder songs. Some of them are beautiful. In a world where children and adults can rarely share culture, Sulkin has created music that both young and old can enjoy. The booklet has suggested activities to go with the songs. The second side is all from the Haggadah, and most of the melodies are traditional or at least familiar. "Ha Lachma" and "Betzait Yisrael," for example, are sung to the well-known tunes of Israeli composer Yedidyah Admon. His Hebrew variant of "Chad Gadya" is also performed. One song that is traditional, but rarely performed is "Al Achat," the passage that follows "Dayyenu." This is the most pleasing of all the recordings aimed at children.

The Art of Jewish Living: The Passover Seder, Chazzan David Silverstein, Zimriyah of Adat Ariel, narration by Dr. Ron Wolfson, Federation of Jewish Men's Clubs, 1988. This tape is intended to be used with the book of the same title. There is a great deal of narration, but it is totally in the way of guiding the listener through the Haggadah. Part of the narration demonstrates the pronunciation of the nonmusical portions of the text. The singing is a bit strained in manner, but includes all the familiar songs; all the simple blessings, including candle lighting, "She-Hecheyanu," wine, "Kiddush," karpas, hand washing, motzi, matzo, maror, and omer; and such rarities as "Ve-Nomar Le-Fanav," which precedes Psalm 113. Besides the traditional version, there is an unusual performance of "Chad Gadya" in which the protagonists are identified by their onomatopoetic sounds (baa, meow, woof, moo, and so on). Your kids will like it. This is an excellent teaching tape.

Celebrate with Us: Passover, "Celebrate with Us" Family, Jewish Family Productions, 1989. There are six English songs here and eight familiar seder songs, as well as the less familiar "Be-Chol Dor Va-Dor" and "Lashana Ha-Ba'ah Bi-Yerushalayim."

A Passover Sing-Along for Kids, The Shining Lights vocalists, Brentwood Music, C-5147N, 1990, with transliterated song sheet. This is a split-track recording with music on one channel and vocals on the other. There are Hebrew versions of "Hineni Mookawn," and two other familiar songs and bilingual versions, actually mostly English, of the four questions, "Avadim Hayinu," "Dayyenu," "Addir Hu," "Echad Mi Yode'a," and "Chad Gadya."

The Paul Zim Passover Seder, Paul Zim, Simcha 33091, 1991. Paul Zim's pleasing, natural singing voice makes up for the presence on this recording of a children's choir, a slightly glitzy production, and a synthesizer. Besides, the choir is exceptionally well-trained. He does all the familiar songs, as well as "Baruch Ha-Makom," "Ve-Nomar Le-Fanav," "Migdol Yeshuot," and "Na'ar Hayiti," from the Grace, "Kol Rinah" and "Pitchu Li," from Hallel, the last with Shlomo Carlebach's melody, "Karev Yom," an elaborate introduction to the ten plagues, and "Lashana Ha-Ba'ah Bi-Yerushalayim Ha-Benuyah" ("Next Year in a *Rebuilt* Jerusalem").

The Complete Passover Haggadah, Cantor Abraham Davis, SISU, 1990s. The most useful material on this amateurish tape is the singing of the complete Grace After Meals and almost all of Hallel. Davis only sings a small part of the Nishmat.

Seder Nights, Paul Zim and the Haggadettes, Simcha 04493, 1993, with transliterated song sheet. Zim's newest Passover tape adds a full orchestra and a well-trained children's choir to Zim's rich voice for a combination of traditional and contemporary musical entertainment. Zim does ten familiar seder songs, including "La-Shanah Ha-Ba'ah Bi-Yerushalayim" and "Mah Lechah Ha-Yom" from Psalm 114; bilingual versions of "Kaddesh Urchatz" and "Chad Gadya"; and seven English-language Passover songs, including "Who Knows One" and "Go Down, Moses."

Besides these recordings aimed specifically at the music of Passover, there are many recordings of Jewish music that include Pesach material. For the most part, these tend to stick to the most obvious choices of material, all of which are well-covered by the Passover recordings listed here. Worth a special mention, however, is the work of Cantor Joseph Rosenblatt (1882–1933), the King of Cantors. It is his voice singing the cantorial portions of Al Jolson's *The Jazz Singer.* A careful search among his recordings will turn up powerful renditions of "Mah Lechah Ha-Yom," "Nishmat," and "Yishtabach," among others.

Sheet Music

B'Shir Orach Chayim, Cantor Herbert Epstein, H.I.E., 1992, 97 pages, spiral bound, plus five fourteen-page transliterated song sheets. A collection of thirty-six new and old melodies arranged to be used as a singing seder.

Songs of the Haggadah, Cantor Binyamin Glickman and Judith Berman, Tara, 1977, 23 pages, transliterated, paper. This booklet comes as a package with the *Goldberg Haggadah,* to which it is keyed by page and line number, and Glickman's *Songs of the Haggadah* recording, for which it provides the musical notation and words.

Songs of the Seder, edited by Howard and Judith Rubenstein, Granite Hills, 1994, 58 pages, transliterated, paper. This book brings together sheet music for twenty-three songs, mostly in familiar versions. It can be used at any seder, but is a companion to their own *Becoming Free* Haggadah.

Chapter Eight

Kol Dichfin Yehseh Ve-Yehchul:
Let All Who Are Hungry Enter and Eat

The Foods of the Seder

Our Passover seder is finished down to the last detail, with all its customs and laws, save for one crucial omission: We have yet to eat our well-earned feast. This would not be a sufficient seder for anyone. For the largest number of seder celebrants, the banquet is the single most essential part of the evening. It is actually a sin to fast on Pesach. Indeed, in 1946 in Jerusalem, on the fourth day of a hunger strike protesting the detention of immigrants to the Holy Land, Golda Meir and fourteen others performed a seder at which only one morsel of matzo was eaten by the participants. They knew that food was central to the celebration of Passover.

> *On Passover, Jews eat history.*
> —Israel Zangwill

The holiday, at once Chag ha-Matzot and Pesach, began as a way for farmers and shepherds to give thanks to God for a successful winter wheat crop and the birth of new spring lambs. The word Pesach literally means to skip. We usually assume that this refers to God skipping over the houses of the Israelites, sparing our firstborn, when he killed all the Egyptian firstborn. We can see in this that the paschal lamb and the Egyptian firstborn are our sacrificial substitutes. Rabbi Moses Leib of Sasov, a Chasidic *tzaddik,* pictured God skipping with joy whenever he reached a Jewish home.

Passover might refer to the Israelites passing over the Red Sea or passing over from bondage to freedom. It may also refer to the way that young lambs gambol in the spring, skipping playfully with unexpected sideways leaps. Intriguingly, Psalm 114, sung just before the meal, refers to the hills skipping like lambs, but without using the word Pesach. The night of the first seder also represented the beginning of the ominous time between that first night of Passover and Shavuot, seven times seven days, when we prayed for *tal* (dew) to ensure a successful barley harvest. When Jews no longer lived the agricultural life, dew came to mean the downward flow of divine blessings. Our proper actions on earth ensure that this flow from the upper *sefirot* is not obstructed by any intermediate sefirot.

The anthropologist Theodore Gaster, however, noticed that this metaphor of skipping or limping occurs in ritual dances performed in ancient times. The priests of Baal, among others, performed such a dance in their contest with Elijah. It is usually associated with mourning, as in ancient Hebrew dirges, which commonly have a limping rhythm, natural enough if they went with a limping dance. These actions would bewail the loss of the god who had died in the fall, but was now being simultaneously mourned and then celebrated at its rebirth in the spring. This is the same drama enacted at Eleusis for Persephone.

Militating against this interpretation, says scholar Chaim Raphael, is the fact that there is no mention in the Bible of any Israelite limping dance; that, for instance, when David leaps and dances before the Lord there is no description of limping; and, in fact, limping made a person ineligible to perform the Temple rituals. This counter-evidence can be explained away if we assume that the original limping metaphor was carried along even though all explanations of it were buried in the Israelite unconscious, replaced with the afterthought of God passing over the blood-spattered doorways in Goshen, a kind of folk etymology obscuring the original one.

Mirth in Funeral   *—Shakespeare*

We have seen how the first half of the seder is full of elements of mourning and anti-demonics, which then lead to the joyous feast. "With unleavened bread and bitter herbs you shall eat it" (Numbers 9:11), and we follow that with postburial hard-boiled eggs. We outwait whatever demons are waiting to join our festivities; and when we have fooled the last ones by pretending to be mourning, we bring out the real feast.

Rabbi Nachman of Bratslav, in his parables, tells of a Jew and a German bumming around the country together. When the night of the first seder arrived, the Jew told the German to stand with him at the back of the synagogue and wait for someone to invite him home to a delicious Pesach meal. The Jew explained the seder ritual, but forgot to mention the bitter herb. Later that night, the Jew asked him how the seder had gone. The German explained that he had eaten a tiny piece of celery dipped in saltwater, had then waited a long time to finally get a bit of dry, unleavened bread, and was next served raw horseradish, which made him run from the house screaming. The Jew then explained that if he had waited just a bit longer, he would have been served a banquet. The German is put in the role of the demon here, weeded out by the ancient shibboleth. He was ignorant of the secret, known to the initiated, of what came after the bitter herb.

As Jews who have grown up with the seder, we have lost sight of its healing and protective qualities. The German hobo did know immediately that he was being given bitter medicine. We only know we like it. We are like the malarial nineteenth-century Englishman adding gin to his quinine to help get it down. A hundred years go by, and the Englishman is now adding quinine water to his gin to help get it down. Like us, he has forgotten that the bitter is medicinal. He only knows he likes it. Our original purpose— whether to confuse the devil into believing we are mourning, not feasting; or to purge ourselves of our sins by eating bitter herbs, to humble ourselves by eating matzo and remembering we were once slaves—has gotten lost over the years as the seder foods have become cherished apart from their symbolism. We forget that, like Henry Bolingbroke, we are "eating the bitter bread of banishment."

Whether or Not I Have Seen It: The Foods Not Present

We have already looked at the symbolism of the foods (primarily in chapters 2 and 3), and we know that all the symbols of the night are expressed through food: three matzot, four cups of wine, saltwater, the six foods on the *k'areh,* and the hard-boiled egg that begins the meal. There is also the symbolism of the foods not present during this Festival of Unleavened Bread. We must search our homes and remove all leaven from them. The search is conducted on the night before the first seder, and *bi'ur chametz* (burning the leaven) occurs the following morning.

For the traditionally observant, regular dishes are put away to be replaced by two sets of Passover dishes, milk and meat, since china cannot be *kashered* for Passover. All crumbs in cupboards have to be eliminated. Every cooking and food preparation area has to be thoroughly cleaned. Stoves and ovens have to be heated until they glow. Even then, metal foil has to cover some surfaces so that Passover utensils will not actually touch them. Metal vessels and utensils must be boiled. This scrupulous approach to ridding one's home of chametz probably had the side effect of making Jewish homes more hygienic than the homes of their gentile neighbors during the Middle Ages. Unfortunately, our immunity from diseases that coursed like wildfire through the non-Jewish population merely engendered murderous pogroms rooted in paranoia and resentment.

If you wish to be as scrupulously observant about Passover *kashrut* as our medieval forebears, talk to a rabbi or a friend who already keeps kosher. The few paragraphs here can only hint at the complexity of these laws. Should you choose to set your own standards of kashrut, though, do not let the complexities of the rules intimidate you. Aim for what feels comfortable and pleasing. Do more only if, and when, you want to.

Whether or Not I Have Removed It

All *chametzdikhe* foods that we want to keep are locked up. We cannot own these foods during the holiday, so they are sold to a rabbi, who in turn sells them, *mekhirat chametz* (selling of leaven), to a non-Jew, who will sell them back for a nominal fee after the holiday. Bread or any other chametz made during the holiday cannot be eaten even after the end of Pesach. Only foods that are kosher for Passover can be eaten during the festival.

We are prohibited from eating any grains other than wheat made into matzo that has been watched to ensure that no leavening took place during its preparation. The prohibited grains are wheat, barley, rye, oats, and spelt, a particular type of wheat. It would be more accurate to say that we can only eat these grains if they have been made into matzo, since there are now oat matzot available from the Satmar Chasidim for those with a wheat intolerance; and as mentioned earlier, the Karaite sect makes barley matzo. Ashkenazim have added these *kitniyot* to the original five grains: millet, kasha, rice, corn, mustard, sesame, sunflower, carob, poppy, fenugreek, cumin, caraway, fennel, cardamom, coriander, and all legumes or pulse—peas, beans, lentils, peanuts, and clover and alfalfa sprouts. Sephardim, more easygoing in general, only follow the specific prohibition of the five grains, though even among the different Sephardic communities there are variations.

Avoiding these may not seem so difficult until you realize that you cannot use grain vinegar or alcohol, corn syrup, cornstarch, corn oil, soy oil, soy sauce, and thickeners made from beans. Almost all processed foods contain one or more of these ingredients, so you have to make everything from scratch or buy foods that have a rabbinic *hekhsher* (approval) for Passover.

It's Almost Like Being in Love

For many Jews today, who do not keep kosher during the rest of the year, there is no incentive to do it for the eight days of Passover. It seems irrelevant and difficult. Although choosing not to follow these restrictions may be easier, however, it also means missing out on a unique cuisine that exists not in a place, but in a time. For those who follow the food laws of Passover in one way or another, it is like traveling to a fantastic realm, a kind of Jewish culinary Brigadoon that appears for only eight days a year. There are strange rules and customs here. Nothing may be puffed up with yeast or baking soda, but eggs can be used to inflate foods like sponge cake, pancakes, and rolls. All of these dishes substitute ground matzo for flour. There is no mustard, but horseradish is used liberally. A strange sideways logic is being applied to the act of eating, and random bits of our usual fare are dropping out of existence.

For those who wish to visit, but not take up permanent residence, there are alternatives to the most scrupulous observance of the food laws. Even if we decide not to change our dishes and *kasher* our stoves, we can still achieve the same end result at the table by only using ingredients that are permitted for Passover. Where we need vinegar, we use cider vinegar; for sweeteners, sugar and honey; for thickeners, potato starch; for oil, olive, almond, walnut, grapeseed, or cottonseed. If we do this, and shop for processed foods at stores carrying kosher for Passover products, we can recreate the meals that our grandmothers used to serve at the seder and throughout the week. If we only want a traditional seder meal, with favorite dishes like *matzo brei* and matzo meal pancakes during the week, we can do it. If we decide to travel to Yaknehaz for the full eight days, we can do that.

De Gustibus Non Est Disputandum: The Flavors of Passover

Every one of the cookbooks listed at the end of this chapter gives recipes for the most familiar and best-loved Pesach treats. Just as every seder gathering has its own peculiarities of performance, so in the area of cooking there are equally extreme opinions on each side of the issues: by hand or machine; oil or chicken fat; light or heavy; salty or sweet. You decide when to fill Elijah's cup and whether the *afikoman* is hidden or stolen, and you have an equal latitude with the traditional Passover dishes. This is not a cookbook, but I have included a few basic recipes and tips aimed at the beginner. Forgive me if I state the obvious.

Horseradish

If you have fresh horseradish root, either home grown or store bought, and a grinder or food processor, you can make your own beet horseradish. It is easy and infinitely tastier than any bottled *chrain*.

Peel the root to get all the dirt off, and cut it into pieces small enough to go in your grinder or processor. Then be prepared to cry like a baby as the radish releases its pungent juices. I had to leave the room twice during the grinding the last time I made it. Supposedly, you can avoid tears if you grind the radish near an open flame. It's worth a try. To color the horseradish, you can either cook a few fresh beets or drain a small can of peeled, cooked beets packed in water. Put these through the grinder along with the pieces of radish. Add a little salt, sugar, and cider vinegar to taste. This is incredibly fresh and potent and has none of the chemical taste of the preservatives used in commercial preparations. You will want to use sliced or grated fresh horseradish for the *maror* and *korekh,* but your own beet chrain for the gefilte fish.

Schmaltz

Schmaltz, rendered chicken fat, is traditionally used in many Passover dishes. It goes without saying that it is high in cholesterol and bad for you. It is also delicious. I allow myself to eat it, as well as too many eggs, for these eight days during the year.

You can get away without using it by substituting vegetable oil. Everything you make with oil will still be delicious, especially if you make a mock schmaltz by frying onions and grated carrots (garlic optional) in oil at a low heat and then straining the oil after the onions have caramelized.

Griventz

If you decide to render the chicken fat, be sure to make *griventz* (fat cracklings) as well. Cook the chicken fat on medium heat, watching to make sure it does not burn. When the fat has melted and the skins rise to the top, it wouldn't hurt to put a sliced onion in as well. Now the bits of skin will fry into chicken cracklings, or griventz. If you can keep yourself from eating these immediately, chop them into your liver along with the fried onion.

Chicken Soup

The most traditional chicken soup is a golden chicken stock. To make this, you can use whole chickens or parts. You might consider adding some turkey necks as well. The more bones (backs, ribs, and necks) and the longer they cook, the more gelatinous and rich your chilled stock will be. I like to make this ahead of time so I can strain it, chill it, and skim off the fat. (The fat can be used in matzo balls and chopped liver. If you do not remove the chilled fat, you end up with a greasy soup.)

The longer it cooks (two hours is enough), the more the meat will tend to fall apart; so once the soup comes to a boil, reduce to simmer for the remainder of the cooking time. While it is simmering, skim off the scum that floats to the top. Kosher chickens produce less scum because they have already been drained of their blood. Whether or not you use kosher poultry, skimming the soup while it is cooking is essential for a clear golden stock. The more painstakingly this is done, the better. Patience is definitely a virtue here.

After it is strained, chill the stock. Separate the meat and skin from the bones and cartilage, which you can throw out. If the skin is intact, you can make griventz from it by adding it to the schmaltz you render. You can either add the meat back into the soup later, or use it for chicken salad or fillings in other dishes.

At this point I deviate from tradition. After I have removed the fat from the chilled soup, I return the stock to the stove and add carrots, parsnips, the stalks and leafy heart of celery, parsley, a whole turnip, a whole onion, a couple of garlic cloves, a dozen black peppercorns, a bay leaf, and a few dashes of paprika. You could do this as part of the first step, but I find it easier to do in two stages. When this has cooked thoroughly, I again strain the soup. I save the carrots, put the rest of the vegetables in a colander, and press the liquid out of them. This is no longer clear and golden, but it makes a delicious chicken and vegetable soup stock.

When you serve the soup, presumably with matzo balls, you can add a bit of chopped fresh dill or celery leaves, your cooked carrots, and any part of the boiled chicken you choose to return to the soup. When I was a boy, I would watch my father clean a kosher chicken and there would often be an egg in the hens. There would also be a number of variously sized yolks in the hen's reproductive tract. My grandmother would put these yolks in the soup on the night of the seder, and we grandchildren would fight over these hard-boiled yolks.

Matzo Balls

Matzo balls, or *knaydlich,* are a constant subject for argument. Everyone talks about light matzo balls, but I find them flavorless. My father liked to eat them with a knife and fork. My son is unhappy unless they skip like tiddly winks or lambs. Some like them on the heavy side, but less dense than these extremes. To make them harder or softer, just add more or less matzo meal than the recipe on the box (which will come out slightly lighter than medium) specifies.

If you like them ultra-light, seltzer is not the answer. It is no better than soup stock and lacks flavor. Instead, separate the eggs, beat the whites and salt, and fold the puffed-up matzo meal and egg yolk combination into this. Matzo balls made this way are quite fluffy. If you want them somewhat heavier than this, follow the recipe on the package, avoid compressing the batter when you form them, and simmer, do not boil, them.

When you are forming the knaydlich, keep your hands wet with cold water to prevent the batter from sticking to you. Don't use oil. Keep the lid on while the knaydlich simmer so they steam and remain moist on their upper surface. Be sure to cook them in water before you add them to the soup, or they will absorb all your stock.

You can make the matzo balls ahead of time and just add them to the soup to heat up. Or add them to slightly boiling water just before the seder begins and transfer them to the soup just before the meal (probably around "Dayyenu," as some old Haggadot direct).

Chopped Liver

Liver presents its own special set of kashrut problems. The traditional way to make chopped liver is to salt and puncture the chicken livers, broil them on a rack in a pan, and then rinse them off. This is to satisfy the laws of kashrut as to the removal of blood from meat. Some go further and insist on grilling them over fire.

If you do not keep kosher, you can sauté the livers with the diced onions, but be sure to fry the onions over low heat, in either schmaltz or mock schmaltz, until they are golden before adding the livers. The onions should be almost entirely cooked when the livers are added. The more finely you dice the onions, the less you have to chop them after they are cooked. The longer the livers cook, the tougher and less tasty they become, although this is less critical with chopped liver than it would be with whole livers.

You can use a grinder or food processor next if you want a pureed sameness of consistency, or you can chop everything by hand in a wooden bowl for a superior nonuniform texture. The eggs are harder to chop with the livers, so you might try chopping the egg fairly fine before adding the liver and onions to the chopping bowl. Chopping is easier a third of a bowl at a time. At the end, mix everything together with a spoon. As for proportions, your own taste should be your guide. I use roughly two medium onions and three jumbo hard-boiled eggs to a pound of chicken livers. You can use calf's liver or beef liver if you prefer, but chicken is tastiest. If you boil the eggs ahead of time and then chill them, removing the shells will be easier because the egg will shrink away from the shell. I sauté a little garlic with the onions and add a small amount of sweet kosher wine, maybe a tablespoon. Season the chopped liver with salt and pepper, put it into a bowl, and sprinkle the top with paprika.

Matzo Brei

There are many variations on matzo brei, fried matzo or matzo French toast, and they are all acceptable. Some people pour boiling water on the matzo. I want the matzo to stay crispy, so I just immerse it briefly in cold water. The matzo has to be at least slightly damp to absorb the egg. Press out the matzo and scramble with eggs. I usually use one less egg than pieces of matzo, but this is another area for choice. I add a little milk and pepper to the eggs. Pour this into hot oil, lower the heat to medium after it browns on the bottom, then toss it until the rest is cooked but still moist. Again, doneness is a matter of personal taste. Some sprinkle cinnamon and sugar on it, or top it with fruit preserves. I just like salt and large quantities of cold milk to wash it down.

Matzo Meal Pancakes

The recipe on the package of matzo meal is perfect for matzo meal pancakes. The only tip I can add is to beware of making them so thick that the eggs are raw in the center. These are also good with cherry and strawberry preserves from Israel and a glass of cold milk.

Sponge Cake

The cookbooks will tell you how to make all kinds of sponge cakes. If you have never made a sponge cake, remember: They have not forgotten to tell you to grease the tube pan. In order for the cake to creep up the sides of the pan, there should be no oil on the pan. If you like powdered sugar on sponge cake, you will need to make it from scratch because commercial varieties contain cornstarch. Put 2 cups of granulated sugar in a blender with 1 tablespoon of potato starch, and blend on high to make your own.

Passover Rolls

We cannot have bread, but we can make Passover rolls or bagels. Combine ⅓ cup of grapeseed or cottonseed oil with ⅔ cup of water and 1 tablespoon of sugar. Boil this mixture so that the sugar is dissolved. Add 1 cup of matzo meal and mix thoroughly. Then add 3 eggs, one at a time, and mix. Be sure each egg is thoroughly blended before adding the next one. Form the batter into bagels (with holes in the center) or rolls.

Whenever you are handling this batter, moisten your hands with cold water. This achieves the same result as greasing your hands and keeps unnecessary oil out of your food. Bake on a lightly greased (Mother's Choice just introduced a Passover cooking spray) cookie sheet at 400 degrees Fahrenheit for fifteen minutes. Turn the oven down to 325 degrees and continue baking for another 45 minutes.

You can fill these rolls with fruit and top with whipped cream for dessert, or fill them with chicken or egg salad for lunches. Most whipping creams have some kind of thickener, which makes them chametz; so you need to find a pure cream with no additives. The same for mayonnaise, which is usually made with chametzdikhe oils and vinegars. There are commercial kosher for Passover mayonnaises, but they are terrible. I urge you to make your own homemade mayonnaise with grapeseed oil, lemon juice, fresh eggs, and herbs. It is really easy and delicious. The recipe is in *The Passover Gourmet,* listed below, but leave out the mustard, which is chametz.

Charoset

We discussed charoset in chapter 2, and some Sephardic versions will follow. If you make the traditional apple-nut-cinnamon-sweet wine variety, figure at least half an apple per person. The proportions can be gauged visually, keeping in mind the intention of making the finished product resemble mortar, or "like clay in straw," according to Maimonides' recipe from his *Mishneh Torah:* "Take dates, dried figs, or raisins and the like, and crush them. Add wine vinegar and mix with shredded stick cinnamon and fresh ginger until it is mixed like clay in straw." This is charoset for the perplexed.

The foods we eat during the meal—horseradish with our gefilte fish or brisket, dumplings made with ground matzo, matzo meal sponge cakes—will all continue to remind us to discuss the

Exodus while we eat. Since we began but did not finish the Hallel before the feast, we might consider the meal itself not as an interruption, but as a part of our praise of freedom.

Passover Cookbooks

There are many Jewish cookbooks and many Jewish holiday cookbooks, but for our purposes we will concentrate on those that are aimed specifically at Passover. You will find recipes for gefilte fish, chopped liver, chicken soup, matzo balls, tzimmes, kugel, matzo brei, sponge cakes, Passover bagels, matzo meal pancakes, farfel, borsht, matzo stuffing, and beet chrain in virtually every one of the following cookbooks. One way of enhancing a seder is to serve a variety of kinds of charoset from all around the world. They all taste different, they generate discussion, and they shine a new light on our standard version.

By way of sampling these cookbooks, we will be presenting a panoply of charoset variations. In all the recipes, unless stated to the contrary, wine is sweet and red, figs and apricots are dried, dates are pitted, apples are cored, and spices are ground. As you will soon see, there are many possibilities for what can be charoset. The important factors are to emphasize fruits, nuts, and spices mentioned in the Bible, especially in the Song of Songs, and to achieve a mortar-like consistency. It can be cooked or raw, sweet, spicy, or tart. Looking over our range of recipes, we can see families of charoset variations, yet no two are exactly alike. If you are inventive, perhaps you can come up with something entirely new.

The same is true for the holiday foods in general. You can make Passover a nostalgic feast, a gourmet experience, a dining discovery, a vegetarian celebration, or a stringent religious observance. Most likely, you will do a little of all of these by picking recipes judiciously from the broad range of available Passover cookbooks.

The Manischewitz Passover Cookbook, Deborah Ross, illustrated by Gene Szafran, Jonathan David, 1982, 186 pages, hardback. Originally published in 1969, this book is based on the recipes created by Ross for Manischewitz from 1957 to 1968. Ross is really a pseudonym, like Betty Crocker, for Edith G. Stoffer, at that time the director of home economics for Manischewitz. Perhaps they felt "Edith Stoffer" was too European, less "modren" than "Deborah Ross." The book is enjoyable reading and contains 318 recipes that will enhance your Passover menus. There are a number of good vegetable dishes and salad dressings worth trying. As my grandmother used to say, "Matzo is very binding."

The weakness of the book is that it constantly prods us to use Manischewitz products instead of starting from scratch. At the same time, it is enjoyably conversational and has an introductory section on Jewish cooking, cleaning the house, setting the table, Passover in many cultures, and Passover menus. It also discusses the fine points of cake baking and variations in matzo balls. Since there is no charoset recipe, I will give her statement on matzo balls:

> When people discuss matzo balls, they usually rhapsodize about their lightness and delicacy. However, when pressed, many people will admit, if a little shamefacedly, that they were accustomed to firm matzo balls at home and still prefer them.

The Kosher for Pesach Cookbook, edited by Rena Novack of the Yeshivat Aish HaTorah Women's Organization, graphics by Rena Novack and Ellen Yaffe, Philipp Feldheim, 1978, second revised edition 1980, 168 pages, spiral bound, typewriter face. The 281 mostly Ashkenazic recipes gathered together here were all contributed by members of the Yeshiva's Women's Organization as a fund-raising project. In addition to the usual holiday dishes, there are also Jewish versions of Chinese and Italian favorites like Egg Foo Yong and Chicken Cacciatore. An introductory section of the book gives an ultra-Orthodox view of chametz, cleaning up for Passover, putting together a seder plate, and some sample holiday menus.

Here are two unusual charoset recipes:

CHAROSET—SEPHARDIC STYLE

½ lb. dates	⅛ tsp. pepper
1 apple	¼ tsp. cinnamon
¼ lb. walnuts	wine
¼ lb. almonds	

Grind all the above together. Add enough wine a few hours before the seder to make it stick together.

Charoset—Iraqi-Syrian Style

2 lbs. dates	cinnamon
2 handfuls mixed walnuts	wine
and almonds, ground	

Rinse dates, grind, add water to cover, cook on small flame until dry, stirring occasionally to prevent sticking, about 2 hours. Take 1 cup of cooked dates, add nuts, cinnamon, and wine. Use the rest of the cooked dates as jam.

The Passover Feast II, edited by Selma Daner, Susan Lando, and Rachel Turk, illustrated by Hattie Dubroff and Susan Lando, West Orange Chapter of American Mizrachi Women, 1978, 371 pages, hardback, typewriter face. This was done as a fund-raiser. In addition to the 918 recipes, it includes information on the holiday and setting the table, cooking hints, Passover thoughts, and blank pages for your own recipes. There are some unusual dishes here, like calf's foot *pitcha,* raisin wine, and jellied carp, inspired uses of matzo, low-fat variations on traditional foods, Israeli specialties, as well as Sephardic dishes like stuffed squash, *mina,* and brown eggs. It was here that I first discovered Sephardic charoset variations, and these three have become standard at our sedarim:

Israeli Charoset

2 peeled apples, chopped	juice and rind of 1 lemon
15 dates, chopped	1 tsp. cinnamon
2 bananas, chopped	⅓ cup wine
½ cup nuts, chopped	sugar to taste
juice and rind of 1 orange	

Mix and chill.

Iraqi Charoset

¼ cup pine nuts	3 ozs. raisins
grated apple	½ cup sugar
2 hard-boiled egg yolks	cinnamon and allspice to taste
½ cup ground almonds	juice and rind of lemon

Mix and chill.

Yemenite Charoset

15 dates, chopped	1 tsp. ginger
10 figs, chopped	dash coriander
2 tbsp. sesame seeds	dry red wine to bind

Mix and chill. (Sesame and coriander are considered kitniyot *by Ashkenazim and are not eaten by them during Pesach.)*

The Complete Passover Cookbook, Frances AvRutick, Jonathan David, 1981, 420 pages, hardback. There are 503 recipes here, and that does not include innumerable variations and alternatives to the basic recipes. There are five different matzo ball recipes, from bantam through heavyweight, that will please everyone. There are just as many gefilte fish variations, from the original filled fish skins to the ground fish patties we are most familiar with today. This is truly one of the most complete Passover cookbooks currently available. It has all the traditional Ashkenazi recipes plus Israeli, Sephardic, and popular foreign favorites from China, Japan, Italy, Greece, and so on. The book opens with background information on keeping kosher at Passover, setting the table, the seder plate and menus, and includes many tips and conversion and substitution tables. It is enhanced by a conversational style and explanations that go beyond bare lists of ingredients.

Rebbitzin AvRutick provides this unusual charoset recipe:

Sephardic Charoset

4 medium apples, peeled	¼ cup vinegar
1 lb. dates	½ cup wine
2 cups pecans or almonds, coarsely ground	

Combine apples and dates in saucepan. Add cold water to cover. Cook over medium heat until apples are tender and almost all of water is evaporated. Grind apples and dates. Add nuts, vinegar, and wine to desired consistency.

The Spice and Spirit of Kosher-Passover Cooking, edited by Esther Blau and Cyrek Deitsch, Lubavitch Women's Organization, 1981, 95 pages, paper. This is not just a cookbook, but Passover as performed by the Lubavitcher Chasidim. There is a message from the late Rebbe, a great deal of material on kashrut, the special kashrut of Passover, eliminating chametz, the laws of Passover, what foods are allowed, how to make wine, how to perform the seder and set the table, the seder plate symbols, the significance of matzo—all in all, a thorough overview of the festival.

There are 261 recipes, most of which avoid *gebroks,* the moistening of matzo and matzo meal. Since the Lubavitchers do eat gebroks on the eighth, rabbinic, day of Pesach, the last chapter of recipes tells how to make traditional Passover favorites like matzo meal pancakes, matzo balls, matzo brei, and Passover rolls. Somehow these all have to be crammed into one day of eating. Luckily, most of the other Pesach favorites do not need matzo or matzo meal so gefilte fish, sponge cakes, and kugels all show up earlier in the book.

The most unusual element in their charoset has to do with their omission of spices. They use only apples, walnuts, and a small amount of wine since, as their Haggadah says, "For some years already we no longer use ginger and cinnamon for charoset, for fear lest some chametz may have become mixed in, in their processing."

Taste of Passover Cookbook, edited by Barbara Amouyal, illustrated by Stephanie Altneu, preface by Haim Shapiro, Jerusalem Post, 1985, 152 pages, paper. This brings together the results of a contest sponsored by the *Post* and the Sheraton Hotels of Israel—188 recipes from every part of the Jewish world. Many obvious dishes are here, as well as such cleverly named items as Red Sea Onion Soup, Never Say Dayyenu Carrot Pudding, Ki Lo Naeh Fish, Darkness in Egypt Chocolate Mousse Pie, and Pass-(them)-Over Brownies. Besides the familiar Eastern European recipes, there are many specialties from Persia, Greece, Italy, Lebanon, and India, as well as modern Israeli and original recipes. If you are strictly kosher, beware of Sephardic recipes that incorporate beans and lentils. Some of the recipes have metric measurements, but there are conversion tables. Others have ingredients that are hard to find outside of Israel, but a little ingenuity should help you come up with substitutions.

Kathy Ozery contributed this charoset recipe from Yemen (which includes sesame seeds and cardamom, two spices prohibited to Ashkenazim during Passover):

CHAROSET FROM YEMEN

250 gm. sesame seeds, toasted	4 tsp. cinnamon
	½ tsp. cloves

1 kilo dates	½ tsp. ginger
½ kilo raisins	½ tsp. cardamom
1 cup almonds, chopped	½ tsp. salt
1 cup walnuts, chopped	

Toast sesame seeds, stirring frequently in pan over medium flame until evenly browned. Combine all ingredients in pot over low flame, adding water to achieve desired consistency. Mixture should resemble preserves. Continue cooking, approximately 15 minutes, to allow flavors to penetrate, adding water as necessary to maintain desired consistency.

No-Cholesterol Passover Recipes, Debra Wasserman and Charles Stahler, Vegetarian Resource Group, 1986, 52 pages, paper. If the prospect of eating your way through a dozen eggs a day for eight days is a little upsetting, you might want to take a look at this collection of 100 recipes which avoids all meat, eggs, and cholesterol. If this seems odd to you, remember that Franz Kafka, Rabbi Kook, Albert Einstein, S. Y. Agnon, and I. B. Singer were all Jewish vegetarians. You may have to give up twelve-egg sponge cakes, but you can still have cabbage/beet soup, prune and potato tzimmes, sweet potato kugel, and fruit compote, as well as many other inventive variations on traditional dishes.

I cannot say I want to have matzo brei without eggs, but there is certainly a need to eat more vegetables at Passover, to get more fiber, and to reduce our fat intake. Originally, Passover was a brief time to indulge in rich, fatty foods before going back to a meager, regular diet. Today, when our usual eating habits include too much fat, Passover can take us over the top. I am sometimes amazed that I make it through the week without cardiac arrest. If this bothers you too, or if you are a vegetarian, check out this small volume of alternative Passover dishes. Besides the recipes, there is some information on Jewish vegetarianism for those interested in changing their eating habits permanently.

Something Different for Passover, Zell Schulman, foreword by Joanne Schindler, Triad, 1986, 188 pages, paper. The 205 recipes included here are intended both to help you make traditional Passover dishes, and to bring a contemporary gourmet approach to them as well. All the recipes are clear, explicit, and detailed, and will allow you to truly serve something different for Passover. Besides the recipes, there are sample menus for sedarim and the rest of the week, a substitution table, material on using microwave and food processor, and background information on the holiday, Passover kashrut, searching for chametz, setting the table, and preparing the seder plate. The dessert recipes are especially impressive.

Schulman adds grated lemon peel to her Ashkenazic charoset, which she makes in a food processor. I dislike the uniform consistency achieved this way, but if time and muscle strain are factors, use your processor. Here is her unusual Sephardic charoset:

SEPHARDIC CHAROSET

½ cup coconut, grated	½ cup dried apples
½ cup walnuts, ground	½ cup prunes
¼ cup sugar	½ cup dried pears
2 tsp. cinnamon	12 ozs. cherry preserves
1 cup raisins	⅓ cup Malaga wine
1 cup apricots	

Chop dried fruits. Cook everything except preserves and wine in a pot with water to cover. Simmer uncovered, stirring occasionally with wooden spoon, for about an hour. When it thickens, add preserves. Remove from heat, add wine, cool.

The Passover Gourmet, Nira Rousso, Adama, 1987, 189 pages, cloth. There are only 111 recipes here, yet Rousso covers a tremendous amount of ground in a small space. All the traditional Ashkenazic favorites are here, often with interesting personal touches, like her chicken soup with leek and red pepper, or the pancakes made without beating the egg whites. On top of this, there are an equal number of Sephardic recipes, more than in any other Passover cookbook: *babanatza* from Rhodes, *mina,* Moroccan *mahammar, bimuelos,* Tunisian *shakshookah, fritada, keftikas,* Tashkent-style brown eggs, *pastelicos, hammin* (Sephardic *cholent*). Many of these dishes use artichokes, leeks, celery root, and olives.

Part of their appeal is the family stories that Rousso includes. These are not merely recipes found in cookbooks, but memories of specific people and moments. Two dishes in particular have become favorites in our home: the Passover pizza made with the best recipe for a matzo crust I have found anywhere, truly the heights of matzo pizza; and the matzo-chicken turnovers with herbed mayonnaise. Many of the Sephardic recipes involve moistening matzo and working with it like Armenian cracker bread. There are two horseradish sauces, a pineapple-horseradish salad, and carp-horseradish patties. Enhancing the presentation are beautiful color photographs of seventy of the dishes that make you want to cook every one of these recipes. This is one of my favorite cookbooks.

Here are Rousso's five Sephardic charoset possibilities:

DATE-APRICOT CHAROSET

½ cup dates	1 cup apricots
2 cups apples, peeled and diced	½ cup chopped walnuts
	¼ cup wine

Cook dates, apples, apricots together in water to cover for 15 minutes. Strain fruit, chop coarsely with wine, and add nuts.

ORANGE-WINE CHAROSET

¾ cup dark raisins	juice and grated peel of 2 oranges
2 cups dates	⅓ cup wine

Grind raisins and dates, add orange peel, juice, and wine.

GINGER-CINNAMON CHAROSET

½ lb. dates	1 tsp. cinnamon
1½ cups raisins	1 tsp. ginger
2 apples, peeled	¼ cup orange juice
½ cup pecans, chopped	

Chop coarsely.

FIG AND COCONUT CHAROSET

½ lb. dates, chopped	1 tsp. cinnamon
½ lb. figs, chopped	½ tsp. cloves
1 cup grated coconut	1 cup wine
1 cup apricots, diced	1 cup pecans, chopped
1 cup plum preserves	

Cook everything except nuts for about 30 minutes in covered saucepan. Add small amounts of water as needed. Remove from heat and add nuts.

ALMOND-RAISIN CHAROSET

4 apples, peeled and sliced	½ cup ground almonds
½ lb. dates	1 cup wine
½ cup raisins	3 tbsp. lemon juice
2 cups water	sugar to taste

Cook fruit with water for fifteen minutes. Strain, coarsely chop fruit, add rest of ingredients.

The When You Live in Hawaii You Get Very Creative During Passover Cookbook, edited by Judy Goldman and Davida Skigen, illustrated by Wren, Congregation Sof Ma'arav, 1989, 147 pages, paper, spiral bound. Sof Ma'arav means "the end of the west," an appropriate name for this farthest western congregation. This fund-raiser cookbook brings together 206 recipes, both Ashkenazic and Sephardic, many of which required quite a bit of ingenuity to bring off in Honolulu. There are also lists for getting organized for Passover, kashrut, setting the table, the seder plate, menus, how to keep Passover low cholesterol, hints, substitutions, and Hawaiian terms. Many of the recipes call for tropical fruits or substitute mahi mahi and butterfish for whitefish and pike. Most of the recipes can be made anywhere though.

Here is an out-of-the-ordinary version of charoset:

LIVNAT BECHLER'S SEPHARDIC CHAROSET

juice and grated rind of 2 oranges	4½ ozs. raisins
	12 ozs. walnuts
1 lb. large, moist figs	4–5 apples, peeled
1 lb. moist dates	¼ cup wine

Finely chop or grate everything, mix, and add wine.

The Haimishe Kitchen Pesach Cookbook, Ladies Auxiliary of Nitra, C.I.S., 1992 and 1993, 133 pages, paper. A collection of 208 Eastern European recipes, including two pages of special instructions for perfect cakes, this was put together by the Ladies Auxiliary of Nitra, a Talmud Torah in Mt. Kisco, New York. If you are really a pioneer, there is a recipe here for making potato starch from scratch, or more accurately, how to make 2 cups of starch from 25 pounds of potatoes.

The Passover Table, Susan Friedland, photography by Penina, food styling by Erez, HarperCollins, 1994, 96 pages, paper. This cookbook has some of the most beautiful food photography I have ever seen, but there are only forty-six recipes. Still, they manage to include all the important Eastern European favorites as well as many Sephardic dishes: *megina, tagine, mina, anjinaras, birmuelos.* The photos are mouth-watering, with exquisite care given to the table settings, linen, china, glass and silver, beautiful old Haggadot (some of the facsimiles supplied by yours truly), fresh produce, floral arrangements, and the appearance of the concoctions. That must be food styling. There is an almost Zen feeling to some of the images that calls out for a haiku:

> lonely matzo ball
> bit of dill *lechem oni*
> next year in Israel

All joking to one side, the paucity of recipes, the refined aestheticism, the emphasis on presentation, all lead to a feeling of preciousness. Will Passover atrophy into a Yuppie event? As if this were not bad enough, there are a number of errors in the introductory text, the worst being the assertion that there is only one arrangement of the seder plate. Unfortunately, all three photos of seder plates differ from each other as well as from this supposed universal pattern, which omits chazeret. In spite of the sloppiness of the introductory material, this is still a handsome volume of recipes.

Here is Friedland's Sephardic charoset recipe:

SEPHARDIC CHAROSET

1 cup dates	½ cup walnuts, chopped
½ cup raisins	1 tsp. grated fresh ginger
1 apple	¼ cup wine

Combine all dry ingredients. Chop finely. Add wine to make coarse paste.

Chapter Nine

Ha Lachma Anya:
This Is the Bread of Affliction

Shopping for Passover

Besides cooking distinctive *Pesachdikhe* dishes, you may also want to shop for certain specialty items. It is up to you to decide how far you want to go and how much effort and time you want to take to create your own Passover. When effort starts to seem like trouble, you have gone too far.

Pesach, Matzo, and Maror

The three main food items that will enhance your seder table that are not readily available are *shemurah* or watched matzo, a kosher lamb shankbone, and fresh horseradish root. You may also want to buy some commercial Passover foods and wine, as well as special objects dedicated to the performance of the Passover rituals.

Shemurah matzo is easy to get if you live near a Chabad house or a Lubavicher synagogue. Barring that, ask your kosher butcher or grocer. If that fails, check with the closest Orthodox synagogue. If all of this is impossible in your geographical location, consider having a box of shemurah matzo shipped to you from Pinsker's, 2028 Murray Avenue, Pittsburgh, PA 15217, or call them at 800-583-2476. Plan ahead to be sure your order gets to you in time for the holiday, and tell them whether you want handmade or machine-made.

If you have a kosher grocery in your town, you should have no trouble getting either a kosher lamb shankbone or chicken neck for the *zero'a*. Kosher butchers usually give shankbones away to regular customers and those placing large Passover orders. The custom today is to strip the meat from the bone so as not to confuse this seder plate symbol with the paschal sacrifice of Temple days. Unfortunately, the splinter that is left looks pathetic on the *k'areh*. I prefer to spend a few dollars for a lamb shankbone that looks like an "outstretched arm." If you have no access to kosher meat, then you do not keep kosher and you may as well use a nonkosher chicken neck or lamb shankbone. Another option is to get a freezer chest, drive to the closest Jewish population center, pick up everything you need for the holiday, and bring it back on ice. Ask other Jewish families what they do and consider pooling your orders, either shopping for some items by mail or driving to a larger town.

Horseradish root should not be hard to find, but often it is moldy, dried up, or rotten. If that is the case, you might do better to use a jar of kosher horseradish than to try to use fresh. Talk to the buyers at the best produce store in your town and see if they can find good quality raw horseradish root. If you have a green thumb, you can grow your own horseradish. It takes at least two years to mature, but it is well worth the wait.

Man Oh Manischewitz: Kosher Wine

Kosher wine, if you accept sweet wine, is easy to get from Manischewitz, Mogen David, Schapiro, Ti-Rosh, Rashi, and Carmel. Their dry wines are terrible, though. For most of us, at least a little sweet wine is nostalgic and cozy. As children, we grew up with it, and our own children will like it more than a dry wine.

Until recently, no one cared about dry kosher wine. Since the Seventies, however, more and more small kosher wineries have sprung up, primarily in Israel, California, France, and Italy, to meet the need for good kosher wines. The major names in this rapidly growing field are Royal Wine (which distributes Baron Herzog, Herzog Selection, Alsace, Menorah, Star of Abraham, J. Furst, Bartenura, Alfasi, Kedem and Chateaux Barbot, Geninf, Le Pin, and Les Sourderies); Gan Eden, Weinstock, Simcha, and Hagafen, all in California; Bokobza and Lionel Gallula from France; and the Israeli wineries of Yarden, Golan, and Baron Edmond de Rothschild. If you have wine merchants in your town, ask their advice—though unless they are Jewish, most will not know about kosher wines. You may have to experiment a little yourself to find decent vintages. The best kosher wines I have sampled were a Baron Herzog Pinot Noir a few years ago, and a magnificent Yarden Merlot, vintage 1990, just this last year. If you can find this Merlot (which was then going for about $15 a bottle), your quest is finished. For a white wine, try Gan Eden's slightly less expensive Fumé Blanc.

Matzo Balls and Gefilte Fish

The big names in processed kosher for Passover foods are Manischewitz, Mother's, Grandma's, Rokeach, Gold's, Goodman's (the oldest, founded in 1865), Horowitz Margareten, Barton's (cookies and candy), and Streit's. Others, some from Israel, include Kemach, Empire, Hebrew National, 999, Carmel, Sinai, Festive, Elite, Ba-Tampte, Season, Polaner, Kineret, Kosherific (I did not make this up), Sharon Valley, and Kedem. Some of the newer matzo companies are Aviv and Yehudah from Israel and the British Rakusen.

You will need to buy commercial matzo, matzo meal, matzo cake meal (more finely ground than matzo meal), and potato starch. If you do not feel ready to make things from scratch, these companies also make chicken soup, soup nuts, mandel cuts, mock schmaltz, matzo balls, gefilte fish, borscht, kishka, macaroons, kugel, blintzes, *kichel,* cake mixes, *schav* (a kind of sorrel or spinach borscht), chopped liver, potato latkes, and farfel. In some cases these products can save you time, but often it is just as easy to make foods from fresh ingredients, especially when you consider the differences in satisfaction and flavor.

Ma Cohen makes processed red and white horseradish that is quite good. Ba-Tampte makes firm kosher dills the traditional way, without vinegar. If you choose to buy gefilte fish—the best is the Rokeach Old Vienna. Other high-quality products are the Sharon Valley fruit preserves from Israel, Streit's canned cranberry relish, and Bartenura balsamic vinegar. Candy tends to be disappointing, with the exception of dark-chocolate covered matzo, Bazooka bubble gum from Israel with the cartoon in Hebrew, and fruit slices, the Jewish version of Chuckles. It would not be Passover for me without white, unsalted, whipped butter on matzo—of course, I salt it—and a red metal can of Swee-Touch-Nee loose tea.

A Sonnet Is a Moment's Monument   *—Dante Gabriel Rosetti*

Deserving of a sentence, if not a sonnet, to itself is Fox's U-Bet chocolate syrup, indispensable for making egg creams:

> In a tall glass
> Pour one inch
> Of Fox's U-bet
> Chocolate syrup
> Add maybe an inch and a half of milk
> Top with seltzer
> Stir but not totally
> You want to achieve
> Something like

A Jewish pousse-café
So that each layer
Is tasty
But unique
Unto itself

Kosher for Passover: Caveat Emptor

When you buy any foods for Passover, be sure they actually are labeled kosher for Passover. Many foods, like wine and matzo, may be kosher all year except at Passover. The special requirements of time and watching are not necessary for matzo eaten the rest of the year. Likewise, non-Passover kosher wine may have yeast added to it. And Fox's U-Bet is only made with sugar instead of corn syrup for Passover. Also check dates and be sure you are getting this year's matzo. All matzo products should be dated—last year's kosher for Passover matzo is this year's chametz. One misleading product is egg matzo. Since it contains added ingredients like eggs and fruit juice, it is considered matzo *ashirah* (rich matzo) and eating it does not fulfill the obligation to eat matzo at the seder. Most people consider egg matzo to be chametz. I dislike its crumbly texture.

The variations in stringency among those who keep kosher have also led to confusion in regard to the labeling of foods. One rabbi's *hekhsher* is approval for some groups and anathema for others. The letter U inside of an O is the symbol for the Union of Orthodox Jewish Congregations, and this is generally accepted by most of those who keep kosher. At least 100 other organizations and rabbis in the United States have their own symbols of approval for various local and national products.

The letter K alone means nothing. It can be put on packaging merely to trick consumers. You need to know which organization is giving its approval. Be sure to differentiate between products having a P as to whether it stands for pareve (neither meat nor milk) or Pesach.

All of this depends on how stringent you intend to be. The best advice I can give is to talk to your rabbi and decide what keeping kosher means to you, why you are doing it, and what you want to achieve by following the traditional food laws. You can write to the Union of Orthodox Jewish Congregations at 333 Seventh Avenue, New York 10001 or call them at 212-563-4000 for more information and to find out about their publications, which give detailed information on commercially processed kosher foods.

Hallelujah: Ritual Objects for the Seder

When Moses and the Israelites praised God after their deliverance at the Red Sea, they proclaimed, "This is my God and I will glorify Him" (Exodus 15:2). The Talmud understands *hidur* (glorify) to mean beautify. There should be an aesthetic element in worship. We can use whatever plates, glasses, napkins, and candle holders we want to for the seder, or we can buy or create special ritual objects intended solely for use during Passover. It is traditional to put one's best china, glass, and silver on the table for the seder.

The most common ritual objects associated with the holiday are the seder plate; matzo cover; cup of Elijah; *afikoman* bag; wine cups and decanters; candle holders; *kippot; kittel;* cushions for leaning; and basin, ewer, laver, and towel for hand washing. Some of these can be used for Shabbat and festivals during the rest of the year, while others are only used at Pesach. For those who keep kosher, metal and glass items that are used during the year for eating and drinking need to be re-*kasher*ed at Passover. Again, check with your rabbi on how to do this.

If you have artistic ability, you can make what you need. The most common homemade objects have always been textiles created by Jewish women, although today that should not bar men from sewing and other fabric arts. Indeed, in my grandparents' generation, so many men were tailors that it was more common for men to sew than women. You can look at books on Jewish ritual objects to get ideas or actually get patterns from the books on Jewish needlepoint. These will allow you to make your own coverings for the cushions, matzo covers, afikoman bags, towels, kippot, and kittel. The traditional decorations for these objects are either the symbols of the holiday, associated biblical verses, benedictions recited while using the ritual objects, or key words associated with the objects. You might want to look at some books on Jewish calligraphy. The letters of the Hebrew *alef bet* are not only intrinsically beautiful, but they are full of nostalgic and kabbalistic meaning. As stated before, it is these very letters that were used by God to bring the universe into being. Unlike our streamlined Roman letters, they still retain the complex texture of handwritten forms.

A towel might include the *berakhah* for washing the hands. Matzo covers could have the Motzi Matzo benedictions or the three words of Rabban Gamaliel—Matzo, Maror, and Pesach. One of the standard forms for the matzo cover is a bag with three separate pockets for each of the matzot. These three pockets are usually detachable from the cover so that they can be easily laundered.

Herald of Your Glory

If, like most of us, you cannot make your own ritual objects, you can still look for well-made Jewish arts and crafts at museums and gift shops. Most traditional versions of the ritual objects are in the baroque style. There were Jewish art objects from before that time, but few have survived. If we could bring together all of the extant ritual objects from before the fifteenth century, we would only need a small box to hold them. Everything else was destroyed by the successive enemies of the Jewish people. If it was made of precious metal, it was melted down. As it says in the Hallel, "Their idols are silver and gold" (Psalms 115:4). Because of this lost past, most ritual objects have been copies of those baroque pieces that were most familiar to people.

The most common Jewish symbol today is the Magen David (shield of David), but this only became popular in the nineteenth century. Before that, the most common emblems on Jewish ritual objects were the two tablets of the covenant, Torah, pomegranates, seven-branched menorah, tree of life, zodiac, shofar, crowns, supporting lions, eagles, bears, and stags, and the twisted pillars of Solomon's Temple. Some of these were also used in medieval heraldry; but where the heraldic symbol was used to trumpet the pedigree of a human being, the Jewish use of the same symbols glorified God. Where a herald might assign a coat of arms to some insignificant baronet for a fee, the Jews were adorning the Torah with shields. When the nations of the world put crowns of gold and silver encrusted with precious jewels on their kings, the Jew was doing the same thing with the scrolls of the law. With this shift of emphasis, we indicate that knowledge and wisdom, not pedigree, are to be esteemed.

Other possible Jewish decorative motifs relevant to Passover are borrowed from the history of Haggadah illustration. Using objects displaying these symbols at the seder reinforces the content of the texts:

> depictions of the Exodus story, such as the crossing of the Red Sea, the ten plagues, or Moses and Aaron before Pharaoh

> references to the text of the Haggadah, such as the four sons, the rabbis at Bene-Berak, or Chad Gadya

> drawings of the rituals and preparations, such as the search for chametz, the baking of matzo, and the fifteen steps of Kadesh Urchatz

If you have craft abilities, you can go further and make your own metal, stone, glass, plastic, wood, or ceramic seder plate, cup of Elijah, wine cups and decanters, and candelabra. Besides the motifs already referred to, you can use reinforcing symbolism on these seder ritual objects. Since we drink four cups of wine, it is traditional to show the four children on the cups, either on separate cups or on four faces of the same cup. This emphasizes the repetition of fours at the seder. An eighteenth-century Polish silver gilt *kos Eliahu* features a set of ten droplet-shaped cartouches, each one containing an illustration of one of the ten Plagues. The pictures of the plagues set into the form of drops refers to the ritual action of removing a drop for each plague.

The most elaborate seder plates are those that combine the matzo cover and k'areh by creating a three-tiered container for the matzot topped by a platform that holds containers for the six symbolic foods. This contraption was originally round with doors or curtains, allowing the matzo to be concealed and revealed as necessary during the seder. In the nineteenth century, after the invention of machinery to make unleavened bread, which introduced the square matzo, some of these three-tiered plates were made in the square format. The most romantic feature, though, is the containers used to hold the foods. These are in the shape of wheelbarrows for the *charoset,* with buckets, mortar-mixing troughs, and other objects connected to the bondage in Egypt for the other foods.

Form Follows Function

In the twentieth century, both the Arts and Crafts movement and the Bauhaus have had an impact on Jewish art, producing new forms for the old objects. In line with that, you might consider commissioning contemporary artists and craftspeople to create personalized items for your seder table. Depending on what materials are used, this does not have to be that expensive. In objects intended for ritual use, form should follow function. Working with an artist will allow you to have input on the final form of your seder plate or cup of Elijah, avoiding many of the mistakes, lost opportunities for symbolism, and lapses of taste that characterize the most commonly produced Jewish ritual objects. As mentioned in an earlier chapter, few commercially produced seder plates follow any of the traditional patterns for the placement of the symbolic foods.

It is also possible to buy an inexpensive vinyl insert that turns any plate into a seder plate. This is made by Shulsinger, and shows the objects in the correct positions. Shulsinger also makes a full line of matzoware—paper products imprinted to look like matzo. There are cups, variously sized napkins and plates, tablecloths, invitations, cloth matzo covers and afikoman bags, Haggadot, jigsaw puzzles, and even an inflatable matzo beach ball. This is a funny novelty item that makes a good afikoman prize.

There are two other Passover products that should be mentioned here. Mesifta Beth Shraga, a yeshivah in Monsey, New York, puts together bedikat chametz kits with a feather, candle, wooden spoon, and card with blessings. Of course, you can assemble your own kit, but this makes it easy.

A measurement guide for the seder from C.I.S. for the uncertain, shows how much wine, karpas, maror, and matzo to be eaten to fulfill the various Passover mitzvot.

You do not have to buy everything the first year. As you grow into Pesach, you will learn what you want and what you need. Until that becomes clear to you, keep it simple and inexpensive.

Besides buying food and objets d'art for ourselves at this season, it is traditional to provide *me'ot chittim* (wheat money) for the poor so that they may be able to buy matzo, wine, and the other foods needed to celebrate the festival. This can be done through synagogues, temples, or any of the Jewish charity agencies. Once I left home, my grandfather always sent me a me'ot chittim check just before Pesach so that I could buy wine and matzo. For many years, spring would roll around and I would do nothing about Passover except miss it. Still, he sent the checks. He never asked me what I did with the money, but I would like to think that, in the long run, his investment paid off with interest.

Chapter Ten

Ve-Higadetah Le-Vinchah:
And You Shall Tell It to Your Children

Children and Passover

Our primary task at the seder is based on the positive biblical commandment, "and you shall tell it to your children" (Exodus 13:8). Yes, but without becoming boring, smarmy, or pompously didactic.

Four Questions: Preparing Your Children

Before we even begin to tell our children, though, we should ask ourselves at least four questions: What do we ourselves like and dislike about the seder? What do we remember fondly about our childhood experiences of Passover and what do we remember painfully? When were our questions answered and when were we left, not wondering, but in ignorance? What do we enjoy in the seder as adults and what leaves us bored, confused, or feeling left out?

In answering these and any other questions along the same lines, we can begin to create a seder that will fulfill the mitzvah of truly telling our children the story of the Exodus. To do this you must prepare the children before the seder, and present the seder and Haggadah in such a way that they can enjoy and understand it.

If you have followed me this far, you know that the Haggadah is not interested in telling the story of Moses, nor is it interested in telling the particulars of the Exodus story in a linear, connected way. What it does attempt to do is to display certain symbols representing bondage and deliverance and to allow these to connect with certain pregnant poetic statements. Out of this we create meaning. This meaning is in us and not in the text or ceremony. That is why we say, "In every generation we must all see ourselves as having personally been redeemed from Egypt."

Our first task, then, is to know the Exodus story and the seder ceremony and text. During the month from Purim to Passover, there are many preparations for the holiday: cleaning, shopping, cooking, and study. Be sure to include selecting the right Haggadah for your seder group and reviewing that Haggadah (see the list of Haggadot in chapter 5). Besides knowing the story, you will also want to decide what to cut out, what to emphasize, and what to do so as not to stumble around when performing the seder rituals. Nothing is as boring, especially for children, as watching someone deciding what to do at the seder. A confident *ba'al ha-seder* puts everyone at ease. Your enthusiasm or the lack of it will convey itself to your children. If duty and obligation loom larger than enjoyment and excitement, our little human polygraphs will give the lie to any assertions on our part to the contrary.

Just as you are studying the Haggadah to prepare for the seder, take some time to teach the four questions to the youngest child. Depending on age and how many children you have, you might teach the youngest in English, the next youngest in Hebrew, and so on, increasing complexity as they get older. I can still remember when I was in the second grade and my brother taught me the words and traditional chant from a transliteration in a children's Haggadah. The next year I went to Hebrew school and was able to read them in Hebrew at the following seder.

By preparing children ahead, you accomplish a number of things: involvement and participation in the big production that the adults are planning; actually answering the questions ahead of time so that they know the answers as they ask them (this allows you to provide knowledge up to the capacity of the child); resolution of fears about holiday changes; and creating the natural expectation that they will not be shy when they perform because they are prepared and everyone expects it. Alternatively, you will be able to find out if they are afraid to perform, in which case you can alter their solo to a group sing in which they lead, or modify the expectations so that they only read in English the first year.

Four Children: Involving Young People

Do not be afraid to abridge the Haggadah to suit your needs. Better a brief, enjoyable seder than one that is painfully long and drawn out. "The Torah speaks of four types of children," and as your children grow up, change, and take on these four personae, new elements can be added to your seder each year. At the same time, do not be afraid to perform the whole seder because someone will not like it or children will become fidgety. This brings us back to preparing our children. First, teach them about the holiday. When you begin your preparations, include them in. Listen for their questions and seize upon them as opportunities to explain the holiday and build up their anticipation. Explain to them why you are cleaning the house, what the special foods are that you buy and prepare, how all of this is leading up to the great seder celebration.

Involve them in your activities. Children may not have our stamina, but they like to do adult things. If you are cleaning, they can clean, either with you or in their own rooms. Explain about eliminating *chametz* so that cleaning becomes a treasure hunt leading up to the final hide-and-seek treasure hunt of the formal search for chametz on the night preceding the seder. Be sure to burn the chametz that you found the night before on the following morning. This allows the children to do two things they enjoy: going outside (where spring has arrived) and watching a fire. Make a bonfire, if local ordinances allow it, or just burn the chametz in the backyard barbecue.

Take the children with you when you shop. Let them choose

Passover treats that they will like: *Pesachdikhe* candy, bubble gum, soda pop, potato chips. If you are observing the food laws for the full eight days, and obligating them to give up foods they normally eat, let them see that there are compensatory treats. Have them make and mail invitations. Let them assist you in cooking, setting the table, creating the seder plate. Making *charoset* is one of the cooking chores you can turn over to the kids. When it is done, have them shape it into a pyramid and explain to them why they have done it. Encourage them to decorate the table with place cards or to make matzo covers and other decorated textiles. You can buy textile crayons that they can use to draw on cloth, and the designs can be ironed in permanently. Although we may be intimidated by the idea of making our own ritual objects, our children will not be. In some communities the Lubavicher Chasidim provide opportunities for children to participate in the baking of matzo. No one, child or adult, can walk into a complicated ritual unprepared and give it meaning. What we tell them ahead of time is what allows them to give the rituals meaning. The more they are involved in the holiday changes, the more excited and less disoriented they will be. Likewise, the more Passover is part of a full Jewish life and year, the less it will seem like an intrusion into the child's secular life and year.

Every Child May Joy to Hear   —*William Blake*

Buy appropriate books that explain the holiday. You can also borrow books from your synagogue or public library, but stories have more meaning when children own their own books. Also, borrowed activity books that cannot be written in and other texts that children have to handle carefully are merely frustrating. If you must borrow books, consider photocopying so that kids can draw on the copies. For the youngest child, get stiff board books. Move on to simple storybooks and coloring and activity books.

Provide them with their own Haggadot, whether you use them at the seder or not. When they are very young, you may want to use an abbreviated Haggadah aimed at children. There are many of these, and you can upgrade every year as they get older. Within the Exodus story, there are many elements that appeal to children.

The story of Moses begins with his rescue from the basket in the bulrushes. All children can get involved in the larger story when you begin with a baby. Do not ignore the major role of Moses' big sister, Miriam. Little girls will be as interested in her as little boys are in Moses. Tell the story within the context of the special role that Moses' family has: father Amram, mother Jocheved, brother Aaron, sister Miriam, and baby Moses. The performance of miracles and the triumph of the underdog also appeal to children. Notice the elements that catch your children's attention and emphasize them.

Besides books that tell the Exodus story and the meaning of the seder, there are also children's cookbooks, audio and video tapes, and software. The audio tapes allow them to learn both songs and stories. One computer game from Davka, *Crumb Eater*, lets the kids play a Pac Man-like game of gobbling up bread crumbs. The most important thing is to create a sense of anticipation, excitement, and participation. On the afternoon of *erev* Pesach, be sure that those who need naps get them. Also, allow substantial late-afternoon snacks because dinner is usually quite late.

Once the seder actually begins, aim it at the children. Rabbi Akiba always had treats like nuts on the table for his children. If they become restless let them work on a Passover activity book or read a Passover story while the ceremony proceeds. If they fall asleep at the table, let them snooze. The important factor is that they are with you as the seder is created and begun. If they drop in and out occasionally, they will still pick up a tremendous amount of information. Each year they will learn more. The seder is organized in an overlapping pattern so that the same material might be presented at one moment in a song, at another in a type of food, and then later in a ritual. All work together to create the total seder experience, a set of overlapping motifs that reinforce one another from multiple perspectives.

Four Cups of Wine: Holding Children's Attention

Drop the idea that the seder is a bore that you will have to struggle against to keep your children interested. Around the globe and through 3,300 years of history, Jewish families have developed ways to keep children's attention at the seder and most of them have sprung from the Haggadah itself, a repository of entertaining, curiosity-arousing, and attention-getting activities: singing our way through the meal; rhymes; poems; moments to show off, like the four questions; stories and legends; a parable about four children; mnemonics; horrific material, like the ten plagues; refrains, like "Dayyenu"; acrostics; counting songs, like "Echad Mi Yode'a"; "House that Jack Built"-types of songs like "Chad Gadya."

We grab our children's attention as well by performing every-day actions in an unfamiliar way: the drama of lighting candles; children being treated as adults and getting to drink wine; ritual hand washing; removing drops of wine with our fingertips; leaning while we eat; eating strange foods in ritual ways; hiding or ransom-ing the *afikoman;* prizes; dramatic performances such as opening the door for Elijah or carrying the afikoman on our shoulders. Far from being resentful about imposed restrictions, children love the magic of ritual.

One children's Haggadah tells the story of the Exodus with stick puppets. There is also a glove of five finger puppets of key Passover characters, Pharaoh in the middle where he belongs. One year we asked our usually reticent son to tell us what he knew of the story of Pesach. Wearing this glove, he began to discourse like a *maggid.* He had been listening after all. Some families add dramatic presentations that they have created.

Two parts of the seder need to be thought through carefully so that no one's feelings are hurt: the four questions and the hunt for the afikoman. When the youngest reads the four questions, be sure that you are not putting too much pressure on a shy personality. One way to avoid this is to allow a few chantings of "Mah Nishtannah," either using different melodies or different languages—Hebrew, English, Yiddish, Ladino, whatever. Decide ahead of time what each child can do and is willing to do so that no egos are bruised. You might have some of the children sing in chorus or lead the whole group in chorus. As for the search for the afikoman, it is important to have a reward for everyone, not just the one who found it. Let them see themselves as a team in which all share in the prizes when one of their number finds it. If the children hold it for ransom, encourage them to do this as a group and share in the reward.

Children always love money as a reward, but consider along with the shiny silver dollars and crisp new bills the following suggestions for afikoman prizes:

> A classic Jewish book to reinforce the themes of the seder.
>
> An inflatable matzo beach ball. Excellent prize.
>
> A glove with five finger puppets that invite your children to dramatize the story. Excellent.
>
> Jigsaw puzzles of either a matzo abstract or a seder plate. Excellent.
>
> A Seder card game from BYLS that teaches the steps of the seder.
>
> Passover buttons, one with either white or blue ribbons showing who found the afikoman; one with a slice of bread in a red circle with a red line through it.
>
> Pencils saying, "Happy Passover" or having one end shaped into a Magen David.
>
> T-shirts in various sizes saying, "I found it."
>
> Passover place mats that educate and some that can be colored, washed off, and colored again.
>
> Puffy stickers of Passover symbols.
>
> Afikoman loot bags with Passover cartoons on them.

Finally, there are many inexpensive accoutrements to your seder table, such as cloth matzo bags, afikoman bags, and vinyl inserts that turn any plate into a seder plate. There is Matzoware from Shulsinger—paper printed to look like matzo, which includes invitations, cups, tablecloths and various sizes of plates and napkins. Any of these items will increase your children's interest in the holiday proceedings.

Make Me a Child Again Just for Tonight

After the seder, remember that the holiday continues for eight days. Be sure to make *matzo brei,* matzo meal pancakes, and sponge cakes during the week. When lunches are packed for school, include matzo crackers in place of bread and Pesachdikhe candies and snacks. Continue to read Passover stories, listen to Passover music, and watch Passover videos with your children during the week. Encourage them to engage in Passover crafts and activities and to help prepare Passover foods.

Handled correctly, the changes from the normal can seem magical and special, a Jewish game, instead of limiting, upsetting, and restrictive. At the same time, stop short of becoming obsessive and monomaniacal. Try to aim for naturalness and let your children's questions and interests lead you. If you can reach the place where you can see the seder through their eyes, Passover will mean more to you and them.

A Catalogue of Children's Books for Passover

The most important part of the holiday is the transmission of our culture from one generation to the next, the way we "pass over," the *Chabad,* the *Ch*ochma (wisdom), *B*inah (understanding), *Da*'at (knowledge), and especially the memories of more than 3,000 sedarim. How we ate the first matzo with our loins girded and our staffs in our hands, what they said in Bergen-Belsen when they had no matzo, when the revolt began in the Warsaw

Ghetto on the night of the first seder in 1943, and who liked their matzo balls hard and who liked them soft—these are all part of the Passover story.

Like all books for kids, Jewish children's books have to contain all the things in the big world: fiction, biography, legends, poetry, and so on. They also have to do this for everything Jewish: holidays, history, Bible, Holocaust. Over the years they have often failed because they were sanctimonious, moralistic, doctrinaire, or boring. Recently, Jewish children's books have begun to change, with excellent illustrators and fine storytellers coming together to create beautiful, engaging, and informative works. Not every Passover book is that good, but the tide is turning.

People often ask about reading levels. Some books can be read by ten year olds on their own, or read aloud to five year olds. Reading level varies according to who is doing the reading and how much work the adult is willing to put into getting the book across. The following listing identifies the books by type and age level and gives recommendations. Incidentally, children's books contain a good deal of information and are an excellent way for Passover *greeners* (novices) to begin to learn about the holiday.

Stiff Board Books for the Youngest Children

I Have Four Questions, Madeline Wikler and Judye Groner, art by Chari Radin, Kar-Ben, 1988, 10 pages.

My First Passover, Tomie dePaola, Putnam, 1990, 12 pages.

My First Seder, Madeline Wikler and Judye Groner, art by Katherine Kahn, Kar-Ben, 1986, 10 pages.

Where Is the Afikomen, Judye Groner and Madeline Wikler, art by Rosalyn Schanzer, 1989, 10 pages.

ABCs and First Readers

Everything's Changing—It's Pesach, Julie Auerbach, art by Chari Radin, Kar-Ben, 1986, 24 pages, paper. A good early rhymed reader that explains to children why things are changing and what the changes are.

Make-Me-a-Match Pesach, Diana Lederman, Gefen, 1988, 10 pages, spiral bound. Pictures of ten Passover objects and symbols must be matched with their Hebrew-English words using two sets of flip cards. Nicely done.

Passover, Miriam Nerlove, Albert Whitman and Co., 1989, 22 pages, paper. Rhymed story of holiday for youngest child. Nice color art.

Passover A–Z, Smadar Sidi, art by Aharon Shvo, Adama, 1989, 43 pages, cloth. Actually *alef* to *tav,* this book gives fairly detailed explanations of fifty-four Hebrew terms relating to Passover with beautiful watercolor illustrations.

Riddles about Passover, Susan Poskanzer, photos by Rob Gray, Silver Burdette, 1991, 30 pages, cloth. Photos and rhymed riddles explain holiday.

What Is Passover?, Harriet Ziefert, art by Lillie James, HarperCollins, 1994, 16 pages, cloth. As children lift flaps, they find the answers to questions about Passover.

Storybooks with Passover Themes

Carp in the Bathtub, Barbara Cohen, art by Joan Halpern, Kar-Ben Copies, 1972, 48 pages, paper. When Mama buys a carp for gefilte fish a week early and keeps it in the bathtub, Leah and Harry try to keep it as a pet. Good story.

Farfel the Cat that Left Egypt, Rabbi Norman Geller, Geller Pub., 1987, 31 pages, paper. Farfel the cat leaves Egypt with the Israelites.

Ike and Mama and the Once-a-year Suit, Carol Snyder, art by Charles Robinson, Jewish Publication Society, 1978, 47 pages, paper. Cute story of Ike's Mama in 1918 Bronx shopping for fourteen suits for all the boys in the neighborhood just before Passover.

Magician's Visit, adapted from an I. L. Peretz story by Barbara Goldin, art by Robert Parker, Viking, 1993, 32 pages, cloth. A magician arrives in town just before Passover and provides a seder feast for a poor old couple. In reality, he is Elijah the prophet. Beautifully illustrated.

Matzah Ball, Mindy Portnoy, art by Katherine Kahn, Kar-Ben, 1994, 32 pages, paper. What happens when baseball and Passover pass over each other.

The Passover Parrot, Evelyn Zusman, art by Katherine Kahn, Kar-Ben, 1984, 40 pages, paper. A parrot named Hametz learns the four questions and steals the afikoman. Nicely done.

The Passover Passage, Susan Atlas, Torah Aura, 1989, 96 pages, paper. Rebecca's adventures aboard her grandparents' boat, the *Diaspora,* as they celebrate Passover in the Caribbean. Well told.

Cookbooks

Matzah Meals, Judy Tabs and Barbara Steinberg, art by Chari McLean, Kar-Ben, 1985, 72 pages, spiral bound. Seventy recipes, graded for difficulty, that kids can make for themselves at Passover. Gives background on holiday, how to set table, make seder plate, prepare symbolic foods, make Passover crafts, and how to make chocolate-covered matzo, macaroons, matzo pizza, *tzimmes,* passover rolls, matzo brei, matzo meal pancakes, chicken soup, and matzo balls. Quite complete.

Activity Books for Children Who Can Read and Write

Many of these activity books have ideas that can be used before or during the seder to increase your children's interest. If your children become restless or disruptive during the seder, let them have an activity book so that they can be busy, but still focused on the holiday.

The Animated Haggadah Activity Book, Janet Zwebner, Shapolsky, 1989, 45 pages, paper. Companion to videotape, *The Animated Haggadah.*

Creative Activities for Passover, Dori Gerber, Contemporary Designs, 1987, 24 pages, paper.

Fun-in-Learning about Passover, Alfred Kolatch, art by Gabe Josephson, Jonathan David, 1972, 64 pages, paper.

Let's Learn about Passover, Sol Scharfstein, art by Arthur Freedman, KTAV, 1986, 32 pages, paper.

My Pesach Play and Learn Book, translated and adapted by J. Bennet from material by Leah Sonnenfeld, art by Chani Sonnenfeld, Feldheim, 1993, 38 pages, paper.

Passover Activity Book, Contemporary Designs, 1991, 44 pages, paper.

Passover Activity Funbook, Robert Garvey, art by Gabe Josephson, KTAV, 1956, 32 pages. A stamp book, but there is no glue on the stamps so buy a glue stick.

Passover Fun Book, David Adler, Hebrew Pub., 1978, paper. Puzzles, riddles, magic, and information on Passover.

Passover Fun for Little Hands, Katherine Kahn, Kar-Ben, 1991, 21 pages, paper.

Passover Puzzler, Sol Scharfstein, KTAV, 1978, 32 pages, paper.

Passover Puzzles and Fun, Linda Schwartz, art by Beverly Armstrong, Hanucraft, 1988, 16 pages, paper, comes with envelope for mailing.

Pesach, A Holiday Funtext, Judy Bin-Nun, Nancy Cooper, Ruth Sternfeld, art by Heidi Steinberger, UAHC, 1982, 32 pages, paper.

Pesach Seder Coloring and Activity Book, art by Shepsil Scheinberg, Feldheim, 1992, 32 pages, paper.

Pesach Shpiel, Shmuel Kunda, Kunda Pub., 1989, 32 pages, paper, comes with box of eight crayons.

The Santa Cruz Haggadah Kids' Passover Fun Book, Karen Roekard, art by Nina Paley, Hineni, 1994, 56 pages, paper. Children's companion volume to *Santa Cruz Haggadah.*

Shalom Sesame, Comet, 1994. Set of four items featuring characters from Sesame Street and Shalom Sesame (Kippi and Moishe Oofnik): (1) *Coloring Book,* paper. *Sesame Street* characters celebrate Passover in oversized coloring book. (2) *Kippi and the Missing Matzah,* Louise Gikow, art by Tom Brannon, 30 pages, cloth, with tape narrated by Anne Meara. (3) *Passover Overpass,* board game. Players begin in ancient Egypt and try to get to Israel. Variant of snakes and ladders using snakes and Moses' staff. (4) *Playing Cards.* Passover card game featuring *Sesame Street* characters.

The Story of Passover, Barbara Soloff-Levy, Watermill, 1989, 32 pages, paper. Nicely done coloring and activity book, except for one flaw. On the page where the Israelites mark the doorposts and lintels of their homes with the blood of the paschal lamb, this book says they were told to mark their doorposts with an X. In the first place, that is not in the Bible. In the second, Jews have traditionally been scrupulous in *avoiding* the cross or X as a magical or protective sign. We do not cross our hearts, for instance. When Jewish immigrants arrived at Ellis Island and were asked to sign their names, those who could not write their names in English put their marks—a circle, not a cross. This was so prevalent, that it is assumed to be the source of the anti-Semitic term "kike" for a Jew, since "circle" in Yiddish is *kikel.*

The Story of Passover, Rabbi Charles Wengrov, art by Emanuel Schary, Shulsinger, 1981, 28 pages, 1990 edition, 16 pages, paper. The new edition has a glitzy color cover, but part of the framing narrative and ten of the pages to color have been sacrificed.

The Story of Pesach Coloring Book, Shepsil Scheinberg, Feldheim, 1992, 32 pages, paper.

Bible Storybooks

Exodus, adapted by Miriam Chaikin, art by Charles Mikolaycak, Holiday House, 1987, 32 pages, cloth. Beautiful full-color illustrations of the Exodus with well-told story.

Festival of Freedom, Maida Silverman, art by Carolyn Ewing, Simon and Schuster, 1988, 32 pages, paper. Tells Exodus story and ends with description of seder.

Moses in the Bulrushes, Warwick Hutton, Macmillan, 1986, 32 pages, paper. Story of the baby Moses nicely illustrated in color.

A Picture Book of Passover, David Adler, art by Linda Heller, Holiday House, 1982, 32 pages, paper. Story of Exodus ending with the seder and why we celebrate it. Well-told, good illustrations.

The Ten Plagues of Egypt, Shoshana Lepon, art by Aaron Friedman, Judaica, 1988, 32 pages, paper. Colorful, funny illustrations and rhyming story of ten plagues.

Holiday Storybooks

Although many of the following books have a story, their primary purpose is to explain the holiday of Passover or the seder ceremony. At the same time, most of them give at least a cursory telling of the Exodus story.

The Book of Passover, Edythe and Sol Scharfstein, art by Siegmond Forst, KTAV, 1953, 42 pages, paper. It is difficult to be objective about the book from which one learned the four questions. Here are all the brightly colored pictures telling the story of the Exodus, the games, riddles, and puzzles, songs like "Go Down, Moses," and, of course, the four questions in Hebrew, English, and transliteration. Quaint, but still charming after all these years.

But This Night Is Different, Audrey Marcus and Raymond Zwerin, art by Judith Brown, UAHC, 1980, 38 pages, cloth. This book begins with one of the basic features of the Passover seder, the asking of questions. The child asks, "Why do we do this?" and the answer is the story of the holiday.

Children love repetition, and by using "But this night is different" over and over, a comfortable structure is created that helps the child to enjoy what is different about Passover. The pictures and the text are equally inviting, and along the way a good deal is learned about how and why we celebrate this holiday. Seven blessings are given in Hebrew and transliteration. Well-paced and cozy, this is one of the best first books about Passover to read to your child.

Dayenu, Rosalind Schilder, art by Katherine Kahn, Kar-Ben, 1988, 32 pages, paper. Aunt Helene is exhausted at just the prospect of the work needed to perform the seder. Uncle Murray convinces her to just do one thing, to clean, and it will be enough. One thing leads to another and pretty soon they have done everything. This is one of my favorite Passover books—in fact, it was a big influence on this book. What is sufficient for Passover? However you answer that question, you and your kids will love this beautifully conceived, well-written, charmingly illustrated, and still simple story. Even the dog, who gets no lines, is good. The key element of the most famous of all Passover songs, the repetition of the word Dayyenu, becomes the structure for this new story of sufficiency. A Passover concept is used cleverly to make a point without becoming moralistic. Something new and clever is added to something old and familiar. The result is this unpretentious charmer about preparing for Passover.

A Family Passover, Anne, Jonathan, and Norma Rosen, photos by Laurence Saltzmann, Jewish Publication Society, 1980, cloth. Photographs from a little girl's point of view show the preparations for Passover and performance of the two seders.

A First Passover, Leslie Swartz, art by Jacqueline Chwast, Simon and Schuster, 1992, 23 pages, paper. Beautifully illustrated, touching story of a Soviet Jewish boy's first Passover in America.

The Four Questions, Lynne Sharon Schwartz, art by Ori Sherman, NAL Penguin, 1989, 36 pages, paper. This was Ori Sherman's first published work. Chanukkah and creation stories followed, establishing Sherman's greatness after his early death from AIDS. This explanation of the Passover seder features a menagerie of Aesopian animals acting out the standard four questions of the youngest child. The answers by Schwartz, a well-known novelist, are excellent, and Sherman's vibrant, magical gouache paintings make this the most beautiful of all Passover kids' books. Nor are these paintings merely good in their own right. They reflect Jewish tradition, harkening back to the *ushpizin* plaques put up in *sukkot*. There are two unfortunate errors, though. One of the four questions suggests that we dip the herbs twice into saltwater. In fact, we dip our green herb in saltwater and our bitter herb in charoset. The last plate shows the fifteen steps of the seder, but compresses them into twelve images. The text does not make clear that there are actually fifteen steps. It would be nice if these slight errors could be corrected.

Just a Week to Go, Yeshara Gold, photos by Yaacov Harlap and Yeshara Gold, Mesorah,1987, 32 pages, paper. Photo essay of Orthodox boy in Old City of Jerusalem preparing for holiday.

Not Yet, Elijah, Harriet Feder, art by Joan Halpern, Kar-Ben, 1988, 28 pages, paper. Rhymed story of Elijah impatiently waiting to get in throughout seder.

One Little Goat—Had Gadya, Betsy Teutsch, Aronson, 1990, 28 pages, cloth, Hebrew-Aramaic-English. Excellent calligraphy but mediocre illustrations and no color. Music included, and beautifully done tables comparing words of lyrics in Aramaic, Hebrew and English. Allegory of nations devouring nations given as explanation of song.

Only Nine Chairs, Deborah Miller, art by Karen Ostrove, Kar-Ben, 1982, 38 pages, paper. Cute rhymed story of too few chairs at the seder.

Passover, June Behrens, photos by Terry Behrens, Childrens Press, 1987, 32 pages, paper. Photo essay showing American Reform family getting ready for Passover, having seder, and telling Exodus story.

Passover As I Remember It, Toby Fluek with Lillian Finkler, Random House, 1994, 32 pages, cloth. Toby Fluek and her mother were the only Jews from the Polish village of Czernica to survive the Holocaust. In this, and her previous book, *Memories of My Life in a Polish Village,* she, with the help of her daughter Lillian, brings that vanished world of rural Eastern European Judaism to life again, both in her simple text and in her touching naive paintings. Here we see that Passover was not a mere eight-day holiday, but served as a focus for the whole Jewish year. A beautiful book and a valuable document of otherwise lost customs and traditions.

The Passover Journey, Barbara Goldin, art by Neil Waldman, Viking, 1994, 56 pages, cloth. Goldin's *The Magician* was also a Passover story. Here she tells the Exodus story with many details drawn from midrashim and explains the seder and Haggadah with fascinating detail. Beautifully illustrated and well told.

Penny and the Four Questions, Nancy Krulik, art by Marian Young, Scholastic, 1993, 32 pages, paper. Penny shares the singing of the four questions with Natasha from the Soviet Union who has never been able to celebrate the Jewish holidays.

A Taste for Noah, Susan Topek, art by Sally Springer, Kar-Ben, 1993, 24 pages, paper. Noah finds, while learning many other things, that although charoset looks like mush, it tastes good. Kar-Ben does it again with fine color art and story and low price.

Toby Belfer's Seder, Gloria Pushker, Judith Hierstein, Pelican, 1994, 31 pages, cloth. The only Jewish family in a small Louisiana town shares Passover with a gentile friend.

Children's Haggadot

The Animated Haggadah, created in clay by Rony Oren, Shapolsky, 1989, 48 pages, cloth, Hebrew-English. A complete Haggadah with illustrations from the excellent *Animated Haggadah* video.

Art Scroll Youth Haggadah, translated by Rabbis Nosson and Yitzchok Zev Scherman, art by Yosef Dershowitz and Dovid Sears, Mesorah, 1987, 64 pages, paper, Hebrew-English. Complete Haggadah, although the translation is paraphrastical. This is all right here, since the goal is to convey the meaning to children, but it is common in all Mesorah translations and makes them seem less than trustworthy. Annotated with midrashic material and profusely illustrated in color.

Boruch Learns about Pesach, Rabbi Shmuel Kunda, Moznaim, 1983, 32 pages, paper. Color pictures and rhymed telling of the steps of the seder. Simple.

Building Jewish Life, Joel Grishaver, photos and art by Grishaver and Jane Golub, Alan Rowe and Lisa Rauchwerger, Torah Aura, paper. A set of six individually sold books and booklets about Passover: (1) *Haggadah,* 1989, 46 pages, Hebrew-English. Almost complete Haggadah, simplified and explained clearly. (2) *Passover,* 1988, 48 pages, Hebrew-English. Overview of seder, its connection to Exodus, and our attempt to realize our involvement in that event. Companion video listed below. Includes three unusual charoset recipes. (3) *Passover Activity Book,* 1987, 31 pages. Activity book to involve youngest in holiday changes and seder. (4) *Mastering the Four Questions,* 1991, set of fifteen 8-page pamphlets and teacher's guide, Hebrew-English. Aid to teaching four questions and their meaning. (5) *Seder Symbols and Their Stories,* 1989, set of fifteen 4-page pamphlets with eight stickers and teacher's guide. Simple introduction to seder symbols and meaning. (6) *15 Steps to Freedom,* 1986, set of fifteen 4-page pamphlets, 2-page questionnaire and teacher's guide. Simple introduction to steps of seder. Grishaver worked on *The Art of Jewish Living: The Passover Seder* with Ron Wolfson. They are both superb educators who remove our fears of the unknown and seemingly complex. Grishaver's Haggadah is only slightly abridged, yet it is simple, clear, and inviting. The rest of these materials are just as good. The packets are more appropriate for the classroom or for distribution to fifteen children from a number of families. There is also a video, which is listed below.

A Children's Haggadah, Howard Bogot and Robert Orkand, art by Devis Grebu, CCAR, 1994, 72 pages, paper, Hebrew-English. Gorgeous, imaginative companion to the *New Union* Haggadah. Music, fold-out pages, and marvelous graphics present the seder and the story beautifully. Detailed.

The Children's Haggadah, edited by A. Silbermann, translated by Isidore Wartski and Rabbi Arthur Super, art by Erwin Singer, Boaz House, 1963, 99 pages, cloth, Hebrew-English. A classic Jewish children's book, originally published in Germany in 1933. Besides the text translated with children in mind, versified passages, quaint color illustrations, music, and large type, there are five early pop-up or interactive illustrations that are charming. We have lost the innocence that would allow us to pull a strip of paper and drown the Egyptians. A blast from the past.

A Child's First Haggadah, Susan Weis, Shulsinger, 1993, 22 pages, spiral bound, stiff paper. All the steps, some of the story, and some clever ways of getting kids into the text, like making them turn the book. Simple.

The Discovery Haggadah, Rabbi Kerry Olitzky and Rabbi Ronald Isaacs, art by Arthur Friedman, KTAV, 1992, 79 pages, paper, Hebrew-English. A fairly complete Haggadah with lots of extra information, puzzles, games, and ideas for reflection. Excellent combination of traditional Haggadah, unusual customs and new concepts. Besides the familiar songs, you will also find the "Ballad of the Four Sons" (sung to the tune of "Clementine"): "Said the father to his children, 'At the seder you will dine, you will eat your fill of matzo, you will drink four cups of wine.' "

The Feast of Freedom Coloring Book, Rachel Rabinowicz, art by Dan Reisinger and Arnold Young, Rabbinical Assembly, 1984, 32 pages, paper, some Hebrew. Companion to the *Feast of Freedom Haggadah.* If you use that, you can give this to your children so that they can follow along, yet stay busy. Detailed.

Mah Nishtanah, Shaul Meizlish, art by A. Taub, photos by Ayalah Avidar, Shai, 1985, 72 pages, cloth, Hebrew-English. Photos show a family seder in Israel, while art tells the ancient story. Detailed.

My Haggadah, Ila Cherney, art by Jana Paiss, Behrman, 1986, 32 pages, paper, Hebrew-English. A Haggadah activity book and Hebrew workbook. Detailed.

My First Haggadah, Lois Rakov, Templegate, 1978, 36 pages, spiral bound. Homemade looking but charming. Detailed.

My First Passover Haggadah, Sol Scharfstein, art by Arthur Freedman, KTAV, 1986, 64 pages, paper. Activities, music, comics, vocabulary, history. Detailed.

My Very Own Haggadah, Judyth Saypol and Madeline Wikler, art by Chaya Burstein, Kar-Ben, 1983, 32 pages, paper, some Hebrew. First done in 1974 and revised slightly in 1983, this has become enormously popular, especially in conjunction with Kar-Ben's *Family Haggadah.* It has pages to color, familiar and new songs, recipes, crafts, and a detailed Haggadah.

Read Me the Haggadah, Chavie Freund, art by Tova Leff, C.I.S., 1990, 38 pages, cloth, Hebrew-English. Bright, colorful art and a rhymed Haggadah. Detailed.

The Story Haggadah, Sol Scharfstein, art by Arthur Freedman, KTAV, 1990, 83 pages, paper, Hebrew-English, a companion 48-page *Skill Text* activity book is also available. An almost complete Haggadah plus a great deal of additional narrative illustrated in color.

Uh! Oh! Passover Haggadah, Janet Zwebner, Yellow Brick Road, 1994, 48 pages, cloth, Hebrew-English. Incredibly complex pictures have hidden objects in them. Each picture has a different premise. Along the way, kids pick up many clever jokes and informative material as they scour the pages looking for hidden objects. Complete Haggadah runs through every other two-page spread. Unique.

Tapes, Records, and Book-Tape Combinations

Passover, sung by Emanuel Rosenberg, KTAV AY-107. This 45 rpm record was originally done as two records and has been put together out of order here. Nonetheless, Rosenberg has a beautiful voice and sings all or parts of eleven familiar seder songs.

Passover Play and Learn Set, Adam Fisher, art by Katherine Kahn, Jody Wheeler, Marlene Ruthen, Susan Dworski, and Richard Rosenblum, Behrman, 1987, comes with tape and two booklets. The *Passover* booklet explains the holiday simply for the youngest child. The *Passover Activity Book* provides stories, games and puzzles. The tape has two stories from the books and a variety of songs, including an English-language four questions set to a Latin rhythm, and two other seder songs.

Passover Pop-Up Book and Tape, Sol Scharfstein, KTAV, 1987. The book has seven paper sculptures that explain the seder and Exodus story to the youngest child. The tape goes into more detail and includes a child singing the four questions. Of true interest is a version of Kiddush sung beautifully by tenor Emanuel Rosenberg.

Software

Some of the following items are for adults, though if you are like me, your children will have to show you how to use them.

Afikoman Adventures, Davka, 1983. All the *Davka* software is available for IBM or Mac. In this children's game, you take whatever you need from today and travel back to ancient Egypt to find the lost seder afikoman. Many possible dangerous adventures before you find it and return.

All About Passover, Davka, 1983. Color graphics, animation, and sound explain the Exodus story, seder, and instruct on specifics.

Crumb Eater, Davka, 1983. The Muncher, a small yellow bird, has to eat all the crumbs before Passover. Arcade game.

Jewish Compu-Chef, Davka, 1984. Comes with basic recipes, software, and supplemental Passover recipes disk.

Hyperseder, Davka. The seder explained on computer.

Videos

The Animated Haggadah, Scopus Films and Rony Oren, 1985, 24 minutes. Excellent claymation of seder and story of Passover. Fun for the whole family, imaginative and not sanctimonious. Still the best kid's Passover video. Book and activity book are available.

The Joy of Passover, Institute for Creative Jewish Media and Ron and Marlynn Weinstein, 1987, 30 minutes, includes 16-page booklet with background, recipes, and songs. A video of the highlights of one family's seder including singing.

My Exodus, Torah Aura, 1984, 30 minutes, includes 1-page teacher's guide. Companion to Torah Aura's *Passover.* Children relive Exodus, cartoons by Joel Grishaver, music video finale.

Parpar Nechmad: Lovely Butterfly: Passover, Israel Educational Television, 1989, 30 minutes. Hebrew only with puppets, games, songs, and stories. We see an Israeli family's seder, which is the most interesting part of the show, and a Passover story is read.

Passover at Bubbe's Boarding House, Pan-Imago and Jean Doumanian, 1990, 30 minutes. The Mishuga puppets have a seder at Bubbe's with a talking Haggadah that takes them back to the Exodus.

Passover in Story and Song, Israel Music, 40 minutes. The strength of this tape is in its images: the baking of *shemurah* matzo, dancing and gathering the omer of barley, Israeli wildflowers, and many beautiful photos and illustrations of aspects of Passover beyond the seder.

Shalom Sesame Passover, Children's Television Workshop, 1991, 35 minutes. This Jewish episode of *Sesame Street* focuses on Passover; features Sarah Jessica Parker, Anne Meara, Alan King, and Mary Tyler Moore; and is the source for all the songs on one side of the tape that comes with *Kippi and the Missing Matzah,* listed above. Is the Israeli muppet, Kippi, a *kippod* (porcupine) because native-born Israelis are *sabras* (prickly pear cactus, thorny on the outside, but with sweet hearts)?

Chapter Eleven

Mi-Bet Avadim: Out of the House of Bondage

Women and Passover

Passover is supposed to be the Season of Our Freedom, but my mother often remarks that by the time she sits down to the seder table, she is completely exhausted. I can remember my grandmother spending more time in the kitchen than at the table. Must the women do all of the shopping, cleaning, cooking, and serving? Not in our house, and increasingly not in many houses. In a world where the father worked and the mother stayed home with the children, the traditional division of labor might have made sense. It is more common today to find both parents working or the children living with only one parent or any number of other household situations. Since Passover is the original liberation holiday, we should be able to find a way to share the work and free women from the traditional drudgery.

Women of Valor

It is not as if women were absent from the original Passover story. We are told in the first chapter of Exodus, even before we reach the birth of Moses, that Pharaoh commanded the Hebrew midwives, Shiprah and Puah, to kill all the Hebrew baby boys. But they feared God and disobeyed Pharaoh. They told Pharaoh that the Hebrew women were vigorous, not like the weak, pampered Egyptian women, and that they gave birth before the arrival of the midwife. Then Pharaoh bypassed the midwives and decreed that all Hebrew baby boys should be thrown in the Nile. This emphasis on midwives and birth continues in the story of Moses and establishes a motif that is sustained, not only in God's taking retribution on the Egyptians by killing their firstborn, but also in the birth of the Israelites as a nation when they pass through the birth canal of the Red Sea.

By the time his father Amram and mother Jocheved had Moses, they were forced to hide him for three months to keep him from being thrown in the Nile. A midrash says that Moses was born three months prematurely, allowing Jocheved that much time to hide him. After these three months, Jocheved got a wicker basket and caulked it with pitch and bitumen, a tar-like substance used in mummification. (There are echoes here of the dying and reviving god Osiris in his coffin in the Nile.) She placed Moses in the basket and put the basket in the Nile among the bulrushes. Jocheved posted Moses' older sister Miriam nearby to see what would happen.

Soon Pharaoh's daughter, named Bithiah (1 Chronicles 4:19) or Thermutis (in midrash) came down to bathe in the Nile. When she opened the basket and saw the beautiful baby Moses, her heart went out to him. She wanted to raise him as her own.

With perfect timing, Miriam rushed forward and offered to find the princess a Hebrew wet nurse. Of course, that wet nurse turned out to be Moses' own mother, Jocheved. She raised Moses (the midrash explains that he was told that he was a Hebrew), until he was grown up (whatever age that is), and then brought him to the princess, who named him Moses.

Mosheh, Moses, means "born of" or "drawn forth from the water." Moses has that slight aura of illegitimacy that is attached to so many mythic heroes whose fathers are wandering gods just passing through town. The name Moses also suggests that the Hebrew etymology is only there to obscure the Egyptian origins of the name, since the suffix *mosis* can be found in many Egyptian names like Tut-mosis and Ra-mosis, or Rameses, meaning child of the Nile. Oddly, Exodus 6:20 tells us that Jocheved was Amram's father's sister, that is, his aunt.

When Moses reached the age of forty, he was forced to flee to the desert of Midian to escape the wrath of Pharaoh. He had been seen in the act of killing an Egyptian taskmaster for beating a Hebrew slave, one of his kin folks. In Midian he aided the daughters of Jethro, who were being kept from watering their flocks by another tribe of shepherds. Jethro rewarded Moses with the hand of his daughter Zipporah. Following the subsequent incident of the burning bush, Moses, now eighty, set off for Egypt to free his people. At this point we find one of the oddest events in the whole Bible. While camped for the night, God encountered Moses and attempted to kill him. To save her husband, Zipporah realized that she must circumcise their son Gershom. She then touched the foreskin to Moses' legs and twice swore that he was a bridegroom of blood to her. This saved Moses' life. In just these first four chapters of Exodus, then, there have already been six heroines.

A Living Doll, Everywhere You Look —*Sylvia Plath*

The ancient rabbis noticed the importance of women to the Exodus story. The Haggadah includes the verse where Abram (not yet Abraham) is told that "your offspring shall be strangers in a land not theirs, and they shall be enslaved and oppressed four hundred years" (Genesis 15:13). Yet the actual period in Egypt was only 210 years, according to biblical chronology. The time off for good behavior was the result of the Israelite women, as the Talmud says, "Due to the merit of the righteous women in that generation, we were delivered from Egypt."

The Talmud and midrash relate that when the Israelite men, following Amram's lead, separated from their wives so as not to bring babies into an infanticidal world, Miriam argued her father out of this behavior. The Egyptians, like the South African gold mine owners, separated the enslaved men and women. In spite of this, the Hebrew women brought warm food to their men in the fields. They consoled them with their belief in God's promise of redemption. That encouraged the men to believe in a future into which it was worth bringing children. When it was the women's time to give birth, they went out to the apple trees and delivered their babies in silence so that the Egyptians would not know that a Hebrew baby had been born. This is hinted at in lines from the Song of Songs, and is one of the reasons our *charoset* contains apples.

Our ancient foremothers were just as zealous as every other generation of Jewish mothers has been to preserve Jewish culture. Even though women were not given the education that men were, they were responsible for the sanctity of the home, both through ritual immersion and the observance of *kashrut*.

Ironically, though separated from men at the synagogue, discouraged from learning Hebrew, and considered unclean during menstruation, it has been women who have always taken responsibility for ensuring the transmission of Yiddishkeit. Knowing all of this, many women and women's groups and collectives have created women's Haggadot and sedarim. Many of these have been published, and are listed in our review of Haggadot in chapter 5. They offer creative Jewish women a number of ways to make the holiday more meaningful. One option that is open to women is to carry out their own rituals without men. These are often second or third sedarim, done following the traditional first and second evenings, which are usually attended by a wide range of family and friends of both genders. Some men volunteer to cook and serve at these women's ceremonies, while other groups prefer to do everything themselves.

If you do not want to separate from the men, you can still share in the creation of the Haggadah and seder by looking at the Passover themes from a woman's perspective. The Haggadah text can be made gender neutral or even feminized. The *berakhot* can be addressed to the Shekhinah. Simply emphasizing the kabbalistic interpretation of Passover brings out the feminine elements within the ceremony and text. You might try conducting the ceremony and see how the men like doing all the shopping, cleaning, cooking, and serving.

Divide and Conquer

You may be perfectly happy with everything about Passover except for the amount of work that seems to get dumped on the women. The answer to this problem is planning and communication. Sit down with your significant other, male or female, and write down everything that needs to be done and when it needs to be done. Include not just the preparations before and during the seder, but after as well. Then divide up the tasks equitably. Do not begin your preparations on the day before Pesach. Careful planning should allow you to take the whole month from Purim to Passover to shop, cook, and clean.

The sharing of tasks can be extended to include guests as well. Most people appreciate being invited to a seder and are happy to assist in a variety of ways. Turning the meal into a potluck takes some of the pressure off the hosts. Although soup and matzo balls may be hard to transport, gefilte fish, chopped liver, sponge cake, bottles of wine, seder plate symbols, matzo, and hard-boiled eggs can easily be given legs. Guests are usually happy to help with serving and cleanup as well, although my own advice is to clear the table but leave the dirty dishes until after the guests are gone. Paper plates, napkins, cups, and tablecloths, and plastic cutlery, are labor savers. Of course, it is nicer to have china, glass, and metal, but not at the expense of enjoying the holiday. Perhaps a better solution to the cleaning problem, though, is to use paper plates not for the seder, but before the holiday to save time, and again during the holiday for lunches. Another way to save time is to cook ahead and freeze foods. Cookies, casserole entrees, and soup stock, for instance, can all be frozen without any loss of flavor.

Ultimately, that must be your major consideration: At what point does the effort push you past the point of enjoyment? Especially when you are just getting started with having sedarim, keep it simple. What is missing will stand out in high contrast, allowing you to know just what to add on every year. If you try to do everything at once, you will never know what is missing, but you will know that you are unsatisfied. You can always do more next year. If you start with sweet kosher wine, jars of gefilte fishlets, beet horseradish, and matzo ball soup served in paper plates and cups to a few close friends, your seder can only improve over the years. As your cooking and ceremonial skills develop, you will look back fondly on your first rudimentary seders, knowing how far you have moved beyond them.

Chapter Twelve

Be-Chol Dor Va-Dor: In Every Generation

Creating Your Own Family Haggadah

We have examined the seder ceremony and the traditional Haggadah from a variety of points of view, and we have looked at the varieties of Haggadot that are currently available. Still, you may be unsatisfied with your choices. If so, you should consider creating your own Haggadah.

Good to the Last Drop: The Traditional Text

During the pre-Gutenberg years, having any Haggadah was difficult. Handwritten manuscripts were expensive, and many people counted on the memory of whoever was leading the seder. Considering that, it is amazing how uniform Haggadot from a wide range of times and places are. If you pick up a facsimile of a fourteenth-century manuscript like the beautiful *Sarajevo Haggadah,* you will find it as familiar as your grandparents' *Maxwell House* edition. The big changes in texts have taken place in the twentieth century, when Haggadot have been aimed at specific audiences and organized around specific themes.

Assuming that none of these work for you, you should still acquire at least one good traditional text of the Haggadah to use as a basis for your personal text. Then photocopy the whole thing and begin cutting and pasting the parts you like and want to include back into your Haggadah. Some sections will be excluded, some will need retranslation, and new material will need to be added either from your reading or from your own or your family's experiences.

Are You Now or Have You Ever Been: Family Traditions

One way to create your own family Haggadah is to ask everyone in the family about their seder memories. If your grandparents or great-grandparents are alive, *kineahora,* you can ask them for their earliest memories of Pesach. Barring that, ask your parents, aunts, and uncles. For that matter, compare your own memories with those of your siblings or with family friends who were seder regulars.

This book has described many variations in custom. Try to find out what your family's custom was. Did they have parsley or potato for *karpas?* When did they fill the cup of Elijah? Did the *ba'al ha-seder* hide the *afikoman* or did the children steal it and hold it for ransom? Was the *maror* horseradish or romaine lettuce? Were the matzot handmade or machine-made? Did they search for *chametz* and burn it the next morning? Did they dip the karpas in saltwater or vinegar? Were the drops of wine removed with the fingertip or poured out? What melodies do they remember? Did the leader wear a *kittel*? Were the four questions done only in Hebrew or in Yiddish as well? Was the family Ashkenazic or Sephardic? If your family had its own customs, add them to your seder. The Jewish expression is, "A custom in Israel is as binding as law."

If no one can remember anything, or if there is no one to ask, then it is up to you to establish custom for yourself and your children. Read a traditional Haggadah and decide what symbols and rituals make the most sense to you.

You may feel that I have included everything that could possibly be said about Passover in this book. Hardly; in fact, what I have attempted to include are those elements of the holiday that fit together into a coherent system of thought, that I felt were meaningful. Especially as regards dietary laws, I have merely skimmed the surface. I have not mentioned that you should avoid starch (which is chametz) in your tablecloth, or that you should feed your dog and cat non-cereal foods during Pesach. Anyone for whom these rules are important will find them out from other sources.

She Came to Test Him with Hard Questions   —*1 Kings 10:1*

Beyond that type of stringency, I have not found an occasion to mention, for instance, the customs of the Falashas, or Beta Israel (House of Israel), as the Jews of Ethiopia prefer to be called. They believe they are the descendants of Manasseh, the son of King Solomon and the Queen of Sheba. They abstain from leaven for three days before the week-long festival of Fasika, subsisting solely on dried peas and beans until the eve of Passover. From that point, they fast until their high priest slaughters their paschal lamb on the altar in the courtyard of their synagogue. They then sprinkle the blood around the entrance. During the holiday they eat nothing leavened or fermented or which has been kept overnight. They call their unleavened bread *qita* and drink only coffee, *celqa* (a drink made from flour, water, and seeds), and milk straight from the cow. They believe that when milk stands, it ferments. They desist from work during the seven days of the festival, but visit relatives and friends during the five intermediate days. When the holiday ends, the first beer brewed and the first bread baked are brought to the synagogue as an offering.

Although those customs are strikingly unique, we have seen many variations within the traditional framework of Judaism. The Lubavicher Chasidim do not wear the kittel, say Nirtzah, or sing the concluding *zemirot*. The Vilna Gaon only used two matzot instead of three. Most Sephardim do not eat hard-boiled eggs before the meal. The Jews of Yemen do not have the cup of Elijah. You are free to create the symbol system that works for you. Try to arrive at it naturally, so that your system is not merely an arbitrary mental construct. Whatever novelties you create will be the customs of the next generation of your family. Will they be strong enough and coherent enough to last for millennia?

Depending on your own level of knowledge, you may want to alter a number of things in a traditional Haggadah. Since fewer people today have a thorough acquaintance with Hebrew, you may want to enlarge the Hebrew text, easy to do on today's photocopiers. For the same reason, you may want to transliterate all, most, or the key parts of the Haggadah. It is amazing how little transliteration is available in most Haggadot. If you are musically literate, you may want to add notation for the song texts. Many Haggadot that do include transliteration and notation put them in a separate section in the back of the book. This just confuses people, making them fumble and feel self-conscious. By making your own Haggadah, even if you only make design changes, you can put everything where you want it. You can not only number pages, but lines as well, making it easier to call on people to read and for them to find their place. You can isolate discrete parts of the text so that the arrangement of the material on the page conveys the structure of the content. Do not worry if these suggestions and additions increase the bulk of the Haggadah. Most guests will be glad to see you whipping through the pages rather than taking forever to read a page.

According to the level of your Hebrew skills, you can either make your own translations or browse various Haggadot in search of good translations. Many parts of the Haggadah come from classical Jewish texts—Tanakh, Mishnah, Talmud, midrash, *siddur.* You can look at various translations of these sacred books to get more ideas about the original content of these writings. Even if you do not retranslate the whole Haggadah, you may want to eliminate antiquated expressions like Thee, Thou, Thy, Thine, and so on, and at the same time make the text gender neutral. Today, whether you are a feminist or not, all the references to our forefathers, fathers, and sons feels exclusionist. There is no loss of meaning, and certainly an increase of meaningfulness for at least half of our people, if we substitute ancestors, parents, and children. With computers, desktop publishing, and Xerox machines, the mechanics of creating your own Haggadah can be physically easy. Still, it is a serious responsibility:

> *It is dangerous to leave written that which is badly written. A chance word, upon paper, may destroy the world. Watch carefully and erase, while the power is still yours, I say to myself, for all that is put down, once it escapes, may rot its way into a thousand minds, the corn become a black smut, and all libraries, of necessity, be burned to the ground as a consequence. Only one answer: write carelessly so that nothing that is not green will survive.*
> —William Carlos Williams

Good to Eat a Thousand Years *—Allen Ginsberg*

We should know by now that the Haggadah is attempting to do more than tell the linear story of the Exodus from Egypt. If all we do is to transform the Haggadah from a complex, provocative, sacred text into a clear, straightforward narrative, we may create something devoid of mystery, good for a few sedarim, but not forever. The same is true of the ritual complexities, symbols, and music. Most of these have been around for centuries if not millennia. To arbitrarily change them may mean the loss of key psychical triggers. It might be better to experience the traditional seder and Haggadah for a few years, even if in an abbreviated form, than to throw it aside precipitously for an unknown quantity.

Still, if you decide to make major changes, take inspiration from the fact that the Haggadah as we know it today would have been quite unfamiliar to most of our people throughout our earliest history. An occasional passage from the Torah might catch their ear, but they would not get too excited until Hallel began. This they would have heard whenever they took their paschal sacrifice to Jerusalem. It was only after the destruction of the Temple in 70 C.E. that the Mishnaic core of the Haggadah as we know it came into being. The zemirot at the end of our Haggadah are the most recent additions, dating from the late Middle Ages or even the early Renaissance.

Just as this book has added one layer after another to what is Passover, so each generation of Jews has added layer after layer to the Haggadah and seder. This was not done methodically, first creating symbols, then ritual, text, music, and food. Instead, as new elements bubbled up from the Jewish unconscious, they were added to the festival proceedings. If they resonated with what was already there and with the ongoing experiences of our wandering Aramean kinfolks, they had a chance to become permanent parts of our tradition. If not, they were forgotten or laid aside. You can do the same with your own family Haggadah. Throw it on your computer and edit it anew every year. Eliminate whatever you can no longer say with feeling, and over the years you will create your Haggadah of the future.

Background Books

Besides the Haggadot reviewed in chapter 5, you might want to look for more background information in the following texts. You would do well to own an English translation of the Bible like the Jewish Publication Society *Tanakh;* a Hebrew-English Bible like the Koren from Feldheim; a Pentateuch with *haftarot,* either the Hertz from Soncino or Aryeh Kaplan's *Living Torah* from Moznaim; a translation and commentary of the Song of Songs, either with the classic commentaries of the Netziv or Alshekh that view the lovers as God and Israel, or Marcia Falk's modern, erotic translation; a good *siddur* like those edited by Philip Birnbaum and published by Hebrew Publishing or the Hertz from Bloch, which includes the *Ethics of the Fathers;* a Passover *machzor* like those from Birnbaum, Metsudah, or Mesorah; a *Code of Jewish Law,* like the Ganzfried from Hebrew Publishing; and a current Jewish calendar such as the beautiful one done annually by Hugh Lauter Levin showing the holidays, new moons, Torah portions, and candle-lighting times.

The Art of Passover, compiled and edited by Rabbi Stephan Parnes, with essays by Bonni-Dara Michaels and Gabriel Goldstein, MacMillan, 1994, 199 pages, cloth. Another production of Hugh Lauter Levin Associates, this one has fifty-four color plates displaying 800 years of Jewish art in paintings, illuminated manuscripts, seder plates, wine goblets and other seder artifacts. They range from magnificent and famous artifacts to a heartbreaking wooden seder plate made at Theresienstadt concentration camp. Text gives insight into the Jewish approach to making beautiful objects for the glory of God.

Laws of Pesach: A Digest, Rabbi Abraham Blumenkrantz, C.I.S., 1994, 27 individually numbered chapters, paper. Revised annually, this small volume includes just about everything you need to know to fulfill the laws of Passover from the most stringent point of view. There are long lists of foods, beverages and wine, kitchen products, cosmetics, and medications that are and are not kosher for Passover. Along the way we are told about the feeding habits of tuna, the difference between true endive and witloof chicory, and how much rodent hair and feces the USDA allows in our food. Almost every possible eventuality is considered. For instance, what would you do if you found a piece of chametz on Shabbat after chametz was burned on Friday morning, as could have happened in 1994?

> It may not be thrown into the bathroom because it is Muktzeh (not to be touched the whole Shabbos). However, it may be moved only in a way that one handles something that is Muktzeh. . . . In order to throw it into the bathroom, one has to kick the Chometz with his foot or elbow, or lift up the piece of Chometz with his elbows and throw it in the bathroom and immediately flush the water.

I see the makings of a new Olympic event here. For the most observant, this is a useful book. I could not put it down.

Mishneh Torah Hilchot Chametz U'Matzah, Moses Maimonides, translated by Rabbi Eliyahu Touger, Moznaim, 1988, 198 pages, cloth, Hebrew-English. The single most important commentary to Jewish law is

Maimonides' *Mishneh Torah.* This volume deals with the eight mitzvot of Passover having to do with ridding our homes of chametz, eating only matzo, and telling the story of Exodus at the seder. To fulfill that last commandment, Maimonides furnishes us with his Haggadah, which is almost identical to the Haggadah of Rav Amram Gaon as well as to our own, demonstrating the continuity of tradition over 1,100 years.

Passover, Mordell Klein, Leon Amiel Publishing, 1973, 120 pages, cloth. Brief but comprehensive, Klein covers history, laws, and customs of Passover, Haggadah, and seder. This excellent work is derived from material in the *Encyclopedia Judaica.*

Passover Anthology, Philip Goodman, Jewish Publication Society, 1961, 496 pages, paper. This volume in Goodman's excellent series on holidays brings together a wide range of materials about Passover to give a multifaceted view of the holiday that roves through all Jewish space and time. It includes this often reprinted benediction written by rabbis imprisoned at Bergen-Belsen in 1944, when there was no matzo and the inmates were forced to eat chametz during Passover: "Our Father in heaven, behold it is evident and known to Thee that it is our desire to do Thy will and to celebrate the festival of Passover by eating matzo and by observing the prohibition of chametz. But our heart is pained that the enslavement prevents us and we are in danger of our lives. Behold, we are prepared and ready to fulfill Thy commandment: 'And ye shall live by and not die by them.' Therefore our prayer to Thee is that Thou mayest keep us alive and preserve us and redeem us speedily so that we may observe Thy statutes and do Thy will and serve Thee with a perfect heart. Amen."

Passover: Its History and Traditions, Theodor Gaster, Greenwood, 1949, 102 pages, cloth. Gaster evidences his linked conception of ritual and story: The story of Passover tells us about the seder meal, just as much as the meal tells us about Exodus. The most interesting material deals with possible meaning of the word Pesach.

The Passover Seder: Afikoman in Exile, Ruth Fredman, University of Pennsylvania, 1981, 168 pages, cloth. Scholarly look at a holiday that celebrates the end of exile, but is observed in exile. A beautiful appreciation of the cycle of Jewish life from an anthropologist who is as passionate as she is intelligent. Shot through with brilliant insights and deep feeling for subject. One of my favorites.

The Pesach Seder: A Practical Guide, Rabbi Label Sharfman, National Conference of Synagogue Youth, 1985, 32 pages, paper, Hebrew-English. Brief but quite comprehensive Orthodox guide to what you need to know to carry out the seder ceremony.

Tractate Pesahim, edited and translated by Rabbi I. Epstein and Rabbi H. Freedman, Soncino Press, 1990, 121 folios (242 pages of Talmud), cloth. The ancient rabbinical disputations that established how we would celebrate Pesach in the Diaspora. Each two-page spread includes a facsimile of a folio page of the Talmud in Hebrew and Aramaic from the standard late-nineteenth-century Vilna edition of Widow Romm and Brothers, with facing English translation of Mishnah and Gemara, but not Rashi or later commentators, although copious notes often draw from these sources.

Special Needs

A Curriculum Guide and Suggested Activities and Experiences for Teachers of Children with Retarded Mental Development in Jewish Religious Schools: Holiday Cycle: Passover Unit, Hershel Stiskin, Jewish Education Committee, 44 pages, paper.

If you are visually impaired or blind, contact the Jewish Braille Institute of America, 110 East 30th Street, New York, NY 10157-0105. They will lend the *Haggadah of Philip Birnbaum* and the *New Union Haggadah* in large print, tape, or Braille, at no charge when you provide a doctor's letter stating your condition. Write for more information.

If you have a wheat allergy and need oat matzo, contact the Satmar Matzo Bakery in New York City at 718-388-4008; or call E. Kestenbaum in England at 011-44-1-455-9476 or 6550, or fax him at 011-44-1-455-5245.

La-Shanah Ha-Ba'ah Bi-Yerushalayim: Next Year in Jerusalem

The Cycle of the Jewish Year

This last chapter brings us full circle, from one to thirteen and back again. Originally, I thought this chapter would be a summing up of what has gone before, an answer to why we celebrate Passover year after year. For instance, we know that the story of the Exodus epitomizes the Jewish experience in history: strangers in a strange land, enslaved, persecuted, genocide in the offing, and then freedom, departure for our own land:

> *All its further destinies are prefigured in its origin.*
> —Franz Rosenzweig

The Holocaust and the subsequent creation of the State of Israel are only the most recent enactment of this central myth of our people. Perhaps we can best understand the mixture of mournfulness and celebration that characterizes the holiday if we project contemporary events backward onto the past. Certainly the words, "In every generation each of us should personally feel that we have been brought out of Egypt," take on new meaning in this context. Even though on this night we are free, we cannot easily forget 210 years of Egyptian bondage any more than the return to Zion can make us forget the 6 million:

All of humanity would do well to celebrate the spirit of
Pesach. Shall we forget it?
—Chaim Zhitlowsky

Keeping Passover

On the calendar Passover represents the beginning of spring. When we were shepherds and farmers, this was the time of harvesting winter wheat, the birth of new lambs, and looking forward to the barley harvest seven weeks later at Shavuot. These symbols, a part of which were offered to God as a sacrifice, became concatenated with the events surrounding our origin as a people: the matzo, wheat, both the bread of affliction and of freedom that the Israelites had no time to let rise; and the paschal lamb, its blood smeared on the doorposts of the house as a sign to God to pass over the homes of the Israelites. Animistic, agricultural, cultic, political, communal, and spiritual elements are all wrapped up in the celebration of Passover. And history. Perhaps the story tells of our nomadic Semitic ancestors settling in Egypt during the reign of the Hyksos, intruding Semitic rulers of Egypt; our lowered social and economic status when native Egyptian pharaohs regained the throne; and the long period of wandering back to Canaan that followed. Of course we want to eat and drink, to sing and laugh, but we also want to remember why we are celebrating. That question has been answered frequently throughout the preceding pages. Some of the recurring themes include:

> Initiation of the youngest into the tribe through ritual drama, and reinitiation of older participants, just as there could be a second initiation at Eleusis or as Australian aborigines recircumcise on a regular basis;
>
> Reconnection with fellow Jews, Jewish family, and past through a specifically Jewish event;

Commemoration of the liberation from bondage in
Egypt and the Exodus from there;

These lead to identification and a sense of obligation
toward the stranger, outsider, enslaved, homeless, persecuted, because we have been strangers in a strange land;

A longing for freedom and a hatred of tyranny, as well
as a sense of freedom even under tyranny;

A love for the Land of Israel and a hope for a redemption
that includes peace and freedom for the whole world;

An awareness of the reawakening of spring and our connection to the earth and its cycles;

A time to take stock of ourselves, to put our lives in
order, to be reflective and humble, to puncture our
pomposity;

An opportunity to sweep our homes and our psyches
clean of accumulated debris:

Now, in the time of spring (azaleas, trilliums, myrtle, vibur-
nums, daffodils, blue phlox), between that disgust and this,
between the things that are on the dump (azaleas and so on)
and those that will be (azaleas and so on), one feels the puri-
fying change. One rejects the trash.
—Wallace Stevens

These all seem like positive results; but stating them glibly can
only begin to convey the profound complexity that is achieved
when these themes, conveyed through food, song, ritual, symbol,
and text, interact with one another, with our life experiences, family past, and knowledge of Jewish history. Although we have mentioned many meanings, we cannot assign final limiting meanings
to any part of the Passover experience. To nail down the meaning

of a piece of literature, a painting, or a moment of life is a reductionist strategy. We reduce experiences to control them, to hold them at arm's length, to keep them from affecting us:

> . . . *to drive the dagger in his heart, to lay his brain upon the board and pick the acrid colors out, to nail his thought across the door, its wings spread wide to rain and snow, to strike his living hi and ho . . .*
>
> —Wallace Stevens

Instead of closing ourselves up by fixing meanings once and for all, we need to be open to the seder experience so that its magic can work repeatedly. We have talked about the seder as a magical ceremony, how it allows us to have an affect upon the universe. At the same time, it works its magic on us. It distracts our minds for a moment, gives them an enormous quantity of food for thought as well as sustenance, while simultaneously asking us to perform a wild repertoire of *mishegaas,* as if we were required to explain the theory of relativity while simultaneously patting our heads and rubbing our stomachs. Somewhere along the way, we give up trying to sort it all out and just let it take over. One year the seder is tremendously moving, the next it is a bore, then again it is *haimish* or heartfelt or funny or simple or sad. And that is as it should be. We are not in charge. If we derive a meaning from it, that is fine, but that does not control what it might be like the next year, or even the next night. Many a second seder has seen the completion of an incubation that began the night before.

Yes, we can think, read, study, talk, even write about it in a pure, cerebral way. That is not the same as keeping Passover. When we engage with it as ritual, we lose or give up control. Maybe you bring off the ceremony flawlessly, everyone joins in enthusiastic singing, the banquet is superb, old friends and family are present after long absence. Or maybe the matzo balls are too light or too heavy, someone cancels at the last moment, a child cries because he or she did not find the *afikoman,* a guest makes a thoughtless remark that hurts your feelings. A seder will more likely be a conglomeration of both sets of experiences, success and failure, pleasure and pain, the sweet and the bitter. We prefer success, the *charoset,* but we can be equally moved or taught by the bitter herb of failure. The seder has structure and protection, but, as in vodoun rituals or the Japanese tea ceremony, these provide the safety net that allows for chance, the unexpected, for meaning:

> *Everything in this world can be imitated except truth,*
> *for truth once imitated is no longer truth.*
> —Menachem Mendel of Kotzk

The real question, however, is not why do we keep Passover, but how do we continue to keep Passover year after year and keep it from becoming stultified? How can we be privileged to plan it so that, as Rabbi Kook put it, "the old may become new and the new may become holy?"

Will the Circle Be Unbroken: Holidays for Gladness, Festivals and Seasons for Rejoicing

One way we keep Passover is by carrying it into the rest of our year, making it the center of our Jewish life. At the conclusion of the formal seder, before the concluding *zemirot,* we say, *"Le-Shanah ha-Ba'ah Bi-Yerushalayim"*—"Next Year in Jerusalem!" We say this at one other time of the year: at the close of Yom Kippur services. In both cases, at the moment of saying it, we have just completed painstaking rites that make us complete before God. We have carried out our part of the covenant and expect God to reciprocate. At Passover we have rid our homes of *chametz* and carried out our elaborate seder. At Yom Kippur we have abstained from food and drink for twenty-five to twenty-six hours while performing five heartfelt prayer services. If we look at the Jewish calendar, we can see that the cycle of the year revolves around two poles, Passover at the vernal equinox and Rosh Ha-Shanah/Yom Kippur/Sukkot at the autumnal equinox. The remainder of the holidays are all in relation to these twin poles.

Although both holidays have contradictory elements in them, Passover is basically a celebratory event ushering in the new year in the spring. We put ourselves into coherence with the seasons following the dull winter months. After being cooped up and in the dark, we shake ourselves out of our winter lethargy and wake up to the new life. We do this at the equinox, the moment when light and dark are perfectly balanced, but with light in the ascendant. Half a year goes by, and we again need to bring coherence into our lives after an equally dull, uneventful summer. Like our tires, we need balancing and alignment. We notice that the days are beginning to dwindle and we think about our lives in relation to the limited amount of time available to us. Although we are able to celebrate the new year in the fall, there is a greater sense of awe and solemnity. We worry about what the approaching year has in store for us. Rosh Ha-Shanah and Yom Kippur allow us to enter this down side of the year with some introspection and soul-searching. Again, this occurs at the equinox, but now the dark is in the ascendant. Balanced between these two poles, these moments of transition, lie all the other holidays of the Jewish year, strung out like a chain of islands in time.

The year as a whole is marked off into twelve lunar months by the slightly off-balance reappearance of the moon every twenty-nine and a half days. This is noted by Rosh Chodesh, the new moon. Special prayers and additional services are said, Half-Hallel is read, a pertinent Torah portion on the new moon ritual in the Temple is chanted, and we may not fast or mourn. It is a little holiday but also a "little day of atonement," Yom Kippur Katan. The kabbalists of Safed made it a day for spiritual renewal. From the third to the fifteenth day of the month, usually just after Shabbat, we can sanctify the new moon through a celebratory custom from talmudic times. A minyan gathers outdoors and rejoices in the swelling proportions of the waxing moon, a sign of abundance and happiness. Even more powerful than the new moon is the regular marking off of each phase of the moon by the regular weekly recurrence of Shabbat, an oasis of peace and rest in a desert of drudgery, a time in which we are forbidden to work so that larger realms can be given time in our lives. Punctuating the comforting regular return of the Shabbat and Rosh Chodesh are the less obvious patterns of *yom tovim*.

Exactly two months to the day before Passover, we celebrate the minor holiday of Tu bi-Shevat on the fifteenth of Shevat. This represents a dividing line between winter and the coming spring. All fruit grown before that date was produce of the preceding year. All fruit after that date, the New Year of the Trees, was considered produce of the new year. The Safed mystics saw the relation between Passover and Tu bi-Shevat, and they created a seder for the minor holiday complete with a special Haggadah whose ritual included the eating of a large number of different fruits, many associated with Israel, and four cups of wine. The wine was drunk in a unique pattern: the first cup was white for winter; the second, white with a little red; the third, red with some white; and, finally, a cup of wholly red wine, in honor of the coming spring of ripe fruit and blooming flowers. It is traditional to eat preserves made from the *etrogim* (citrons) used at Sukkot.

Purim, Jewish carnival, comes one month later, on the fourteenth of Adar, although in Jerusalem and other ancient walled cities, it is celebrated on the fifteenth. Like Passover and Chanukkah, Purim celebrates a political victory over an oppressor. This is a time of excess, when we are to get so drunk we cannot distinguish between the villain Haman and the hero Mordecai, when people don costumes and men and women are allowed to cross-dress. It parallels the ancient Near Eastern festival of Marduk and Ishtar (in our historicized version, Mordecai and Esther), in which a substitute king must die to ensure the fertility of the land. In our story Mordecai is the first substitute king, when Haman leads him around town wearing the king's clothes and riding on the king's horse. Later, though, Haman takes Mordecai's place on the gallows. Similarly, on Passover, the Egyptian firstborn take our place. Tradition has it that Haman was hanged on Passover, as we learn from the poem by Kallir sung at the second seder (text v). Indeed, he is said to have ascended the gallows on the second day of Passover, so Kallir's *piyyut* is especially appropriate for the second seder.

After the passage of another month, Pesach arrives on the fifteenth of Nisan, our third full moon holiday in a row. Following carnival and its excess, Passover is a period of restriction. The month between the two holidays is used to prepare for Pesach. The text of the Haggadah and the laws of the festival are studied. Especially relevant prayers, readings, and Torah and *haftarah* portions, are recited before, during, and after Passover. Somewhere during this period, the Song of Songs is chanted according to the traditions of the various Jewish communities. The house must be cleaned, the kitchen changed over, chametz must be disposed of, locked up, sold, and burned. Some use the palm frond from Sukkot to sweep up chametz. Bits of the candles and wicks left over from Chanukkah are used to start the chametz bonfires, a burning up of winter. Special food and wine for the eight days must be set aside. On the day after the search for chametz, the fires for the baking of matzot are started using the willows left over from Sukkot. We are making a connection between the vernal and autumnal equinoxes. That evening we have our first seder.

On the following night, we have a second seder. The reason for two sedarim in the Diaspora is that, before the calendar was fixed, Jews outside of Israel could not be sure of the exact date of the holiday. To avoid missing the correct moment of performing the seder, the rabbis added a second day of yom tov outside of Eretz Yisrael. The second seder also gives families the chance to celebrate each seder with one set of in-laws or with different sets of friends. It can be a smaller, more intimate, cozy event for immediate family and a friend or two. It removes the pressure of having just one chance to get it right, while also allowing us to introduce an element of variety into the seder by singing alternative melodies to the familiar songs or adding supplementary readings. We begin the counting of the omer at the second seder.

Recently, some have added the custom of a third seder focused on some particular concern in contemporary Jewish life: equality for women; Jewish-gentile relations; Jewish-African-American coherences; Jews living under the imminent threat of destruction, as with the Jews of the former Soviet Union or the Falashas of Ethiopia; peace between the Israelis and the Palestinians. Some have added a fifth cup of wine, a fourth matzo, or an empty place setting at their regular sedarim in sympathy with those of our tribe who cannot openly carry out our ancient traditions. If these ideas appeal to you, they can be made as personal or all-encompassing as you like. Many recent Haggadot provide readings that can be used with these ceremonies.

The first two and the last two days of Passover are full holidays. We light candles in the evening before each of these days. The middle four days are *chol ha-moed* (half-holidays), on which many of the holiday restrictions, though none of the food laws, are lifted. Although full Hallel is recited on the first two days of Pesach, only the Half-Hallel is recited during the morning service on chol ha-moed and the final two full holidays. This is out of respect for the Egyptians who drowned in the Red Sea. In fact, it is assumed that the crossing of the Red Sea took place on the seventh day of Pesach. The song sung by the Israelites at the Red Sea is chanted in the synagogue, and there is a custom of gathering that evening at a body of water or before a container of water to commemorate the miracle.

Jewish tradition has it that all the water in the world, even that in bowls and vessels, split at the same time as the Red Sea. On the final day, Yizkor (memorial prayer) is recited in Ashkenazic synagogues.

The Jews of North Africa conclude the Passover holiday with the Maimuna celebration. The name comes either from the Arabic for "good fortune" or the Hebrew *emunah* (belief), indicating faith in a future redemption in Nisan. It is also associated with the commemoration of the death of Moses Maimonides' father, Maimon, who died on the last day of the holiday. At sunset, at the end of the eighth day of Passover, the table is set with dairy foods and various symbols: sheaves of wheat, flowers, and greenery; a dish of flour with wheat stalks, beans, coins, and paper money; a bowl of yeast, sometimes immersed in the wine from the cup of Elijah, which will be used to make the first loaf of bread after Passover the next day; and a live fish in a bowl of water, a symbol of fertility. When friends and relatives visit throughout the night, they are given a leaf of lettuce dipped in honey, symbolizing spring, new crops, and sweetness, as well as sweetness overwhelming bitter herbs. The following day there are picnics in the country.

As soon as the first day of Pesach is over, we begin to count the omer. The order that begins at the seder continues into the year. The first week of the counting of the omer ends on the last day of Passover. Six more weeks of counting go by until Shavuot is reached, seven weeks of seven days of counting. This ominous forty-nine-day period is punctuated on the thirty-third day of counting by Lag Ba-Omer, a momentary release from the semi-mourning period. The wheat harvest and liberation from bondage are followed by the prayer for dew on the first day of Passover, which eventually culminates in the barley harvest and the receiving of the Torah at Sinai. Freedom, the creation of a people, is linked, by the counting off of the days until Shavuot, to the giving of the Torah at Sinai. Freedom is completed with law.

The year rolls along through the nontransitional summer without differentiating the days until midsummer and the fast of Shivah

Asar be-Tammuz, the seventeenth of Tammuz. On that day Nebuchadnezzar breached the walls of Jerusalem. A three week period of
mourning follows, capped by Tishah Be-Av, the ninth of Av and the
saddest day in the Jewish year. On this day both the first and second
Temples were destroyed. It is the custom to fast and sit on the floor,
as we do when mourning, reading the Book of Lamentations. The
ascending part of the year is poised at its zenith for the beginning of
its descent. In the following month of Elul, in the weeks before the
New Year, *selichot* (penitential prayers) are recited.

The lamentations and penitence lead up to Rosh Hashanah,
the first of Tishri and the New Year, when we pray to be inscribed
in the book of life for a good year. The first of Nisan is also the beginning of the year, so the year begins at two points, emphasizing
the circular, nonlinear, Möbius-strip nature of Jewish time. The
world's creation, when the Spirit of God hovered over the face of
the deep, began at Rosh Hashanah. The creation of the Jewish people began at Passover, when they came through the Red Sea. The
world and the Jewish people are born out of purifying water. Indeed, on the first day of Rosh Hashanah, we go to a running stream
of water to perform Tashlikh, the emptying of our pockets of bread
crumbs, as a symbolic way of washing away our sins. Just as we
searched out crumbs and eliminated them with fire at Pesach, so
now we eliminate them with water at Rosh Hashanah.

An ominous period of ten days follows until Yom Kippur, the
Day of Atonement. Just as we wear the *kittel* at Passover, so we wear
it again at Yom Kippur. Just as we begin our telling at the seder
with the Aramaic Ha Lachma Anya, so we begin Yom Kippur with
the Aramaic Kol Nidre. We say, "Next year in Jerusalem!" at both
holidays. A midrash tells us that the King of Nineveh who repents
in the Book of Jonah, which is read on Yom Kippur, is none other
than the Pharaoh of the Exodus story. After his failure in Egypt, he
was still able to gain employment in the family trade by pulling up
stakes and relocating to Assyria. When Jonah arrives, he has already
learned his lesson and repents immediately.

On the full moon comes the Festival of Booths, Sukkot, the autumnal equinox, exactly six months after Passover. Both holidays are seven days long (eight in the Diaspora). This holiday is associated with the forty years in the wilderness, when the Israelites lived in booths, as well as the fall harvest, when the people lived in the fields in makeshift structures. The last ceremony of Sukkot is the triplicate beating of the willows from the four species in a final plea for atonement. The palm frond from the four species will be saved to sweep up chametz on the night before the first seder, while the willows will be used to start the fires of the matzo oven on *erev* Pesach. On the final day of Sukkot, the two-day holiday of Shemini Atzeret begins. This has the same concluding function as the final day of Passover. Simchat Torah, a celebration of the Torah, when people dance in the synagogue with the five scrolls, takes place on the second day. The circularity of the year is emphasized by completing and beginning again the annual reading of the Torah. All three of the pilgrimage holidays are linked together, agriculturally and historically.

The final holiday of our cycle is Chanukkah, which falls close to the winter solstice. Now the days are at their shortest and darkest, so we light candles, one on the first day and so on until, on the last day, we light eight candles. By imitative magic, mimesis, we urge the sun to begin to increase in strength. We also celebrate the Maccabbean victory over the Seleucid Syrians. Interestingly, almost exactly six months from the fast of Tammuz in midsummer, comes the fast of Asarah be-Tevet, the tenth of Tevet, in midwinter. It commemorates Nebuchadnezzar besieging Jerusalem. At this point the year reaches its nadir and begins to turn around again:

> *If winter comes, can spring be far behind?*
> —Percy Bysshe Shelley

Not only does the year rotate around Passover, but the actual days of the festivals fall according to the days of Passover. The first day of Passover can never fall on a Monday, Wednesday, or Friday. That means the first seder can never be on Sunday, Tuesday, or

Thursday night. If we look at the first days of the other holidays, we find that Tishah Be-Av will always fall on the same day of the week as the first day of Passover. (This connection between Tishah Be-Av and Passover illuminates one of the reasons for eating the hard-boiled egg at the seder: mourning for the Temple.) Shavuot will fall on the same day as the second day of Passover; Rosh Ha-Shanah, the third day; Simchat Torah, the fourth day; Yom Kippur, the fifth day; and Purim, the sixth day. Passover is linked in this way to most of the other holidays.

Passover begins the cycle of the Jewish year, commemorating the liberation from bondage in Egypt and the Exodus towards Eretz Yisrael. On the seventh day leaving Egypt, the Israelites crossed the Red Sea. On the fifty-first day, they received the Torah on Mount Sinai. That is Shavuot. In the fall, when we celebrate Sukkot, we are commemorating the forty years in the wilderness after the Sinai revelation. The year then begins its downward swing, which will paradoxically lead to a new beginning. As we approach that new beginning, each successive Passover, we eagerly anticipate redemption, our return to Zion, an end to our wandering in the wilderness. Since we were first redeemed in Nisan, so will we be redeemed in a future Nisan.

By synchronizing our life cycles with the natural cycles of the seasons and the heavens, by observing and keeping the rest of the cycle of the holidays, we extend the meaning of Passover. We place Passover within the context of the year and the year within the context of Passover. Does this mean we have to do everything at once? We can give the same answer as Franz Rosenzweig, when asked if he prayed wearing *tefillin:* "Not yet." Keeping Passover can be the beginning of our growing into an organic, coherent, personally arrived at Jewish practice:

> *If only we were able to perform the mitzvot with simple sincerity. "The Torah was not given to ministering angels" (Berakhot 25 b). A person should choose one mitzvah*

> *and observe it strictly, with all its fine points; all the other*
> *mitzvot should be kept without any stringencies whatsoever.*
> —Rabbi Nachman of Bratslav

The Torah Speaks of Four Children

Passover permeates not only the remainder of the year, but the totality of our lives. It helps us define our sense of ourselves as Jews. The parable of the four children, which is all of us at one time or another, tells us how the wise child thinks and thinks about what it all means, explaining it and reexplaining it, never completely satisfied with the explanations. The wicked child rails against it, denies its call, tries unsuccessfully to break away from it. The simple child is happily Jewish without a great deal of thinking, doubting and considering. The first answer learned remains satisfactory.

But who are the ones who do not know what to ask? That is when we have no questions, are neither angry nor happy. We take being Jewish for granted, attach neither positive nor negative qualities to it, and never look for a meaning in it beyond our own brief lives. It has as much significance as curly or straight hair, left- or right-handedness. We then forget that in Europe, being a Jew was difficult, but knowing how to be Jewish was easy. We understand that in America, being a Jew is easy, but fail to see that knowing how to be Jewish is difficult.

In Europe both the world outside of us and our own people insisted on our Judaism. We suffered, but we had community. The ghetto walls not only kept us in; they kept the non-Jewish world out. In America there is neither ghetto nor walls. Being Jewish can no longer be done passively. How to be Jewish becomes a large responsibility, yet so many of us do not know how to begin. The Haggadah tells us that with the one who does not know what to ask, we must begin, we must open the discussion and say, "This is on account of what the Lord did for me when I went out from Egypt." "This," says the Haggadah, refers to the matzo and bitter herbs before us on the night of the seder. The seder itself is the answer to the question. Even if we sit at the table alone now, at the end of the twentieth century, we must still ask the questions of ourselves.

Ten Rungs

Provocatively, Passover does not allow us to stop with just our own Jewish pride. It makes us go out of ourselves and identify with anyone who is oppressed or alone:

> *You shall not oppress a stranger, for you know the heart*
> *of a stranger, seeing you were strangers in the land of Egypt.*
> —Exodus 23:9

In doing that it stepped outside of any kind of narrow chauvinism. It achieved the authority to speak about the whole human condition. Not only are the Jewish people in exile from the Holy Land, our souls are in exile from God. This is the plight, not just of the Jewish people, but of every human being. Our survival, our perseverance, our triumphs in spite of impossible odds, the painfully won wisdom of forty centuries of wandering, of being uprooted, homeless, and persecuted, can now serve as a guide and an emblem for a world in which those experiences are now the common lot.

The *tzaddik,* Rabbi Menachem Mendel of Kotzk, told the story (a beautiful Jewish elaboration of a detail in a Rosicrucian parable) of how our souls descended from heaven via a ladder. Heaven calls to the souls, but the ladder is gone. Some souls never try to get back, while others leap for the bottom rung of the ladder but fall and finally give up. Still there are those who know the futility of trying, yet never abandon their effort. Sometimes God catches hold of them and pulls them up to that first rung.

You Are There

The seder is God's strong hand and outstretched arm reaching down to help us back to wholeness:

> *Now that my ladder's gone, I must lie down where all the*
> *ladders start, in the foul rag-and-bone shop of the heart.*
> —William Butler Yeats

The Haggadah text and seder ritual and symbols are like a time capsule, or survival kit, or genetic code of everything Jewish, our memories of the past and dreams of the future. Like a time capsule, it contains representative fragments that remind us of each of our incarnations: wandering shepherds and farmers, slaves in a foreign land, wanderers again, a federation of clans, a kingdom of priests, exiles, honeybees carrying the pollen of civilization from culture to culture, further wandering, further descent into bondage, while at the same time creating an invisible democratic, self-governing country of the mind that spanned the globe, the return to our land, all of this repeating and repeating for millennia. Pick up a fragment of an Aramaic invitation from Babylonia, and stuck to it you'll find something to do with the expulsion from Spain in 1492. Another shard from the Middle Ages about a biblical figure is tied up with a bit of medieval philosophy and a Holocaust story. It is a jumble, but somehow everything is evoked. And as we have been privileged to perform it, we are in it too.

Like a survival kit, it contains everything necessary for enduring the most hostile environments. Here are the basic myths, parables, legends and stories, the modes of thought, the paradigms, the symbols and rituals, the questioning, the commentary, the intense analysis, the food and songs, the humor and pathos, that are the Jewish people. In it is everything else that is Jewish apart from Passover as well. All the rest of the calendar, the holidays, the diet, the law, our languages, history, culture and customs, the reverence for learning and love of Israel, all are implicit in Passover.

Like a genetic code, it contains the bare minimum amount of genetic information to allow one generation to produce the succeeding Jewish generation. As long as the seder is carried out, there is the possibility of the Jewish people continuing. As long as we continue to keep it, so will it keep us.

At the end of the Haggadah, we say Nirtzah, asserting that we have finished the seder and we pray that our service will be accepted. The Alter Rebbe, Shneur Zalman of Lyady, the founder of Chabad Chasidism, removed this closing section of the ceremony from his Haggadah. He felt that there could be no end to the seder:

> *To be sure, the illumination of every festival radiates every day; but the festival of Pesach extends continuously.*
> —Shneur Zalman of Lyady

The more we discuss the Exodus from Egypt, the more it will open to us. The more we know its collection of paradigms, stories, riddles, parables, and poems, the more applicable its lessons become to every aspect of our lives. If this were nothing but the performance of an antiquated ceremonial relic, a fossil from the Jewish past, kept out of duty, guilt, to make our elders happy, then we might as well stop keeping it. If we continue to keep it, and we do, it is because of its meaning to our own lives now. "In every generation each of us should personally feel that we have been brought out of Egypt." That is the labor of a lifetime; and in keeping Passover, in the Haggadah and seder, we have been provided with the implements and vessels to accomplish that Great Work.

La-Shanah Ha-Ba'ah
Bi-Yerushalayim!

Next Year in Jerusalem!

Dates of Passover Through 2012

It seems appropriate that this book should end with numbers and the alphabet since the Haggadah ends the same way, with the *zemirot* of chronology, counting, and alphabetical acrostics. So here are the dates of Passover into the next century.

Jewish Year	Latin Year	Date on which first seder night falls
5755	1995	Friday, April 14
5756	1996	Wednesday, April 3
5757	1997	Monday, April 21
5758	1998	Friday, April 10
5759	1999	Wednesday, March 31
5760	2000	Wednesday, April 19
5761	2001	Saturday, April 7
5762	2002	Wednesday, March 27
5763	2003	Wednesday, April 16
5764	2004	Monday, April 5
5765	2005	Saturday, April 23
5766	2006	Wednesday, April 12
5767	2007	Monday, April 2
5768	2008	Monday, April 19
5769	2009	Wednesday, April 8
5770	2010	Monday, March 29
5771	2011	Monday, April 18
5772	2012	Friday, April 6

People are often confused about when to have their seder because the Jewish day begins at sunset on the preceding evening. The dates given here are the dates on which the first seder occurs, in other words, on which the fifteenth of Nisan begins. Have your seder on these specified dates. The following day, until the sun sets, is also the fifteenth of Nisan. The sixteenth of Nisan, the time in which we have our second seder, begins that evening.

Glossary

The following is a list of all the Jewish terms used in the book, as well as many of the names and places, with explanations. Besides explaining these words, a browse through this list should suggest the interconnecting web of meanings that are conveyed when we speak of Jewish subjects in their original languages, not to mention the mixture of everything from the sublime to the ridiculous. We jump from Abrabanel to *Zohar,* move from kabbalah to kugel, and all are bits of the Mosaic mosaic.

For the ten *sefirot,* see the end of chapter 2, where these are explained. For the fifteen seder steps, see the end of chapter 3, where these are listed. For the Hebrew letters, the months of the year, the twelve tribes, the orders of the Mishnah, and the books of the Torah, see chapter 6. For Jewish holidays, see chapter 13, where the cycle of festivals is fully detailed. All terms are Hebrew unless stated otherwise.

Abrabanel, Don Isaac (1437–1508): Member of a distinguished family, and leader of the Spanish Jewish community at the time of expulsion in 1492. He was a statesman, diplomat, financier, scholar, philosopher, and commentator on the Bible and Haggadah. Though exempted from expulsion, joined his people in exile. Various spellings.

Abulafia, Abraham ben Samuel (1240–c. 1291): Ecstatic Spanish kabbalist who based mysticism on permutation and combination of divine names and free association. He accused Pope Nicholas III of responsibility for persecution of the Jews, and was condemned to death at the stake; but the pope's subsequent death led to his release.

Achad ha-Am (Asher Ginsberg) (1856–1927): Hebrew writer, thinker, Zionist from Ukraine, who settled in Palestine. His pen name means "one of the people."

afikoman: From the Greek *epikomion,* after-dinner revels; the larger part of middle (Levi) matzo, hidden by the leader or grabbed by the children. The seder cannot continue until it is ransomed from children so it can be eaten as dessert. It symbolizes the paschal sacrifice.

Aggadah: Legendary, as opposed to legal, material in the Talmud and midrash. From the same root as Haggadah and *maggid,* "to tell."

Agnon, Shmuel Yosef (1888–1970): Hebrew writer and Nobel laureate (1966) who was born in Galicia and settled in Israel.

Ahavat Yisrael: "Love for people of Israel." It is a positive commandment for all Jews to love one another. Ahavah (love) is one of the books of *Mishneh Torah.*

Akdamut Millin: "Prefatory words" that open the Aramaic prayer by Meir ben Isaac Nehorai recited before the Torah reading on the first day of Shavuot.

Akiba (c. 50–135 C.E.): One of the greatest Jewish scholars of all time, this *tanna* (teacher) laid the groundwork for Mishnah, supported the Bar Kokhba revolt, and was tortured and executed by Romans. According to legend in the Talmud tractate Chagigah, Akiba, ben Zoma, and two others engaged in mystical studies. One died, one became apostate, and ben Zoma went mad. Only Akiba entered the garden of mystical speculation and left unharmed.

alav ha-shalom: "Peace be upon him (or her)," said when mentioning the dead.

alef bet: First two letters of the Hebrew alphabet; by extension, the whole alphabet.

Aleichem, Shalom (1859–1916): Pen name of Shalom Rabinovitz, Ukrainian-born Yiddish author, called "the Jewish Mark Twain." (When Twain met him, he said, "I am the American Shalom Aleichem.") His stories of Tevye the milkman are the basis for the Broadway musical *Fiddler on the Roof.* His pen name means "peace be upon you," the standard Jewish salutation; it is also the opening of the Friday evening hymn welcoming the angels of Shabbat. Muslims have almost the same salutation in Arabic, *salaam aleikum.* His granddaughter, Bel Kauffman, wrote *Up the Down Staircase.*

Alenu: "It is our duty," the first word of prayer at the end of synagogue services asserting God's unity. Medieval Christians censored this as being insulting to Christianity.

aliyah: "Ascent," both going up to read from Torah and emigrating to Israel; Plural, aliyot.

Alkabetz, Solomon ben Moses ha-Levi (c. 1505–1584): Member of the Safed mystical community; wrote Shabbat hymn welcoming Sabbath Bride, "Lekhah Dodi."

am ha-aretz: "People of the earth"; refers to unlearned, or less than observant, Jews.

Amidah: "standing," central prayer of every service, said standing, also known as Shemoneh Esreh.

amora: "Spokesman"; Jewish scholars of the third through the sixth centuries who created Gemara. Plural, *amoraim.*

Amram ben Sheshna Gaon (c. 810–874): Head of the Babylonian talmudic academy; his prayer book is the basis of all later Jewish liturgy, including the Haggadah.

anjinaras: Turkish Sephardic dish of sweet-sour artichokes.

apikoros: Skeptic or unbeliever; from the Greek philosopher, Epicurus.

Aramaic: Lingua franca of the Ancient Near East, spoken by Jews from the sixth century B.C.E. to the ninth century C.E. The Dead Sea Scrolls are written in Aramaic. Jesus spoke one form of Aramaic. Many Jewish prayers and parts of the Bible, Talmud, Targum, Haggadah, and *Zohar* are in Aramaic. It is still spoken today in parts of Syria, Turkey, Kurdistan.

arba'ah minim: "Four species" waved at Sukkot: *etrog* (citron), *lulav* (palm branch), two willows, three myrtle twigs. The four species are a symbolic representation of the male organs of fertility, testicle and phallus; by imitative magic, they call forth rain and fertility from heaven when they are waved.

arba kosot: "Four cups" of wine drunk at the seder.

arba kushiyot: "Four questions" or perplexities asked by the youngest child at the seder.

Ashkenaz: Biblical country assumed to be Germany; the term now refers to Jews of Christian lands of Eastern Europe and their descendants, Ashkenazim.

Aviv: "Spring," which begins on the first of Nisan.

ba'al ha-seder: "Master of seder"; the leader of the seder ceremony.

babanatza: Sephardic wine pudding.

baleboosteh: From Hebrew "*ba'al ha-bayit*," master of house; as with most Yiddish expressions, it can as often be used sarcastically.

Bar Kokhba (d. 135 C.E.): "Son of a star"; the leader of the Judean revolt against Rome during the time of Hadrian. Its short-lived success was soon crushed. Akiba supported him.

bar mitzvah: "Son (or inheritor) of commandments." When Jewish boys reach age of thirteen, and girls, twelve, they assume full responsibility for their own spiritual, religious actions. They can be counted as part of a minyan, and they become eligible for aliyah. Sometime after 1400, bar mitzvah, a ceremony of initiation into the world of honoring and reading from Torah, came into being; in the late nineteenth century, a parallel ceremony of bat mitzvah was created for girls.

bat mitzvah: See bar mitzvah.

Baruch ben Jehiel of Medzibezh (1757–1810): Podolian Chasidic *tzaddik,* author, grandson of Ba'al Shem Tov.

bedikat chametz: "Search for leaven"; the ceremonial search for *chametz* on the evening preceding seder.

Beilis, Menahem Mendel (1874–1934): Russian Jew accused in 1911 of killing a Christian boy to use his blood to make matzo. He spent two years in jail, and was finally acquitted. He spent last fourteen years of his life in New Jersey. Bernard Malamud's *The Fixer* is a brilliant fictional telling of his life.

Bene-Berak: City in the ancient Holy Land, near modern Jaffa and Tel Aviv, where Akiba had his academy and where five rabbis met for seder and possibly to plot the Bar Kokhba revolt.

bentsch licht: "Make benediction over light"; Ashkenazic expression referring to the blessing over candles that begins Shabbat, festivals.

ben Zoma, Simeon (second century): A *tanna,* and a brilliant scholar, who was never ordained and so was known by his father's name, "son of Zoma." Along with Akiba and two others, he engaged in mystical studies that led to his madness and early death.

berakhah: "Benediction"; recited in thanks for food, drink, and so on, and before performing commandments; plural, *berakhot.* Berakhot is the title of the first tractate of Talmud, on benedictions.

Bergen-Belsen: Concentration camp near Hanover, Germany. Though not a death camp, 51,000 Jews, including Anne Frank, died here between 1943 and 1951, when the camp was finally evacuated.

betzah: "Egg"; the seder plate symbol representing Chagigah, the festival offering. Also a talmudic tractate on festivals.

Birkat ha-Mazon: "Blessings for food"; four benedictions of Grace after Meals. As part of the seder, reciting Grace is Barekh.

birmuelos: Also *bimuelos* or *burmuelos;* Sephardic farfel cupcakes, pancakes, or doughnuts. They are also made as potato pancakes with cheese.

bi'ur chametz: "Burning of leaven"; the ceremony on the morning preceding seder where leaven found the night before is burned.

blintzeh: From Russian for "crepe" (Yiddish, *bletlich*); traditionally filled with cheese, but just as often filled nowadays with potatoes or fruit. It is the mainstay of dairy meals eaten at Shavuot.

Bonfils, Joseph ben Samuel (Tov Elem) (eleventh century): French rabbi, scholar, and poet who wrote a long poem from which the Nirtzah section of the Haggadah is derived.

borscht: From Russian for "beet soup"; eaten hot or cold with sour cream, potatoes, cucumbers. Borscht Belt refers to resorts in Catskills that catered to Jewish vacationers and where so many Jewish comedians, like Sid Caesar and Danny Kaye, developed their craft.

bris: Literally "covenant"; but usually refers to the covenant of circumcision, *bris milah,* performed when a boy is eight days old. It is also spelled *brit* and *brith,* as in B'nai B'rith, but is almost always pronounced *bris.*

bubbeh: Yiddish for "grandmother"; from Russian.

Buber, Martin (1878–1965): Austrian-born scholar, philosopher, Zionist. His grandfather was a great scholar of midrash. He called his existential concept of relationship, between people or between people and God, I-Thou. He settled in Israel in 1938, where he worked for peace between Jews and Palestinians. He created the contemporary interest in Chasidism by presenting their stories in *Tales of the Hasidim* and other works.

Caro, Joseph (1488–1575): Legal codifier, mystic, and part of the Safed community. He wrote *Shulchan Arukh, The Code of Jewish Law,* standard to this day. He had an angelic teacher, a *maggid,* who spoke through him.

Chabad: Acronym for *Ch*ochma, *B*inah, and *Da*'at (wisdom, understanding, and knowledge). Refers to the Lubavich Chasidic system, which emphasizes a combination of Torah study and kabbalah.

Chag ha-Aviv: "Festival of Spring"; one of the names for Passover.

Chag ha-Matzot: "Festival of Unleavened Bread"; another name for Passover.

Chagigah: "Festival"; usually refers to the three pilgrimage festivals: Passover, Shavuot, and Sukkot. It is also the title of a talmudic tractate on festivals, with much mystical lore.

chag same'ach: "Joyous holiday"; a holiday greeting.

chai: "Life"; the numerical value of *chai* is eighteen.

challah: When bread was made in Temple times, this was the priestly portion. Today challah is twisted egg bread eaten at Shabbat and festivals, from which a small bit of dough is burned in remembrance of Temple days. This is one of the religious duties traditionally associated with women. It is also the title of a tractate of Mishnah on dough offering.

chalutzim: "Pioneers"; early Zionist settlers in Palestine.

chametz: "Leavened dough," and by extension anything made from the five grains capable of fermentation, other than matzo. Later, for Ashkenazim, it also referred to *kitniyot,* legumes and other prohibited foods.

chametzdikhe: Anything containing *chametz.*

chanukkiyah: Ritual object used at Chanukkah; a candelabra for eight lights plus one for lighting others. Also called menorah. Plural, *chanukkiyot.*

charoset: Substance we dip *maror* in to ameliorate its bitterness. It is made from fruit, nuts, wine, and spices, and is intended to look like the mortar of Egyptian bondage.

Chasidei Ashkenaz: Jewish pietist movement in medieval Germany, mystical, ascetic, ethical. Unconnected to later Chasidism.

Chasidism: Pietistic movement founded on the teaching of Ba'al Shem Tov, noted for fervor and attachment to *tzaddik.*

Chatimah: "Seal"; conclusion of benediction, indicating the fundamental reason for reciting it.

chazeret: Literally, "lettuce"; the second bitter herb, usually horseradish or romaine, on the seder plate; usually used for Hillel sandwich.

chazzan: Cantor or singer of liturgy in synagogues.

cheder: "Room"; the room attached to the synagogue where children were taught; Hebrew school.

cholent: Like kugel, this dish would go into a slow oven on Friday night, and be eaten after shul on Saturday for lunch: the original crock pot. Many are complete meals in themselves, with meat, barley, beans, potatoes, carrots, onions, even *knaydl* or a kugel. Of course, at Pesach we leave out beans and barley. Besides allowing a hot meal on Shabbat, *cholent* can turn a tough piece of meat, chicken gizzards, or even a leather belt into a tender gourmet treat.

chol ha-mo'ed: Intermediate days of Passover, Sukkot; half-holidays when essential work may be performed, but all other rules of the holiday are in force. Mo'ed Katan is the title of a talmudic tractate on intermediate days of festivals.

chrain: Yiddish for "horseradish."

Chumash: From Hebrew for "five," the first five books of the Bible, the Torah text; plural, Chumashim.

chuppah: "Bridal canopy" under which the bride and groom stand during a Jewish wedding.

chutzpa: Yiddish for a combination of nerve, presumption, and arrogance.

Cordovero, Moses ben Jacob (1522–1570): Member of the Safed mystical community, a disciple of Caro and the teacher of Luria.

Da'at: "Knowledge," a kind of eleventh *sefirah* reconciling male and female wisdom and understanding.

daven: Ashkenazic term for "to pray."

derash: "Interpretation"; one of the four methods of exposition of scripture, in this case, the homiletical method.

Diaspora: Greek for dispersion; those Jews outside of the Land of Israel. The term has been adopted by African-Americans to refer to their dispersion outside Africa.

Dov Baer, the Maggid of Mezhirech (d. 1772): Volhynian *maggid,* one of two main disciples of Ba'al Shem Tov, who transformed the charismatic personality of the Besht into the system of Chasidism.

Eleazar ben Azariah (first–second centuries): A *tanna,* Mishnaic sage, and leader in post-Temple times in creating Pharisaic Judaism. When, at eighteen, he was named head of the Sanhedrin, his hair turned white overnight as a sign of maturity. That is why he says in Haggadah that he is like one who is seventy years old.

Eleazar ben Judah of Worms (c. 1165–c. 1230): Mystic, scholar, poet, part of Chasidei Askenaz at the end of the movement. His wife and daughters were killed by Crusaders in 1196.

Eliezer ben Hyrcanus (first—second centuries): One of the five key disciples of Johanan ben Zakkai at Jabneh. *Tanna,* teacher of Akiba, later his colleague, and a creator of Exilic Judaism.

Elijah ben Solomon Zalman, the Vilna Gaon (1720–1797): Rabbi, scholar, and one of most brilliant minds in Jewish thought. He had a photographic memory, and knew the Bible by heart at age three. He settled in Vilna, had few students, and preferred study companions. He wrote on the Bible, both Talmuds, and the Code of Jewish Law. A master kabbalist, he opposed Chasidism; and in this we can see beginnings of antipathy between Litvaks (Lithuanian talmudic intellectual Jews) and Galitzianers (Polish Chasidic emotional Jews of Galicia).

emunah: "Faith," or "belief."

Epstein, Marc: Contemporary scholar of Jewish iconography, his article on the hare in Jewish art and midrash appeared in *Orim* 2, no. 1 (Autumn 1986).

Eretz Yisrael: "Land of Israel."

erev Pesach: The twenty-four busy hours preceding Passover, during which we search for *chametz,* burn it, sell it, *daven,* hear the conclusion of a tractate of Talmud, bake matzo, go to *mikveh,* daven again, and go home to perform the seder!

etrog: One of the four species of Sukkot, the citron, a lemon-like fruit; plural, *etrogim.*

Falasha: Old Ethiopic for "wander," or "emigrate"; the Jews of Ethiopia, or Beta Israel, as they call themselves. They follow the Bible literally, and believe they are descended from Manasseh, son of Solomon and Sheba. Most are now in Israel.

farfel: Broken pieces of matzo used for stuffing, and so on. Farfel is also the name of ventriloquist Jimmy Nelson's dummy dog.

fier kashes: Yiddish for "four questions" or "perplexities."

Finkelstein, Louis (1895–1991): Contemporary conservative rabbi and scholar. His speculative essays on "Pre-Maccabean Documents in the

Passover Haggadah," *Harvard Theological Review* 31 (1941) and 36 (1943), pushes dating of parts of Haggadah back before destruction of Temple.

fleishikh: Yiddish for "meat," as opposed to dairy.

fliegle: Yiddish for "wing," as, for instance, of a chicken, or a human arm.

forshpeis: Yiddish for "appetizer."

fritada: Sephardic frittata, baked not fried, usually made with spinach, leek, or Swiss chard, and matzo. Served as an appetizer at the seder.

galut: "Exile"; Jewish people separated from the Land of Israel.

Gamaliel ha-Zaken, Rabban (first century C.E.): The Elder, grandson of Hillel, president of the Sanhedrin.

Gaon: Heads of Babylonian talmudic academies from the sixth to eleventh centuries; plural, *geonim.*

Gaster, Theodore Herzl (1906–1992): Son of rabbi and scholar, Moses Gaster, authority on Samaritans. He was a scholar of comparative religion, folklore, and anthropology, and a follower of Cambridge ritualists. He translated the Dead Sea Scrolls, wrote on Purim as ritual theater, and edited Frazier's *Golden Bough.*

gebroks: Dishes in which liquid is added to matzo or matzo meal.

gefilte fish: Literally, "stuffed fish," since originally ground fish patties were put back into fish skins; usually eaten with beet horseradish. There is no truth to story that they are found swimming with sliced carrots on their heads.

Gemara: Aramaic for "completion"; Aramaic texts of rabbinic discussions of Mishnah carried on in academies in Babylonia, Jerusalem. Mishnah and Gemara together are Talmud.

gematria: From Greek "geometry"; Jewish system of assigning numeric value to letters, then connecting words of equal value.

get: Aramaic divorce document that dissolves the marriage bond. Gittin is the talmudic tractate on divorce.

ghetto: Walled-in section of a city where Jews were confined to live. The term was first used in Venice, where it referred to the Jewish quarter near the foundry, or "ghetto." Later used for urban concentrations of Jews created during Holocaust in Warsaw, Vilna, and other cities. The term was later adopted by African-Americans to refer to urban concentrations of blacks.

Glick, Hirsh (1922–1944): Born in Vilna, this Yiddish poet wrote "The Partisan Song," "Mir Zaynen Do," "We Are Here," the battle song of the Vilna partisans. He died in the Holocaust.

Goldberg, Isaiah-Nissan Hakohen (1858–1927): Yiddish, Hebrew writer
from Belorussia, he took the pen name Yaknehaz.

golem: A *hapax legomenon,* a word that occurs only once in the Bible, in
Psalm 139:16, meaning "formless matter," with the implication that it is
on way to becoming a being. Over centuries, the concept developed of a
subhuman being created by wonder-working rabbis to protect the Jewish people. In one version a rabbi creates a being by inscribing *emet*
(truth), on its forehead. When the golem becomes larger, and potentially
dangerous, the rabbi erases the first letter, *alef,* leaving *met* (death). The
golem crumbles back into clay and falls on the rabbi, crushing him.
Here we can see roots of the *Frankenstein* story. The theme was picked
up by alchemists as the basis for the homunculus, a tiny human form
created in the alchemical vessel by the alchemist when he accomplishes
the Great Work. In the late nineteenth century, various golem legends
became agglutinated around the figure of Rabbi Judah Loew, Maharal of
Prague. The clay of the golem was said to be wrapped up in the attic of
Altneuschul, in Prague. In various guises, the figure has remained a fix-
ture in Western thought and literature ever since. H. Leivick wrote the
Yiddish play, *Der Golem,* on this theme; and Gustav Meyrink based his
wonderful symbolist novel, *The Golem,* on these stories. The great German expressionist film, *The Golem,* also retells story. Interestingly,
Prague playwright Karel Capek modeled his invention of robots in
R.U.R. (Rossum's Universal Robots) after the golem, as did the creators
of Superman, Jerry Siegel and Joe Schuster. Later, comic book versions
of the golem itself were created. Jorge Luis Borges noticed that golem
rhymed with Scholem, and appropriately it was Gershom Scholem who
named the computer at the Weizmann Institute Golem I. The term can
also be used sarcastically to refer to a fool.

gorgle: Yiddish for "neck."

gornisht: Yiddish for "nothing," though *gornisht* is far less than nothing.

goy: Literally, "nation"; today the term most often refers to a non-Jew;
plural, *goyim.*

greener: Yiddish for "greenhorn," a newcomer to America.

griventz: Yiddish for chicken skin fried crisp in chicken fat.

haftarah: Portion from Prophets read after the Torah reading on Shabbat,
festivals, and fast days. There is usually some connection between the
haftarah and Torah portion or calendar; plural, *haftarot.*

Haggadah: Book with text recited at the seder, and ritual instructions for
the ceremony; plural, Haggadot.

haimish: Yiddish for "homey," implying comfortable, familiar, cozy, warm.

halakhah: Legal part of the Talmud, as opposed to narrative and legendary material; plural, halakhot.

Hallel: Psalms 113–118, recited on Passover, Sukkot, and Chanukkah. The Half-Hallel omits Psalm 115:1–11 and 116:1–11. This is recited on the last six days of Passover and New Moon. Psalm 136 is the Great Hallel. Reciting Hallel is one of the fifteen steps of the seder.

hammin: Sephardic *cholent.*

Havdalah: "Distinction"; ceremony in which we bless God for distinguishing light from dark, Israel from nations, Shabbat from six days of work, sacred from profane. It is performed at the end of Sabbath and festivals, usually with wine, spices, and a special torch-like Havdalah candle. Many folk customs are associated with this ceremony.

Hebrew: Language used by God to create the world; Semitic language of the Hebrews, Abraham, Isaac, and Jacob, then of the Israelites, of the Bible, and of the nations of Israel and Judah. It continued to be used as a literary language during Exile, and became the language of the Land of Israel again in the twentieth century, especially after founding of the State of Israel.

Heine, Heinrich, (1797–1856): German poet and prose writer who often used Jewish themes, as in *The Rabbi of Bacharach,* which begins with a beautiful evocation of his childhood Passovers. The beautifully illustrated Haggadah he describes there is a 1723 hand-painted copy by Moses Judah Loeb of Trebitsch, Moravia, of the Amsterdam Haggadah, 1695, owned by Heine's great-grandfather, Lazarus von Geldern.

hekhsher: "Approbation" on food products stating that the undersigned rabbi asserts that the food is kosher or kosher for Passover.

Heller, Bunim (b. 1908): Polish-born Yiddish poet, who settled in Israel in 1957.

heseba: Leaning to the left during the seder, a combination of Hebrew for "sitting down to a meal," *heysave,* and Yiddish for "bed," *bet.* In other words, sitting down to a meal as if you were in bed.

Hillel the Elder (first century B.C.E.–first century C.E.): Greatest rabbi of the period of the Second Temple, president of the Sanhedrin, and ancestor of a dynasty of presidents that lasted for six centuries. He contrasted with the more severe Shammai in conflicts between human and property rights. He is famous for saying, "What is hateful to you, do not do unto your neighbor," and "If I am not for myself, then who will be for me? And if I am only for myself, then what am I? And if not now, when?"

Israel ben Eliezer Ba'al Shem Tov (c. 1700–1760): Podolian-born healer, wonder-worker, and founder of Chasidism. Although he left no writings, his legends are collected in *Tales of the Besht* (an acronym for Ba'al Shem Tov, Master of the Good Name). At his death there was no Chasidism, disciples created the movement.

Isserles, Moses ben Israel, the Rema (1525 or 1530–1572): Polish rabbi and legal codifier, he annotated Caro's Sephardic *Shulchan Arukh* with his *Mappah* (tablecloth) for use by Ashkenazim, making it the authority on Jewish law for all communities to this day.

Jericho: Oldest town in Israel, and perhaps the world. Its walls came tumbling down when Joshua marched around it seven times, blowing shofars. Now it is a West Bank Palestinian town, the center of Palestinian self-government.

Joshua ben Hananiah, (first–second centuries C.E.): *Tanna,* one of five key disciples of Johanan ben Zakkai, and a creator of post-Temple Judaism.

Judah bar Ilai (c. 100–c. 180 C.E.): *Tanna,* pupil of Akiba and Tarfon, this is the Rabbi Judah who created the acrostic of the initial letters of the ten plagues.

Judah Loew ben Bezalel, Maharal of Prague (c. 1525–1609): Chief Rabbi of Prague, scholar, last of pre-Lurianic kabbalists, had an audience with Emperor Rudolph II. In the late nineteenth century he became associated with legends of the *golem.*

kabbalah: "Received tradition"; Jewish mystical tradition that began in Southern France and Northern Spain in the twelfth century. By extension, it is the whole body of Jewish mystical thought, brilliantly delineated in Gershom Scholem's *Major Trends in Jewish Mysticism.*

Kaddish: Aramaic for "holy"; the Aramaic prayer recited as the concluding hymn at services, and also as a mourner's prayer.

Kallir, Eleazar (flourished 600–630): Cantor in the Holy Land, the greatest composer of *piyyutim,* liturgical poems. Many are still in the *siddur,* especially prayers for dew for Passover, and rain for Shemini Atzeret.

Kaplan, Mordechai (1881–1983): American Conservative rabbi who founded the Reconstructionist movement in Judaism, but his influence went far beyond that movement. His key Reconstructionist work is *Judaism as a Civilization.* He created the first American bat mitzvah for his daughter.

Karaite: "Scripturalism"; a schismatic fundamentalist Jewish sect dating from the eighth century. Small communities still remain, primarily in the Crimea and Israel. They opposed the Talmud and sought to interpret the Bible literally.

k'areh: The seder "plate" containing symbolic foods of Passover.

karpas: "Parsley"; the green vegetable eaten at seder.

kasha: Russian for "porridge"; buckwheat groats. It puns with Hebrew for "difficulty," a puzzle, "in the soup," something perplexing, as in the *fier kashes,* the four questions.

kasher: "Fit," "proper"; to make kitchen or utensils kosher.

kashrut: Jewish dietary laws. Not eating milk with meat; eating only clean animals: mammals that have split hooves and chew their cud, fish with scales and fins, domestic birds (pigeon, chicken, turkey, goose, duck, some game birds); eating only birds and mammals that have been ritually slaughtered. Certain parts of clean animals are also forbidden. By extension, separate sets of dishes and cooking utensils must be used for milk and meat.

kavvanah: "Directed intention." Mystical intention used to focus the mind when performing commandments; plural, *kavvanot.*

ka-zayit: Amount equal to the bulk of a *zayit,* an olive. An extremely vague unit of measurement, especially when translated into quantity of matzo, *maror,* and *karpas;* plural, *ka-zeytim.*

Kedushah: "Holiness"; the third benediction of Shemoneh Esreh, that part of Amidah said standing when repeated by reader during services. When this is chanted, we are joining our prayer with that of the angels in praising God, carrying out the neo-Platonic idea of upper and lower worlds being congruent. Also one of books of the *Mishneh Torah.*

keftikas: Sephardic ground meat and vegetable meatballs or patties.

Kelal Yisrael: "Community of Israel"; the whole of the Jewish people.

Keneset ha-Gedolah: "Great Assembly" or "Great Synagogue." The Men of the Great Assembly, lead by Ezra, were Jewish leaders at the beginning of the Second Temple period.

ketubbah: From Hebrew for "writing"; the Aramaic marriage contract, often beautifully illuminated, specifying the husband's duties and obligations to his wife; plural, *ketubbot.* It is also a talmudic tractate on marriage contracts.

Khetuvim: "Writings"; the third section of the Bible, containing scrolls and wisdom literature.

kibitz: Originally this Yiddish term referred to someone who gave gratuitous advice during a card game. Today it usually just means to chat or chatter. Those who kibitz are kibitzers.

kibbutz: Collective agricultural communities, central to the return of Jewish people to Palestine in the twentieth century; plural kibbutzim.

kichel: Puffed-up egg cookies coated with crystallized sugar.

Kiddush: "Sanctification"; prayer usually recited over wine to consecrate Shabbat, festivals. Kiddushin is a talmudic tractate on marriage.

kineahora: Combined Yiddish-Hebrew word meaning, "There shouldn't be an evil eye," uttered whenever something positive or complimentary is said.

kippah: Yiddish for "cap," usually referring to a skullcap; plural, *kippot.*

kishka: Russian for "intestines," referring either to human intestines or to stuffing-filled intestinal casings made by Ashkenazim.

kitniyot: Foods added to the list of prohibited foods at Passover by the Ashkenazim, since they were used as flour substitutes: primarily rice, corn, millet, and legumes.

kittel: White robe worn at the seder, on Yom Kippur, by the groom at the wedding, and as a shroud.

Klein, Abraham Moses (1909–1972): Canadian Jewish poet, novelist, translator, and essayist.

klezmer: Compression of *kell zemir,* "vessel of song"; the secular music of the Ashkenazim.

klippot: "Shells"; shards of broken vessels that had been intended to receive divine light in the worlds that were created before our own. These worlds had too much severity, Gevurah, the fifth *sefirot,* so they shattered. Remnants of those attempts at creation exist in our world as evil mixed with sparks of divine light. Our task is to raise these sparks mired in shells back to their divine source.

knaydl: One matzo ball; plural, *knaydlich.*

Kohen: "Priest" in the Temple, descendants of Aaron, the first High Priest. Also the upper of the three matzot at the seder.

Kol Nidre: Aramaic for "All vows"; the opening words of the Aramaic nullification of vows that begins Yom Kippur. Often misunderstood, it does not nullify vows between people, but allows a fresh start in spiritual development. Without nullification of vows, if we swore we would never get angry, overeat, gossip, or waste time, and then fell off wagon, we would never try again. It wipes the slate clean, and allows us to make New Year's resolutions afresh.

Kook, Abraham Isaac (1865–1935): Rabbi, scholar, Zionist, and mystic, Kook was the first Ashkenazic Chief Rabbi of Eretz Yisrael. He sought to include rather than exclude, and in turn was beloved by all segments of the Jewish population of Palestine, from Orthodoxy through secular Zionists.

korekh: Hillel sandwich of matzo and *maror* eaten just before the seder meal.

kos: "cup."

Kos Eliyahu: "Cup of Elijah," poured in expectation of the prophet's visit to our sedarim heralding the coming of the Messiah.

kosher: "Fit" or "proper," as regards food.

kosher le-Pesach: Those foods that are both kosher and free of chametz and so are "kosher for Passover."

Kotzk, Menachem Mendel of (1787–1859): Polish Chasidic *tzaddik* who locked himself in his room next to his students' study room for the last twenty years of life. He was the disciple of Simchah Bunem of Przysucha. He was uninterested in gaining a large group of followers, and represented a return to Torah study in Chasidism.

Krakovsky, Levi I.: Twentieth-century kabbalist, a student of Rabbi Yehudah Ashlag, who had founded a yeshiva for kabbalistic studies in Israel in 1920. Krakovsky wrote *The Omnipotent Light Revealed.*

kugel: Baked pudding, usually noodles or potatoes; actually the pan in which the pudding is baked. Since no cooking could be done on Shabbat, the pan would be put into the oven at the lowest heat on Friday, before the Sabbath began. By lunch on Saturday, it would be ready to eat.

Ladino: From the word "Latin," it is the Judeo-Spanish (Castilian) language of Sephardic Jews.

Lapide, Pinchas (1922–): Contemporary scholar of Jewish-Christian relations.

latke: Potato pancake usually eaten at Chanukkah, but good at Pesach as well.

L'chayim: "To life!" The quintessential Jewish toast.

Leib, son of Sarah: Disciple of the Ba'al Shem and the Maggid of Mezhirech; a hidden *tzaddik.*

Levi: One of Jacob's sons; one of the twelve tribes. Moses was a Levite. Levites assisted priests in Temple service. They had no territorial inheritance, but received tithes from other tribes. Also, the middle matzo of three at the seder table.

Levi Yitzhak ben Meir of Berdichev (c. 1740–1810): Rabbi, Chasidic *tzaddik,* disciple of the Maggid of Mezhirech, active in Poland. A popular figure in Jewish legend and fiction.

Lipkin (of Salant), Israel ben Ze'ev Wolf (1810–1883): Rabbi, founder of Musar movement.

Lubavich: Town in Belorussia where Dov Baer (1773–1827), son of Shneur

Zalman of Lyady, settled. The town became the focus of the Chabad movement, and followers are called Lubavichers.

lulav: Palm branch that gives its name to the assemblage of palm, myrtle, and willows shaken, along with the *etrog,* at Sukkot.

Luria, Isaac ben Solomon Ashkenazi (1534–1572): Known as the Ari, the Lion, an acronym for Holy Rabbi Isaac. Member of the Safed mystical community. He transformed the kabbalah of his time, and all kabbalah after him is Lurianic.

Lydda: Important Palestinian scholarly community, seat of the Sanhedrin in the first and second centuries.

Maccabee: Name given to the hero of the Chanukkah story, Judah Maccabee, then to his brothers and their Hasmonean dynasty, which began the rebellion against the Seleucid tyrant Antiochus IV Epiphanes in 168 B.C.E. The Hasmonean kingdom survived as an autonomous state until it was defeated by Rome in 37 B.C.E. The story is told in the apocryphal Greek books of Maccabees. Handel wrote an oratorio about Judah, and today a kind of Jewish Olympics, Maccabiah, is held every four years in Israel. Maccabee is usually translated "hammer," but the etymology is uncertain.

machetunim: Yiddish for "in-laws."

machzor: "cycle," festival prayer book.

maftir: "One who concludes"; the person called up to read the close of the weekly Torah portion and then *haftarah.* Also, the closing verses of the Torah portion.

Magen David: "Shield of David"; an ancient magical symbol composed of superimposed male sulphur and female mercury triangles. It has been a Jewish symbol since the seventeenth century, and a Zionist symbol since the late nineteenth century. It is used on the Israeli flag, and in red, as the Israeli version of the Red Cross.

maggid: "Teller"; an itinerant preacher; the narrative portion of the Haggadah; an angelic teacher. Rabbi Joseph Caro had such a maggid who spoke through him, mediumistically, in a high-pitched voice.

mahammar: Moroccan vegetable and egg mold.

Maimonides, Moses the Rambam (Rabbi Moses ben Maimon) (1135–1204): One of the greatest Jewish scholars, rabbis, legalists, philosophers, and doctors. His great works are *Mishneh Torah,* a clear presentation of the whole of Jewish law, and *Guide to the Perplexed,* a reconciling of Judaism with rational Aristotelianism. He formulated the thirteen principles of faith.

Maimuna: North African Jewish celebration of the end of Passover and the anniversary of the death of Maimonides' father, which occurred on the preceding day.

makkot: "Strokes"; the ten plagues God inflicted on the Egyptians. Also, a talmudic tractate on flogging.

Malamud, Bernard (1914–1986): American Jewish novelist who wrote *The Fixer* about the Beilis blood libel.

mama-loshen: Combined Hebrew-Yiddish for "mother tongue," "Yiddish." Certainly both mothers and fathers of the *shtetl* spoke Yiddish, but since women were rarely taught Hebrew, Yiddish became associated with mothers.

mandel: "Almond"; as in *mandelbrot,* "almond bread," an almond cookie.

maror: "Bitter herb"; a seder plate symbol, usually horseradish or romaine.

Marrano: Probably derived from Spanish word for "swine," referring to the secret Jews of Spain and Portugal, who outwardly converted to avoid the exile of 1492. They celebrated Passover on sixteenth of Nisan so as not to be caught by the Inquisition.

Masada: Herodian fortress in the Judean desert where Jewish resistance to the Roman occupation ended in 73 C.E., when Zealot defenders committed mass suicide after a long seige.

masorah: "Passed-down tradition," as opposed to kabbalah, "received tradition." The Masoretes were scribes responsible for safeguarding the text of Bible. Their version of the Bible is referred to as Masoretic; their marginal notes are masorah.

matzo: As Fats Waller said of jazz, "If you don't know by now, don't mess with it." "Unleavened bread," made with only flour and water. There is a positive commandment to eat it at seder.

matzo brei: "Fried matzo," scrambled with egg.

mavin: "Understanding"; originally a judge or expert that one came to for decisions, now more commonly sarcastic or facetious.

megillah: "Scroll"; usually refers to the scroll of Esther read at Purim, but can also be applied to Song of Songs read at Passover; Ruth, at Shavuot; Ecclesiastes, at Sukkot; and Lamentations, at Tishah be-Av. It is standard to include Jonah, read at Yom Kippur, in printed editions of the five scrolls. Also, a talmudic tractate about Purim.

megina: Sephardic layered matzo and meat pie.

mekhirat chametz: "Selling of leaven"; which is done in the morning on the fourteenth of Nisan. Everyone in the community sells *chametz* to the rabbi, who in turn sells it to non-Jews for a nominal fee. After Passover it is sold back to the rabbi, who in turn resells it to community.

menorah: A candelabra, either a seven-branched oil lamp of the Tabernacle and Temple, or an eight-branched lamp of Chanukkah. This, not the Magen David, was the most widespread Jewish symbol of antiquity. It appears on the Arch of Titus, and in our century it reappeared as the symbol of the State of Israel.

me'ot chittim: "Wheat money," raised for the poor before Passover so they can afford matzo for the seder.

mezuzah: "Doorpost"; a parchment scroll with the Shema and other Torah verses that instruct us to have the mezuzah on the doorposts of our homes. Also, a minor tractate about *mezuzot* added to the Talmud.

middot: "Measures"; the thirteen divine qualities of mercy. Also, a tractate of Mishnah about the measurements of the Temple.

midrash: The rabbinic methods of interpretation of the Bible, from the same root as *derash.* Also, various collections of rabbinic material using these methods developed from *tannaitic* times to the tenth century and collected from 400 to 1550. Midrash is best known in the form of stories that expand the bare details of biblical narrative. The connection between the four cups of wine and the four forms of redemption is from *Midrash Rabbah,* the "Great Midrash."

mikveh: "Gathering of waters"; a ritual bath of immersion, used by women following their period. Immersion renders clean that which has become unclean. It can also be used for vessels and by men, as well. Also, a tractate of Mishnah on ritual bath.

milchikh: Yiddish for "dairy," as opposed to meat.

mina: A Sephardic layered matzo and meat pie.

minhag: "Custom." There are 613 commandments, and the way we observe them is based not only on talmudic interpretation, but on the customs of our ancestors. In some cases we observe custom even in absence of law.

minyan: "Number"; the quorum of ten adults necessary for various religious ceremonies, such as reading from Torah, saying Kaddish, weddings, circumcisions. When ten pray together, the Shekhinah hovers over them.

mishegaas: Yiddish for "craziness"; from Hebrew *meshuga* (insane).

Mishnah: "Repetition"; Oral Law as opposed to Torah, Written Law. When it became too cumbersome for memorization, around 200 C.E., Rabbi

Judah ha-Nasi in Palestine organized the material into the Mishnah. It is the core of the Talmud.

Mishneh Torah: "Repetition of the Torah," also known as *Yad ha-Chazakah* (strong hand), since *yad* equals fourteen, the number of books in it. It is Maimonides' comprehensive, logical codification of Jewish law.

Mitnaggedim: "Opponents" of Chasidism, in particular Lithuanian Jews devoted to the Talmud as opposed to the *Zohar,* and who kept the Polish prayer book instead of adopting the Lurianic Sephardic customs, as the Chasidim had.

Mitzrayim: "Egypt"; also "limitation," "boundary," "narrow straits."

mitzvah: "Commandment," "duty," "obligation," "good deed"; plural, mitzvot. There are 613 commandments, 248 positive and 365 negative.

Moses Leib of Sasov (1745–1807): Chasidic *tzaddik,* scholar, rabbi, and composer. A disciple of the Maggid of Mezhirech.

Mount Gerizim: Mountain near Nablus in the Holy Land, sacred to the Samaritans and the site of their paschal sacrifice.

Mount Sinai: Mountain on which Moses received the Torah. Identification is uncertain, but it is popularly believed to be at the site of the sixth-century St. Catherine's Monastery.

Musar: "Ethics"; a late nineteenth-century movement aiming to strengthen the connection between Jewish law and ethical behavior.

Nachman ben Simchah of Bratslav (1772–1811): Great-grandson of the Ba'al Shem Tov, rabbi, Chasidic *tzaddik,* and founder of Breslov Chasidism, known as dead Chasidim because they never chose another *tzaddik* after him. He was a great storyteller, creator of parables, and author of thirteen beautiful mystical fairy tales. Often despondent, he believed he possessed the soul of the Messiah, but either his failure or that of Jewish people prevented that from becoming actualized.

Nevi'im: "Prophets"; the second division of the Bible, containing writings of major and minor prophets.

niggun: "Melody"; among the Chasidim, usually wordless.

notarikon: Greek word for a method of interpreting scripture by reading the first or last letters of the words of a biblical phrase.

omer: "Sheaf"; a measure of barley offered on the second day of Passover in the Temple. It is still counted today for forty-nine days, the omer period, between Passover and Shavuot.

pareve: Food that is neither meat nor dairy, such as vegetables, fruit, grains, eggs, and fish.

pastelicos: Sephardic meat-filled fried potato dumplings.

Peretz, Isaac Leib (1852–1915): One of the greatest Yiddish writers, especially famous for his mystical short stories influenced by Chasidic legends.

Pesach: "Passover"; but also the paschal sacrifice itself and another name for the shankbone on the seder plate. Pesachim is a talmudic tractate on Passover.

Pesachdikhe: Foods and kitchen utensils acceptable for Passover.

pidyon ha-ben: "Redemption of firstborn"; a ceremony on the thirty-first day after birth in which the child is redeemed by giving a Kohen five silver coins. Since the firstborn were spared when God passed over the houses of the Israelites, they must forever after be redeemed. Children of Kohanim or Levites are still exempted from this since they were dedicated to service in the Temple.

Pirke Avot: "Chapters of the Fathers" popular Mishnaic tractate, read a chapter a week every Shabbat afternoon during the omer period, contains no law or legend, only pithy wisdom of the sages from the Great Assembly to *tannaim.* Often included in *siddurim,* known as *Ethics of the Fathers* or *Wisdom of the Talmud,* source of quotes used here from Hillel and Tarfon.

piyyut: Liturgical poem; plural, *piyyutim;* composers are called *piyyutin;* from the Greek for "poet."

Prague: Czech capital, famous for its old Jewish community, Jewish quarter, synagogues, like the Altneuschul, cemetery, and golem legend. It was the home of the Maharal and Kafka. The first illustrated printed Haggadah was made there. When Czechoslovakia was absorbed into greater Germany, 100,000 Jews who lived there were rounded up then interned at Theresienstadt. Eventually 90 percent died or were murdered. Their specifically Jewish belongings were saved to be used in a future museum of an extinct race. Today, these objects, along with synagogues and cemetery, form the collection of the world's largest Jewish museum.

pulkey: Yiddish for "thigh," most often used to refer to chicken's drumstick.

pupik: Yiddish for "navel"; by extension, stomach or chicken's gizzard.

Purim-*shpil:* "Carnival play"; performances that arose at Purim, since everyone was already in costume. Youngsters would go in groups from house to house putting on these skits in return for treats. Out of this came Yiddish theater, and Borscht Belt comedy sketches.

rabbi: "Master"; originally teachers who interpreted the Bible, and created Talmud and midrash. In the Middle Ages, a rabbi was a community leader but not necessarily a *maggid* (preacher) or chazzan (cantor). His leadership was based on his ability to make halakhic (legal) decisions. Today the rabbi is the leader of the synagogue community and functions similarly to minister.

Raphael, Chaim (1908–): Contemporary English Jewish scholar and author, Oxford professor.

Rashi, Solomon ben Isaac (1040–1105): French rabbi, scholar, and one of greatest Bible and Talmud commentators of all time. His commentaries are standard additions to the Torah and the Talmud.

Rav, Abba Arikha (third century C.E.): Babylonian *amora,* student of Judah ha-Nasi, colleague of Samuel. Their work was the foundation of Talmud.

rebbe: Honorific used by Chasidim for a *tzaddik* who may or may not be an ordained rabbi. In the earliest period of Chasidism, it was unusual for a tzaddik to be rabbi. Since later tzaddikim inherited positions, they were not necessarily rabbis either. As time went on and talmudic learning became not only accepted, but desirable, it became more common for Chasidic leaders to have rabbinic ordination, especially after Chasidic *yeshivot* were established.

rebbitzin: The wife of the rabbi.

Ropshitzer, Naphtali Tzevi (1760–1827): Polish Chasidic *tzaddik,* disciple of Yaakov Yitzhak, the Seer of Lublin.

Rosh Chodesh: "New Moon"; the first day of the month, Half-Hallel and additional service recited in synagogue. The blessing can be recited at night any time from third day to the full moon, usually at the end of Shabbat.

Rosenzweig, Franz (1886–1929): German theologian; he influenced Buber, with whom he began a translation of the Bible into German.

Roth, Cecil (1899–1970): Oxford translator, historian of Jewish art, Marranos, Haggadah, Venetian ghetto.

Roth, Leon (1896–1963): English scholar, philosopher, translator, rector of Hebrew University, brother of Cecil.

Ruzhin, Israel Friedmann (1797–1850): Great-grandson of the Maggid of Mezhirech, grandson of Abraham ben Dov the Angel, son of Shalom Shakhna of Probishtch. Founded his own dynasty, and lived in luxury.

Sabra: Aramaic for "prickly pear cactus," thorny on outside but with a sweet heart. Native-born Israeli.

Safed: A town in Galilee; the reputed author of the *Zohar,* Simeon bar Yochai, lived and was buried in nearby Meron. This drew the mystical community to Safed in the sixteenth century.

Samuel ben Solomon of Falaise, Sir Morel (thirteenth century): French rabbi, scholar, member of the school of Talmud commentators begun by Rashi.

Samuel, Mar (second–third centuries): Babylonian *amora,* colleague of Rav. Their work is the foundation of Talmud.

Sanhedrin: Group of seventy-one scholars in Palestine whose word was final in political, legal, and religious disputes during the Roman period until the early fifth century. Also, a talmudic tractate on judges, resurrection.

schav: "Sorrel"; soup made from sorrel or, alternatively, spinach. Traditional at Shavuot, common at Passover.

schmaltz: "Fat," usually from chicken or other poultry. It can also refer to something overly sentimental, schmaltzy.

Schneerson, Menahem Mendel (1902–1994): The seventh *tzaddik* of the Lubavicher Chasidim, a brilliant scholar and charismatic figure, son-in-law of the previous *rebbe.*

Scholem, Gershom (1897–1982): One of the greatest scholars of the twentieth century. He revived kabbalah as an important subject of study, giving it a central place in Jewish thought and history. He was a friend of literary critic Walter Benjamin.

seder: "Order"; the ritualized Passover meal.

Sefirat ha-Omer: "Counting the omer"; demarcation of the forty-nine days between Passover and Shavuot by counting the omer in memory of the omer offering made in the Temple.

selichot: "Forgiveness"; penitential prayers recited from before Rosh Hashanah until Yom Kippur.

Sephard: Biblical country assumed to be Spain, now referring to the Jews of Muslim lands of North Africa and the Ottoman Empire and their descendants, Sephardim.

Septuagint: From Latin for "seventy"; the first Greek translation of the Torah done by seventy-two elders in Alexandria in the third century B.C.E. The rest of the Bible translation was completed over the next two centuries.

Shabbat: "Seventh day"; the Jewish day of rest, beginning at sunset Friday and ending at sunset Saturday. Also, a tractate of the Talmud on Sabbath. In Yiddish, Shabbos.

Shabbat ha-Gadol: "The Great Sabbath"; the Sabbath preceding Passover, when the rabbi's sermon deals with the laws of Passover.

shakshookah: Tunisian tomato stew of vegetables and poached eggs.

shalom: "Peace"; the Jewish way of saying hello and goodbye.

shaygets: "Non-Jewish male."

Shekhinah: "Divine presence"; the feminine aspect of God, which shares the Exile of the Jewish people.

shema: "Hear"; the first word of the Shema, the Jewish declaration of God's unity recited in the morning and evening service, on one's deathbed, and by Jewish martyrs.

shemurah: "Watched," or "observed," referring to matzo made from wheat watched from harvest through milling and baking. It is desirable for the matzot used at the seder.

Shenei Luchot ha-Brit: "Two tablets of the covenant"; the Ten Commandments.

sheytel: Yiddish for the wig worn by Orthodox women after marriage.

shikse: "Non-Jewish female."

Shir ha-Shirim: "Song of Songs"; the scroll recited during Passover.

shmoos: To have an intimate conversation; from the same root as *shema,* "hear" or "listen."

Shneur Zalman of Lyady (1745–1813): Disciple of the Maggid of Mezhirech, founder of Chabad Chasidism, and the author of *Tanya,* which reveals both talmudic learning and deep mystical experiences, a rare combination in his generation. He had a dispute with Vilna Gaon, a representative of Mitnaggedim, who was not opposed to kabbalism, but to *tzaddikism,* the cult of the leader. As Alter Rebbe, he is the first Lubavich tzaddik.

shochet: "Ritual slaughterer," who slaughters clean animals properly so they are kosher. He must use a sharp knife to sever the jugular veins, carotid arteries, esophagus, and windpipe in one stroke so that death is instantaneous.

shofar: "Horn"; the ram's horn blown to awaken us to repent in the month before Rosh Hashanah, on New Year, and on Yom Kippur.

shtetl: "Little town"; plural, *shtetlach.* Little towns of Eastern Europe, often completely Jewish or with Jewish majorities, often virtually self-governing. This is the world of I. L. Peretz and Shalom Aleichem, on the one hand remembered fondly, and on the other remembered for its filth, poverty, superstition, insularity, lack of opportunity, and frequent anti-Semitic intruders.

shtraymel: Wide fur hat worn by some Chasidim. Its thirteen sable tails represent the thirteen divine qualities. It was adopted from the dress of the Polish nobility of the eighteenth century.

shul: Yiddish for "synagogue," from German for school, which may suggest the importance of education in Judaism. Synagogue came into being after the destruction of the first Temple during Babylonian exile.

Shulchan Arukh: "Prepared table"; the feast at the Passover seder; the title
   of Rabbi Joseph Caro's *Code of Jewish Law.*
siddur: "Order of prayer"; Ashkenazi word for prayer book.
sidrah: "Arrangement"; the weekly Torah portion. The Torah is divided
   into fifty-four portions, all of which are read in a year, at the rate of one
   and occasionally two a week.
sidre: "Order"; the six orders or sections of Mishnah.
simchah: "Rejoicing," joyous occasion.
Simchah Bunem of Przysucha (1765–1827): Polish Chasidic *tzaddik,* disciple of Yaakov Yitzhak of Przysucha, the Yehudi (the Jew).
Spira, Israel, the Rabbi of Bluzhov (?–1989): Contemporary Chasidic
   tzaddik, Holocaust survivor. For more on him read Yaffa Eliach's uplift-
   ing *Hasidic Tales of the Holocaust.*
spodik: Tall fur hat worn by the Chasidim of Gur, or Gerer Chasidim.
Sternhartz, Nathan of Nemirov (1780–1845): Disciple, biographer, and
   companion of Nachman of Bratslav. He became the leader of the
   Breslovers after Nachman's death. He collected and published Nachman's work, including the stories.
sukkah: "Booth"; a temporary structure set up for Sukkot in remembrance
   both of wandering in the Sinai for forty years and of harvest booths.
   The sukkah is festooned with produce, and meals are eaten in it; some
   sleep in the sukkah. Also, a talmudic tractate on these booths.
Szenes, Hannah (1921–1944): Poet, Zionist, and resistance fighter during
   World War II. She parachuted into Yugoslavia in 1944, crossed into
   Hungary, and was caught, tortured, and executed.
ta'am: "Flavor"; that special something great cooks put into food.
tagine: Moroccan Sephardic chicken dish made with fruit, nuts, and spices.
tal: "Dew," prayed for from Passover to Sukkot. Also, the beneficence of
   heaven.
tallit: "Prayer shawl"; a fringed garment worn during morning prayers, afternoon prayers on Tishah Be-Av, and all day on Yom Kippur. The
   knotted fringes at the four corners are a commandment of the Shema.
Talmud: "Study," or "learning"; discussions, commentaries of *amoraim* on
   the Mishnah of the *tannaim;* Mishnah in Hebrew, Gemara in Aramaic.
   There is a Babylonian Talmud (Babli), and the shorter Jerusalem Talmud (Yerushalmi). Over the centuries other commentaries have been
   added to Talmud, like those of Rashi and his school, so that discussion
   spans thousands of years. Each page of the Talmud is unique in
   arrangement, 2,500 years of teaching spiraling around itself. Talmud is
   not a code of law, but its methods teach us how to think and make

decisions about the law. By extension, Talmud, like Torah, is all knowledge and learning. For excellent introduction, read Adin Steinsaltz's *The Essential Talmud,* or his English-language Talmud volumes.

Tanakh: Acronym for *T*orah, *N*evi'im, *Kh*etuvim, the three parts of the Bible. Tanakh is the Bible.

tanna: Aramaic for "teacher"; plural, *tannaim.* Palestinian scholars who created Mishnah, c. 20–200 C.E.

Tarfon: *Tanna,* contemporary of Akiba, martyr. He is famous for saying, "The day is short, the task is great, the workers are lazy, the reward is much, the Master is insistent," and "It is not your duty to complete the work, but neither are you free to desist from it."

tashlikh: "You shall cast"; a ceremony on the afternoon of the first day of Rosh Hashanah, in which pockets are emptied of bread crumbs, which are thrown into the sea or a stream of running water. We hope our sins will be swallowed up as the crumbs are by the fish. There is an interesting parallel between the crumbs of Passover and Rosh Hashanah, one destroyed by fire, the other by water.

tchotchke: Yiddish for toy, small present, knickknack, trifle, trinket.

tefillin: "Phylacteries"; two cubical leather boxes containing verses of the Shema and other scriptural passages that tell us to bind God's words on the hand and for frontlets between the eyes. So Orthodox men (and some non-Orthodox Jewish men and women) place these boxes, using leather straps, on their arm and hand and forehead, during morning *tefillah* (prayer) on weekdays. The strap is laid on the arm in a symbolic pattern representing the ten *sefirot* and the name of God, Shadai. Like the mezuzah and tallit with *tzitzit,* tefillin are intended to make us notice, to be conscious of our actions. Also, a minor tractate about tefillin added to Talmud.

terefah: "Torn"; referring to unkosher carrion. Terefah is anything not kosher. In Yiddish, *trayf.*

teshuvah: "Return," meaning repentance.

Theresienstadt: "Model" concentration camp in Czechoslovakia where 150,000 Jews were interned. Less than 10 percent survived. For more on this, read *I Never Saw Another Butterfly* and *Precious Legacy.*

Torah: "Teaching"; handwritten scrolls containing the five Books of Moses, and by extension, all Jewish learning and literature.

Tosefta: Aramaic for "addition"; collection of *tannaitic* material left out of the Mishnah but arranged in parallel order to it.

tuchis: "Under"; buttocks, tail, rear end, behind, posterior, rump. When we speak of a child's, we say tush or tushy.

tuchis afn Tish: This vulgarity literally means "keister on the table," but this tells us nothing. It's more like, let's get to the bottom line, nitty-gritty, skinny.

tzaddik: "Righteous"; the charismatic leader of a Chasidic sect, often supposed to effect miracles, make women fertile, cure illness, and perform other wonders. The tzaddik is linked to the Messiah, since Yesod, the ninth *sefirah* and one associated with Messiah, means "foundation" and "the righteous are the foundation of the world." The tzaddik holds the messianic tendencies in Judaism in suspension. Through him there is hope, but enthusiasm never goes over the edge into false messianism. Through the tzaddik, the community connected to God even if individual members are not.

tzimmes: Various baked dishes of fruits and vegetables, such as carrots, sweet potatoes, apples, prunes, sometimes with meat as well: an attempt to make fruit compote in a world with little fruit. Also, to make a fuss.

tzitzit: Elaborately knotted fringes on the four corners of the prayer shawl. Also, a minor tractate about these fringes added to the Talmud.

ushpizin: Aramaic for, "guests"; the seven guests—Abraham, Isaac, Jacob, Moses, Aaron, Joseph, and David—invited to the *sukkah* on successive days of Sukkot. Plaques are hung in the sukkah picturing them.

Warsaw: Polish capital with a strong Jewish presence for centuries. Almost 500,000 Jews were concentrated in the ghetto during the Holocaust. It took longer to suppress the Jewish rebellion that began there on Passover, 1943, than to conquer any single European nation.

yahrzeit: Yiddish for "time of year," or "anniversary"; the annual commemoration of the death of a parent by lighting a candle and saying *Kaddish.*

Yannai (c. sixth century): Palestinian *piyyutin,* teacher of Kallir.

yarmulke: Skullcap worn by Orthodox Jews always, Conservative Jews when engaged in religious activities, and Reform Jews rarely (though it seems to be making a comeback).

yeshiva: "Academy"; a school for the study of Jewish subjects, especially Talmud; plural, yeshivot. They began after destruction of Temple in 70 C.E., and have spread all over the world.

Yiddish: "Jewish," Judeo-German, common language of Ashkenazim. Starting around 1000 with Jews in Rhineland, Yiddish was carried eastward as Western Europe became more hostile to Jews, then spread throughout Eastern Europe. It is mostly Germanic with a lot of Hebrew, and many additions from Slavic tongues; written in Hebrew letters.

yiddishkeit: "Jewishness."

Yisrael: "Israel"; all Jews who are not Kohanim or Levites. The bottom matzo of the three used at seder.

yizkor: "May God remember"; the opening words to the memorial prayer. Recited on the last day of Passover, Shavuot, Yom Kippur, and Shemini Atzeret.

Yom Tov: "Good day"; festival. In Yiddish, *yontif.*

Yose of Galilee (second century): *Tanna,* student, colleague of Akiba.

Zangwill, Israel (1864–1926): English-Jewish writer of poetry, novels of Jewish subjects, and mysteries. "Zangwill" is Hebrew for "ginger."

Zeman Cherutenu: "Season of Our Freedom," another name for Passover.

zemirot: "Songs," usually table songs sung during Shabbat meals, such as "Eliyahu ha-Novi"; at Passover, the six table songs that follow the formal end of the seder.

zero'a: "Arm"; both God's outstretched arm and the lamb's shankbone, or other bone, on the seder plate.

zeydeh: Yiddish for "grandfather."

Zhitlowsky, Chaim (1865–1943): Russian-born Yiddish writer, philosopher.

zimmun: "Invitation"; the sung invitation from the leader to two others to join in Grace after Meals.

Zohar: A word used in Daniel 12:3, where it means "brightness," "radiance," or "splendor." Written in literary pseudo-Aramaic near the end of the thirteenth century in Northern Spain by Rabbi Moses ben Shemtov de Leon, the *Zohar* was attributed to a *tanna,* Rabbi Simeon bar Yochai. The bulk of it is mystical midrashic commentary to Torah, but its form is like a mystical novel with Simeon wandering around a fantastic Holy Land with forays into heavenly yeshivot. It is the Jewish mystical work par excellence, at times as popular as Bible and Talmud.